Tw[illegible]

Anothe[illegible] Andalucian Life

Victoria Twead

Also by Victoria Twead

Chickens, Mules and Two Old Fools (2009)
Two Old Fools - Olé! (2011)
Two Old Fools on a Camel (2012/3)

Victoria Twead was born and raised in Dorset, England, before moving to West Sussex to pursue a teaching career. In 2004 she nagged poor, long-suffering Joe into relocating to a tiny, remote mountain village in Andalucía, southern Spain.

Published by FAR Publishing, 2011

First Edition

A CIP catalogue record for this title is available from the British Library.

Two Old Fools - Olé!

Another slice of Andalucían Life

by
Victoria Twead

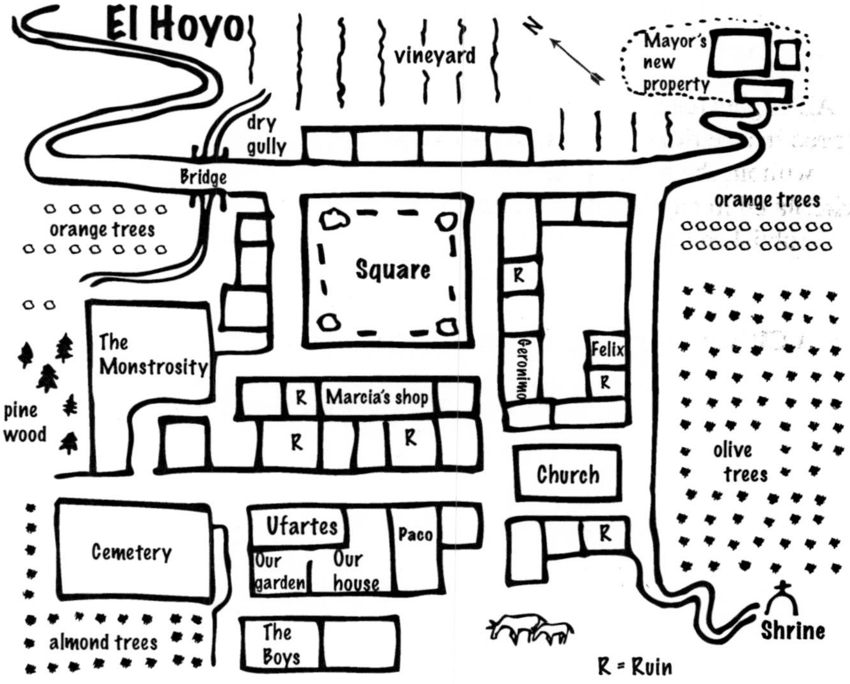

Acknowledgements

Gayle and Iain of Orce Serrano Hams for their constant support along the way. I have shamelessly plundered their knowledge of Spanish cuisine and recipes. If you're looking for traditional Spanish cookware, or something tasty and Spanish, I highly recommend visiting *www.orceserranohams.com*

Carrie Compton from Missouri, who was one of my very first 'fans' and whose loyalty and generosity helped me enormously through the launching of *Chickens* and the writing of *Olé!*

Paul Hamilton, not just for the fantastic *Olé* cover, but for the scores of hilarious 'photographs' he constantly sends me. Take a look at *Celebrities and Other Animals* on my website, or the album on my Facebook page and you'll see what I mean...

Justin and the members of *EyeOnSpain.com,* who gave me so much encouragement when 'Chickens' was launched.

Mindy Sampson for her friendship and proofreading expertise.

Clive Muir for fascinating Spanish wildlife facts. Check out his website - *www.grazalemaguide.com*

Kiersten Rowland, one of my first readers. Living in Spain, we have much in common and sharing experiences with her has been a pleasure and a laugh. *www.kierstenrowland.com*

Sandra Marshall and *Alstrays - alstrays.com* for their help with the cat family that entered our lives unexpectedly. Thanks to their selfless work, countless cats and kittens have been found new forever homes.

Our amazing friends, the Gin Twins, Sue and Juliet. May they long continue to visit us in El Hoyo. The gin bottle will always await their arrival, along with chilled tonic and icecubes.

My son Shealan (my computer guru) and his lovely wife Hannah who've always taken an interest in my small successes.

My daughter Karly for allowing her stories and photographs to be used, (yet again), and for her constant encouragement. And thanks to Cam, Di and Barry for embracing Karly into their family, allowing me to stop worrying about her being so far away.

My wonderful friends Tweek and Al and their daughters Emma, Beth and Meg for always being in the background rooting for me.

Hanna Uehre, one of the sweetest, most thoughtful people I have ever met on the Internet. Twitter name *@Travelmaus.*

The majority of events in the book are true, although some of the people and place names have been changed to protect privacy.

If I have made mistakes in any of the recipes, please forgive me. Similarly, please overlook any Spanish language errors - I still have much to learn.

Email: TopHen@VictoriaTwead.com
www.VictoriaTwead.com

Two Old Fools - Olé!

Another slice of Andalucían Life

by
Victoria Twead

Note to the Reader

I absolutely loved writing *Chickens* from beginning to end, but by the time I reached the last chapter, I was exhausted. "I don't think I'll write another," I said to Joe.

Although *Chickens* was such fun to write, I'm the kind of writer who agonises over every comma, and I endured sleepless nights worrying about the structure and content. Would the things we found funny amuse other people? Would the readers like the characters? Would anybody want to read about two old fools anyway? "Wait and see," said Joe.

Well, we did wait and see, and were completely astonished at how well *Chickens* was received. I never dreamed it would become an Amazon bestseller, nor did I foresee how many friends I would make as a result.

A couple of years ago, I scoffed at Twitter and Facebook, considering them a complete waste of time and 'not real'. I was wrong. Thanks to the Internet (and Twitter and Facebook in particular) I have chatted with literally hundreds of delightful people. Complete strangers who had read *Chickens* emailed me, some with amusing anecdotes of their own. Many others provided help, encouragement and endless laughs. You all spurred me on to write this sequel to *Chickens*, and I thank you for that. Although Joe and I live in a tiny village in the Spanish mountains, we feel we are always surrounded by friends from all over the world.

Ole! was just as much fun to write as *Chickens*, although equally exhausting. Joe and I have a routine: I write a segment, whereupon Joe checks it and makes minor changes or suggestions. I then edit (if I agree with his advice) and carry on writing the next part. At the end, we put the whole manuscript aside for a week or more to 'prove', then print it off. Joe then reads the whole book aloud to me. If he stumbles, we rewrite that part to improve the flow.

Amongst all the praise and fan letters I received, there were, of course, criticisms which I have tried to address in *Ole!* Some said *Chickens* was too short, so *Olé!* is longer. Some said the photographs were too small, so I have increased their size.

But the main criticism came from a handful of American readers who were most affronted by our chickens' names. I am sincerely sorry for that - I never meant to offend. Our American friend, Colton, has since explained to us that the 'F' word is far stronger and more offensive in the States than it is in the UK. Rest assured, the two unfortunately-named chickens are not mentioned in *Olé!* although they did live to a ripe old age, oblivious to the storm of protest they caused. (RIP B & F)

One more thing. For those unfamiliar with the little stick men I've used for scene breaks, they are Indalos, or Rainbow Men, the emblem for this part of Andalucía.

So here it is, my second book. It was a joy to write and, I hope, will be enjoyed by those who are kind enough to read it.

Vicky
October 2011

My first German Reader

For Joe
Without him, I'd have given up long ago.

And for Carrie Compton
For her kindness and support from the very beginning.

Two Old Fools - Olé!

Contents

Spanish Recipes

Quantities in metric and US measures

Page

1
The Fish Van

Joe and I were in the kitchen, drinking coffee and feeling deliciously smug. It was a Monday morning in April and we were remembering what Mondays used to bring, back in the grey old days, before we moved to Spain.

"We're so lucky, aren't we?" I said. "In England, we would've been getting ready to go to work. You'd have been stressing about getting your uniform sorted, or paperwork prepared. And I'd be planning my lessons and worrying about getting reports done, or staff meetings, or whatever."

Joe nodded. "Yep! Instead, we're sitting here, listening to the cuckoo in the valley and Geronimo's donkey singing to his girlfriend in the next village. I might even start writing my book soon."

I was unconvinced. Not a word of Joe's masterpiece had been committed to either paper or word-processor as yet. His book was a bit of a standing joke.

One of the chickens launched into her Egg Song, the triumphant announcement that another egg had just been introduced into the world.

"And new-laid eggs for breakfast," I said.

I sighed, the self-satisfied sigh of the truly content. Five years had passed since we'd left England behind and set up home in El Hoyo. Five years of living in a crazy, tiny mountain village, miles away from the nearest big town.

I stole a glance at Joe across the kitchen table. When you've been living with somebody for a long time, you can sense when something is bothering him. Joe was deep in thoughts of his own.

"You are glad we decided to stay in Spain, aren't you?" I asked, after a pause.

"Of course I am! It's a wonderful life here."

"Then what are you thinking about?"

"Nothing. It's just that sometimes I..."

"Sometimes you what?"

Joe held his hand up, a signal for me to remain silent. "Shh, Vicky... Is that the fish van?" he asked, a puzzled expression creasing his brow.

I stopped and listened. I could hear birds, the chickens scratching outside and, yes, the distant familiar hoot of the fish van.

"That's odd," I said. "The fish van doesn't usually come on a Monday in April. There aren't enough people in the village to buy fish.

Let’s take our coffee up to the roof terrace and look.”

“You’re so nosey,” said Joe, but he followed me just the same, and picked up the binoculars on the way.

On the far side of the valley, we could see the white fish van wending its way down the twisting mountain road, horn beeping to announce its arrival as it always did. But it was not alone, it headed a procession. The convoy consisted of three vehicles. First the fish van, then a largish truck with canvas sides and finally a black minibus. Any traffic in the village during the week was unusual, but a convoy?

“What is that writing on the side of the truck?” I asked.

Joe focused the binoculars and concentrated. “Er, I think it says, ‘Ufarte’ and ‘Almería’.”

We digested this gem of information in silence.

“Ufarte?” I repeated at last. “Are you sure?”

“Yep, quite sure. Ufarte.”

As the three vehicles entered the village, all three drivers leaned on their horns and wound down their windows allowing three different sets of music to blare out into the valley.

Joe and I exchanged glances. Who were these people? What were they doing in our village? We had a bird’s eye view from our roof terrace and we froze in horror as the raucous convoy thundered past the village square, turned into our street, and parked below, right outside our house.

The Ufarte Truck

Nothing much had changed in the five years since we’d made El Hoyo our home. Our ability to speak Spanish had improved hugely but there were only a handful of permanent residents in the village with whom to practice it. However, every Friday evening, the population of the village rose, only to plummet again on Sunday nights as the weekenders returned to the city.

Of the permanent villagers, dear old Marcia had hardly aged at all. Always dressed in black, with her silver hair secured by ever-escaping hairpins, she continued to run the only village shop. The shop was aging faster than she was. The walls were beginning to crumble and the steps had worn away. Luckily, her two strapping sons came up to the village most weekends and carried out basic maintenance.

Uncle Felix, the illiterate, retired shepherd, still shared his two-roomed cottage with his beloved mule and a pair of chickens. Ancient, but like most Spanish peasant folk, he enjoyed rude health and frequently boasted he had never visited a doctor. Although toothless and wizened, he still possessed more energy than either Joe or I.

Every February we relied on Uncle Felix to supervise the pruning of our grapevine. He would arrive, cloth cap pulled low over his eyes, ready to bark out orders. His mule would wait patiently outside in the street, thoughtfully grazing on our window-box, aware that her adored master would rejoin her soon. If the window was open, she'd push her long face into the room, rattle her ears, and snicker for her master.

"Cut there! No, not there... Further up! *¡Madre mía!* Not *that* branch, cut the one to the left!"

Joe and his clippers would dance hither and thither, obeying Uncle Felix's commands. But it was worth it. Every year, the grapevine produced huge, plump bunches of grapes, more than we could possibly eat.

And how could El Hoyo continue to function without Geronimo? Who else would sweep the streets, assist the old folk and give us chicken advice? Along with his three moth-eaten dogs, Geronimo had acquired a donkey, which he often tethered beside Uncle Felix's mule. The mule and donkey were fond of each other and grazed flank to flank while Geronimo sat on the drystone wall, swigging from his bottle, watching them. Geronimo still enjoyed a beer or brandy a little too enthusiastically, but everyone turned a blind eye. Geronimo was part of the fabric of El Hoyo, and arguably Real Madrid Football Club's most devoted fan.

Paco and Carmen-Bethina, the best neighbours in the world, were still very much part of our lives. Every Friday they'd arrive from the city, noisy and exuberant, shattering our peace in the nicest way.

Paco's balled fist would pound on our front door, making us jump. "English!" he'd bellow. "We have tomatoes for you!" (Or cherries, or shiny red and green peppers - depending on the season.) He'd hand us a huge bag crammed with produce while his wife, Carmen-Bethina, stood behind him, a broad smile dimpling her round cheeks.

Of course 'Bethina' wasn't really Carmen's name, but five years ago, when Paco had introduced himself and his wife, he'd said '*vecina*', meaning 'neighbour'. We'd misunderstood his Andalucian accent, (because '*v's*' sound like '*b's*') and assumed her name was Bethina. And so the name had stuck.

Carmen-Bethina frequently baked us cakes, and our waistlines expanded. Their son, Little Paco, had grown tall, but played enough

Spanish Roasted Tomato Salad

Serve as part of an outdoor buffet or side dish with barbecued chicken. This is also a perfect accompaniment to any tortilla dish.

12 large ripe vine tomatoes
3 tablespoons olive oil
2 tablespoons balsamic vinegar
A sprinkle of caster sugar

Halve the tomatoes and place in a single layer in a roasting tin.
Drizzle with the oil and vinegar and mix well.
Roast in a medium oven for around 45 minutes to an hour (adding the sugar after 20 minutes or so).
When they are ready, they will be soft and lightly caramelized.
Serve warm.

soccer in the village square to avoid piling on the pounds, despite his mother's baking.

The same could not be said of Bianca, Little Paco's cocker spaniel. We had watched her grow from sickly puppy to barrel-on-legs and it was easy to see why. Bianca had become the family dustbin. All Carmen-Bethina's cooking scraps and left-over dinners were disposed of inside Bianca. Brown eyes innocent, tongue lolling, she had also become a master thief. Turn one's back on anything vaguely edible, and Bianca snaffled it. She was crafty. As silent as a feather, she could clear untended plates quicker than a blink, and was often banished from the house, tethered and wailing outside.

In our street, Paco's family lived on our right-hand side. The house on our other side had always stood empty, although long ago, we had been introduced to the old man who owned it. He was quiet, and on the rare occasions when he visited his house, we seldom saw or heard him. One day, Paco told us that the old man had died. We were saddened to hear that, and the house next door remained empty, locked and silent.

It is rare for old Spanish houses to appear on the property market as traditionally they are passed down from generation to generation. I guess we shouldn't have been surprised when the fish van, the truck and the minibus drew to a halt outside our house that April Monday morning.

The empty house next door! The old man's relatives had come to claim it. Up on our roof terrace, like unseen birds perched in a tall tree, we stared down at the activity below.

Simultaneously, all three vehicle doors flew open. We recognised the Fish Man immediately - was he a relative of the family? Probably. Everybody else was new to us, we didn't recognise any of them.

Two men jumped from the Ufarte truck's cab and began to roll up and tie the canvas sides, revealing stacked furniture, boxes and household goods. The Fish Man got out of his van to help them.

"Do you think we should go down and introduce ourselves?" I asked Joe. "Perhaps we should offer to help?"

"Pardon? Vicky? What did you say?" The music from the minibus was still blaring.

"I just wondered if we should go down and... Oh, NEVER MIND!" Ordinary conversation was impossible above the blast of the music. I noticed Joe was scratching his nether regions, a sure sign that he was agitated. I followed his gaze to the street below and understood his consternation. The minibus occupants were spilling out into the street...

If you know me, you'll be aware that I'm a list-maker. I can't fight it. I'm compelled to keep records and compile lists. In England, my friends nicknamed me Schindler. Already I was forming a mental list as I spied on our new neighbours. My first impressions were as follows:

Family Member (1) (Later we found out his name was Juan.)
Papa Ufarte: *Surprisingly tall for a Spaniard, handsome, bearded, athletic build, dressed in jeans and T-shirt. Carrying a guitar. Loud-voiced, shouting orders. Probably 35 years of age.*

Family Member (2) (Maribel)
Mama Ufarte: *Attractive, masses of black hair pulled back into a high, swinging ponytail. Wearing jeans and a bright smock top. Maybe early 30's. Lots to say, barely stopping to breathe. Displayed a certain poise and grace, even as she balanced (7) on her hip.*

Family Member (3) (Jorge)
Boy: *Mop of black hair. Lots of energy. Barcelona football shirt. Chewing gum. About 7 years old.*

Family Members (4) and (5)
Twin Girls: *Beautiful, identical. Identical pink sparkly fairy costumes, pink fluffy wings, pink tights, pink shoes, pink shoe-ribbons. Black shiny hair held aside by identical pink flowery hair-slides. Carrying identical dolls and magic wands. Maybe 5 years old?*

Family Member (6) (Carlos - hereafter referred to as Scrap.)
Boy: *A tiny scrap - miniature version of (3) minus the chewing gum. His mouth pursed around a dummy (pacifier) that appeared to be a permanent fixture. Followed (3) wherever he went. Obsessed with kicking. (In that short space of time: kicked car tyre, stone in the street, sister's ankle, our front door.) Probably about 3 years old?*

Family Member (7) (Real name Sergio - hereafter referred to as Snap-On.)

Boy/Girl(?): *Tangle of curly dark hair, bare feet. Maybe 18 months old? Looked old enough to walk but wasn't set down by mother.*

Was that it? No. A pair of high-heeled shoes emerged from the vehicle, followed by a pair of shapely legs, a very short denim skirt, a tight top that left little to the imagination, arms with jangly bracelets and a dark head of hair. She yawned and stretched luxuriously, tossing her mane of hair over her shoulders. Leaning languidly against the minibus, she examined her fingernails. I mentally added her to my list:

Family Member (8) (Lola Ufarte)
Auntie(?): *Maybe a little younger than Mama Ufarte, slim, gorgeous. Dressed to kill, flirtatious. As my mother-in-law would have said, "No better than she should be."*

"Whew," Joe shouted into my ear. "That's a big family! How are they all going to fit into that little house?"

I shook my head, still engrossed by the scene below. If you counted Scrap (6) and the babe in arms (7) we had eight new neighbours! I felt a little sneaky observing from above, unseen, but it was deliciously tempting. We'd often noticed that if we were on the roof terrace looking down, people seldom looked up.

A familiar figure turned the street corner, Real Madrid soccer scarf draped loosely round his neck trapping some of his long curly hair. He was leading his donkey by a rope. Three dogs trailed behind. Geronimo.

"*¡Hombre!*" shouted Papa Ufarte. Geronimo, the Fish Man and the two other men shook hands and clapped each other on the back. Geronimo and Mama Ufarte exchanged kisses. The children danced around Geronimo and patted the donkey. Geronimo swung the twins in the air and pretended to box with the eldest boy. Only the voluptuous young lady leaning against the minibus, examining her nails, held back and I sensed she was choosing her moment.

At last, the young lady straightened and, hips swaying, sauntered over to Geronimo. The effect was instant. Geronimo's head dropped shyly, and his hands hung by his sides. The lady offered her cheeks to be kissed, and toyed with his scarf coquettishly. I could sense Geronimo's embarrassment as he quickly kissed her and backed away, flushing red. A moment ago he'd been greeting the adults and playing with the kids, but this siren had transformed him into a shambling oaf. Geronimo waved a hand and hurried away, his donkey and dogs trotting behind him.

Oblivious to this painful scene, Papa Ufarte rattled the keys in his hand and tried the lock of their house. It opened easily and he disappeared inside, followed by Mama Ufarte and the seductress. The children milled around, went inside, ran out again and amused themselves as children do.

The oldest boy produced a football and began dribbling and kicking it in the street. Scrap tried to join in and kicked a wardrobe in temper when his big brother wouldn't allow him to share his game. The fairy twins settled down in the dust and played with their dolls.

Then a surprising thing happened. The Fish Man suddenly clapped his hand to his forehead, indicating that he had recalled something important. He cupped his hands to his mouth, loudspeaker-style, and roared over the deafening music.

"Juan? Maribel! JUAN! What about Grandmother?"

Olive Oil Infusions

Flavoured olive oils are a favourite here in Andalucía. Add extra flavour and aroma to a bottle of olive oil by simply adding a few ingredients and letting them infuse together. Easy to make and the longer you keep it the more intense the flavour.

Simply add any of the following ingredients to the olive oil. You can add the ingredients on their own or combine them how you like.
Choose from:

- **whole peeled cloves of garlic**
- **sprigs of thyme**
- **sprigs of rosemary**
- **whole black peppercorns**
- **dried chili peppers**

Once the oil has been allowed to rest and infuse (for at least a week), use it to drizzle over salads or pizzas, spice up pasta or simply serve with crusty bread for a true Spanish delight.

2
Kids and Cake

Joe and I were mesmerised. We leaned further over our terrace wall, watching the scene playing out in the street below.

"Your Grandmother!" shouted the Fish Man again, and turned back to his van.

"*¡Madre mía!*" Papa Ufarte shot out of the house with Mama Ufarte close on his heels.

"*¡Madre mía!*" echoed Mama Ufarte, the curly-haired toddler still glued to her hip, her free hand over her mouth.

The Fish Man hurriedly unlocked and swung open the back doors of his van. The smell of fish wafted up to us. The men from the truck stopped unloading furniture into the street and came to assist. We couldn't see the contents from our lofty vantage point until the men hauled something weighty out. It was an armchair.

And that was the first sight we had of:

Family Member (9)
Granny Ufarte: *Grey hair, black clothes, shawl around her shoulders, rug on her knees, heap of knitting in her lap, fast asleep and snoring in the armchair.*

The children continued playing, unconcerned, as the men lifted the armchair, complete with snoring Grandmother, out of the fish van and into street. The old lady twitched a couple of times, then carried on sleeping, head lolling, mouth wide open revealing bright pink gums.

"Vicky, can you believe that?" mouthed Joe and raised the binoculars to his eyes again, training them down on the street below. It was a bone of contention between us that he utterly refused to wear glasses, maintaining that his eyesight had remained unchanged since the 1980's.

"Pardon?" I said, absorbed by the tableau unfolding.

"I said, CAN YOU BELIEVE THAT?" Joe roared above the music.

At that precise moment, Papa Ufarte leaned into the minibus and switched off the music. Joe's shout echoed round the valley. Ten heads lifted to see Joe and I leaning unashamedly over our balcony wall, the binoculars still glued to Joe's eyes and trained down to watch the activity.

Ten mouths gaped up at us. Even Granny Ufarte opened her eyes for a full fifteen seconds before sinking back into slumber.

Joe guiltily dropped the binoculars from his eyes. I struggled to compose myself.

"Er... *Buenos días*," I called down, and was alarmed to hear my voice coming out as a croak. "Do you need any help?"

The two little fairies lost interest and went back to their dolls and make-believe world. The older boy drummed his football against our front door, making me wonder if even a tiny scrap of varnish would remain. His little brother, Scrap, tried in vain to intercept the ball, teeth clamped onto the dummy in his mouth. The Fish Man and workers resumed unloading, lifting out dressers and chests and setting them down in the dusty street. Granny Ufarte slept on, and the temptress was still in the house. Only Papa and Mama Ufarte and the babe continued staring, faces uplifted. The babe pointed a fat finger up at us in wonder. Mama Ufarte's pretty face broke into a smile of recognition.

"Ah, you must be the English!" she said.

Joe and I nodded in unison, a double-act.

"If you need anything, just ask," I said, face still glowing red with shame. Nobody likes to be caught spying.

"*Gracias*," said Papa Ufarte. "Thank you, we most certainly will."

We waved and backed away from the balcony wall, out of sight, ashamed and embarrassed. We weren't to know that we had yet to meet the last, and smallest member of the family, the one that was going to give us more problems than all the others combined.

If we'd continued watching, we'd have seen what was to prove Joe's nemesis being carried into the house next door. Blissfully ignorant, we returned to our kitchen and made more coffee.

"Well!" I said excitedly. "How embarrassing that they caught us staring down at them! But what a family!"

"Goodbye peace and quiet," said Joe, shaking his head miserably.

"But weren't those twin girls just beautiful in their fairy costumes? I bet even their parents have a job telling them apart."

"Hmm... I think our life is about to change," muttered Joe darkly.

"Oh, don't be silly! They're just a lively young family. Except for Granny Ufarte, of course. I don't think she'll be very lively by the looks of her, poor dear."

"How do you know they're called 'Ufarte'?"

"Well, I don't, but that was written on the side of the truck. I'm just assuming they're all Ufartes, even the Fish Man. You know how Spanish families stick together and help each other out."

"You mark my words,' said Joe, tapping the teaspoon against his cup. "Things around here are going to change. Dramatically."

I ignored him and prattled on. "And weren't the two little boys gorgeous? It'll be nice for Little Paco next door to have some more friends to play with."

From the kitchen we could hear the muffled thud of the football hitting our wall in an endless, rhythmic tattoo.

"Soccer crazy," said Joe.

"You're over-reacting as usual. They live next door, not in our house! And they're probably just weekenders like most of the other villagers. They won't affect us. We'll probably hardly see them."

My last words were drowned out by a hammering on the front door. Joe dropped the teaspoon with a clatter, and for a few seconds our eyes met.

"I'll go," I said at last.

Standing on the doorstep was almost the entire Ufarte clan. Only Granny and the seductress were missing. And, of course, the smallest, hairiest member of the Ufarte family who we had yet to meet. I gaped for a second, collected myself and smiled. I hope I looked welcoming, but I suspect I looked a little shell-shocked.

"*¡Hola!* Do come in..." I said, but the fairy twins, the oldest boy and Scrap already had. Over my shoulder I saw them cantering toward the kitchen as though they already knew the way. Papa and Mama Ufarte, still holding their youngest, stayed on the doorstep.

Mama Ufarte bent forward, babe leaning out of the way, and planted kisses on both my cheeks, Spanish style.

"My name is Maribel," she said. She gazed fondly at the baby in her arms and ruffled his curly hair with her free hand. "This little boy is Sergio." The toddler solemnly stared at me, examining every wrinkle on my face. Maribel half turned, indicating her husband. "And this is my husband, Juan."

Juan stepped forward for the kissing ritual, his beard lightly brushing my face.

"Enchanted," he said. I flushed as I caught myself wishing I was a few decades younger.

"Er, I'm Vicky. I must say - you have a lovely family. Please, come in and meet my husband, Joe."

"Later, Veeky," said Juan, in his deep, golden voice. "We have just brought the children to you. We will go down the mountain and do some shopping. The children will stay with you. We have heard you like children."

"Oh yes, we love children, but..."

"They are very good children," smiled Maribel. Even in this moment of confusion I was struck by her typical Spanish comeliness. Her black hair gleamed with health and her skin was the colour of dark honey. She had the grace of a dancer as she disentangled little Sergio's arms from her neck and peeled him off her hip. She held him out to me and I instinctively took him. Sergio wound his fat little arms round my neck, his legs round my waist, and studied my face at close quarters.

"*Abuela* is taking a siesta in her chair in the shade. She won't wake until we get back. And she will guard the furniture that is still in the street." Maribel pointed. I could see Granny Ufarte's armchair parked beside the mound of furniture. "Grandmother sleeps a lot."

"But..."

"We are very lucky to have such fine neighbours. Everybody in the village says you are very good people," said Maribel, and Juan nodded in agreement. "We will see you later, when we have finished our shopping."

Juan nodded again, and walked away down the street. Maribel blew an airy kiss to little Sergio and followed her husband.

"But..." I tried, but got no further, partly because I was lost for words, and partly because little Sergio had pushed a fat, grubby finger into my mouth.

"Well!" I said to Sergio, extracting his finger. "Let's see what's happening in the kitchen. Let's go and find your brothers and sisters."

I heard the activity long before I reached the kitchen. Standing in the doorway, my eyes swept the scene before me. The fairy twins were cross-legged on the floor, Joe squatting with them. Cupboard doors hung open, and most of my saucepans and wooden spoons were already spread all over the tiles. My heart sank. Where was the orderly kitchen I had left just moments before?

"Um, we were just playing Cooking," said Joe, looking up at me a little guiltily. The fairies didn't look up, they were far too busy.

"And the boys?" I asked. I was feeling a little weak.

"Outside. In the garden."

The bang-bang-thud of the football as it ricocheted off the walls and my cherished raised flowerbeds and plant pots made me wince.

"Would you believe it? Their parents have gone shopping," I said in English. "And left all the kids with us..."

"I know," said Joe, beating an imaginary cake mix with my silver soup ladle. "The kids told me."

"It's a bit of a cheek, though, isn't it?' I said, removing little Sergio's chubby finger from my ear. "I guess that young lady went shopping, too. You'd have thought she'd stay behind and watch the kids."

"Not a lot we can do about it," Joe shrugged. "Anyway, it's nice to have little kids around, I suppose. Didn't I tell you things were going to change?"

I sat down with Sergio on my lap and watched the fairies playing. They were totally immersed in their game. Fairy #1 cracked an imaginary egg into a bowl, while Fairy #2 stirred.

"We're making *bizcocho*," announced Fairy #1, glancing up.

"Like Mama's," said Fairy #2.

"You can have some when it's ready."

"But only when it's cooled down."

"Or you'll get a sore tummy."

"Because it's not good for you to eat warm cake."

"But if you're good..." Fairy #1 wagged her finger at Joe and me, "you can lick out the bowl."

"But only if you're *very* good."

"And you must save some for Sergio."

In spite of myself, I was enchanted. These little girls were repeating word for word what they'd heard their Mama say a thousand times as she baked.

"Well, you're both doing a grand job!" said Joe, getting up and stretching. "I can't wait to taste it when it's ready."

I stood up and unwound Sergio's arms from my neck and stooped to place him on the floor beside his sisters. Sergio screwed his face up, sucked in an enormous breath of air, opened his mouth wide and howled.

"You cannot put our little brother down," said Fairy #1 crossly.

"He does not like it," said Fairy #2, shaking her head.

"Can't he walk?" I asked, hurriedly gathering Sergio up again as he took a long, deep breath for the next howl. Aloft again, Sergio's bawls instantly ceased.

"Yes, he *can* walk," said Fairy #1, stirring energetically with my best egg whisk before waving her magic wand.

"But he does not like it," said Fairy #2, busily pushing back a curtain of hair from her eyes.

"He screams when he is put down."

"So Mama always carries him."

"Hmm..." I said grimly. "So I see."

Sergio, restored on my lap, amused himself by fiddling with my hair.

"I shall call you Snap-On," I told him in English. Snap-On stared back at me and thoughtfully stuck his finger up my nose.

"He's like a growth," muttered Joe in English. "I think the only way you can remove him is surgically."

"What are you saying?" asked Fairy #1 suspiciously.

"We do not understand what you are saying," said Fairy #2.

"Oh, we were just saying what a big family you are," said Joe, in Spanish.

"Yes," I chimed in. "There's your Papa, Mama, your *abuela*, big brother..."

"Jorge..." said Fairy #1.

"And your little brother..."

"Scrap," mouthed Joe.

"Carlos," corrected Fairy #2, frowning at Joe.

"Then there's little Sergio here..."

"Snap-On," said Joe, taking a risk.

Snap-On stopped exploring my nose for a moment, sensing he was the centre of attention.

"And the new baby," said Fairy #1.

"In Mama's tummy," explained Fairy #2, patting her own little flat one.

Joe and I looked at each other with raised eyebrows. Another on the way?

"And *Tía* Lola, though she doesn't live with us all the time."

"Ah, *Tía* Lola. Does she have a boyfriend?"

"*Tía* Lola has *loads* of boyfriends."

"I'm sure she does..." said Joe, dryly.

"And don't forget Fifi!" said Fairy #2.

"Oh no, you mustn't forget Fifi!" The fairies were adamant, even stopping their cooking to ensure we didn't forget Fifi.

"Fifi? Who is Fifi? Where is she?" I asked. "Is she another sister?"

The fairies rolled their eyes and shook their heads and wings in unison but an explanation was not forthcoming. I was about to question them further when it suddenly dawned on me that the bang-bang-thud of the football outside had stopped. Anybody who has been a mother, or in charge of children, will relate to this - when children go quiet, alarm bells ring. There is usually trouble afoot. And there was.

Not a sound came from the boys in the garden, no voices, no football being kicked.

"Quick, Joe, take Snap-On." I hissed. "There's something not quite right in the garden. I'd better get out there and take a look."

Mama Ufarte's Lemony Sponge Cake

Bizcocho

This is a very quick sponge, quite dense in texture with a lovely lemony tang.

5 large eggs
150g (6 oz) sugar
150g (6oz) flour
3/4 tsp baking powder
Finely grated rind of 1/2 lemon

Divide the sugar in half. Separate the eggs and beat the whites into one half of the sugar until the mixture is stiff.

Beat the egg yolks into the other half of sugar, then fold the two halves together.

Sift the flour and baking powder. Add the lemon and add to the mixture, little by little.

Place in a lightly greased round baking tin and bake in the middle of a pre-heated oven at 180 degrees for approximately 20 minutes.

Note: The Spanish often eat bizcocho for breakfast with coffee or hot chocolate. It is also delicious as a dessert served with icecream.

3
An Expedition

I thrust the toddler at Joe. Startled, Joe took him. Snap-On's gripping instincts kicked in, and, like a spider monkey, he curled his fat little legs and arms around Joe. The fairies were not concerned, and continued with their baking session on the floor.

I hurried into the garden, very aware of the devastation the Ufarte boys' football had already caused. I averted my eyes from the ruined geraniums with their scarlet petals littering the patio like confetti. I didn't allow myself to focus on the flattened shrubs, some with limbs snapped at crazy angles like broken arms. I was searching for the boys.

Ginger and Regalo

And then I saw them. They stood with their backs to me, side by side, Jorge's arm around his little brother's shoulders. Both were staring into the chicken coop with huge interest. *Ah,* I thought. *They're fascinated by the chickens! How sweet!* I smiled fondly and tiptoed up behind them, not wanting to disturb their rapt concentration.

"They will come out any second, Carlos! Are you ready? Do it like I showed you!" Jorge was speaking in a stage whisper.

On cue, Atilla the Hen, always the leader of the pack, strutted out from behind the hen-house wall, closely followed by Regalo, Ginger and 'Ello Vera.

"*Uno, dos,* NOW!" hissed Jorge, fairly dancing with excitement.

Scrap obeyed. A powerful stream of water shot out, soaking the unsuspecting hens. "BAWKKKK!" The chickens squawked with indignation, and, dripping and flapping, hurtled back behind the hen-house wall, out of sight and out of range.

The hose! I hadn't noticed the hose which I'd foolishly left lying around, complete with its irresistible gun and trigger. I'd left it on the 'Sprinkle' setting to water my precious plants, but of course the little baboons had twisted the nozzle to 'Jet'.

"No!" I said firmly, making the boys jump and interrupting their glee. "No! That's not nice! You are NOT allowed to shoot the chickens!"

Jorge had the grace to look a little guilty. He picked up the football and bounced it self-consciously, avoiding my eyes. Scrap, however, was not going to relinquish his weapon without a fight.

"Give me the hose," I said, holding out my hand.

"No!" said Scrap round his dummy, his face a mask of determination.

"Well, then I'll have to take it from you."

"No!"

Scrap aimed a kick at my ankle, which connected accurately and painfully. Hopping, I tried to prise the gun out of the infant's surprisingly vice-like grip. But that was my mistake.

I prefer to think Scrap didn't aim at me purposely, but in the effort to hang onto the gun, he pulled it into his chest with both hands, and squeezed the trigger. The jet of water that shot out absolutely drenched me.

Jorge stopped bouncing the football and gaped as I wrestled the gun off his little brother. I won, of course, but at a cost. I was soaked to the skin while Scrap remained bone dry.

Seething, I wound up the hose and locked it in the workshop. I left the boys to destroy what was left of my beloved flowers and dripped my way back indoors.

The kitchen was a scene of calm domesticity. The fairies were serving Joe and Snap-On with imaginary cake and invisible hot chocolate.

Joe looked up. "Good gracious!" he said. "I didn't realise it was raining."

I gave him one of my Looks. "Right," I said, stepping over bowls and saucepans and drying myself with a hand-towel. "Give me Snap-On and I'll look after the twins. You take those two urchins to the square to kick their football around. And don't come back until they're exhausted."

"But it's raining..."

"It is *not* raining."

Joe stared at me for a second. His eyebrows may have flicked in surprise, but he had the good sense not to ask questions or argue.

"Soccer in the square? Right! Sounds good."

I reclaimeded Snap-On and Joe departed with the two boys. I was beginning to calm down. I adjusted Snap-On on my damp hip and looked down at the playing girls. This was going to be a good deal easier than entertaining their brothers.

"That's a lovely game you're playing," I said.

Simultaneously, both fairies pushed the kitchen paraphernalia away and got to their feet.

"We don't want to play Cooking anymore," said Fairy #1.

"Because it's no fun without *Tío* Joe," said Fairy #2.

"*Tío* Joe talks funny..."

"But we still understand him."

"And he's very good at playing Cooking."

"And he tastes everything."

So! Uncle Joe had scored a hit with the fairies? I tried not to feel resentful. There he was playing gentle games with the little girls while I'd been outside, wrestling with the devil's spawn, and getting soaked for my efforts. I gently drew Snap-On's finger out of my left nostril and wracked my brains, trying to think of an amazing game that would both entertain the fairies and raise my own status.

"Let's go on a Nature Walk," I said, sounding more enthusiastic than I felt.

"Where?" Fairy #1 narrowed her eyes suspiciously.

"Oh, out in the garden... Maybe round the village?"

"What will we see?" asked Fairy #2.

I had no idea. "Oh, that's part of the adventure!" I said. "We could see *anything!*"

"Sabre-toothed tigers?"

"Um, probably not..." The scathing look the fairies aimed at me told me I was probably going to be a huge disappointment to them, not a patch on Uncle Joe.

"*Tío* Joe said there are sabre-toothed tigers in the woods behind the cemetery," challenged Fairy #1.

"He did?' I narrowed my eyes. *Uncle Joe is going to pay for that!*

"Can we take some nets and traps and things?"

"And some meat, just *in case* we see a sabre-toothed tiger?"

"Excellent idea," I said warmly. With my spare hand, I opened the fridge and took out the steak I was going to grill for Joe's dinner. The fairies brightened and started looking for other essential Nature Walk equipment. Together, we rummaged in the workshop to see what we could find. The result was:

A tennis racquet (for catching flying creatures)
Bucket and spade (for digging out underground creatures)
An old walking stick (in case we needed to rescue a lost lamb)
A long piece of string (to lead the tiger home)
A jam jar (for any other creatures)

Armed with Joe's steak (in case we encountered a sabre-toothed tiger), the expedition was ready.

"*Tía* Veeky, can Fifi come with us?" asked Fairy #1, gazing up at me with dark, soulful eyes.

"Fifi likes Nature Walks," said Fairy #2.

"Er, where is Fifi?" I asked.

"Fifi is outside, with our *abuela*."

"Oh! I didn't see her. Well, why not? Yes, Fifi can come."

The fairies skipped ahead of me, out of the front door, and into the street. I hurried behind as best as I could, laden with Snap-On and most of the Nature Walk equipment. I was very much looking forward to meeting Fifi. Perhaps she would help me carry some of the stuff.

"Fifi! Fifi! *¡Vamos!* We're going for a Nature Walk to see sabre-toothed tigers!" The fairies were very excited, their pink shoes barely touching the dusty street as they ran to Granny Ufarte amidst the heap of furniture.

Granny Ufarte slumbered on in her armchair, mouth working, head lolled to one side, oblivious to the world. But the mound of untidy grey wool on her lap suddenly wriggled and sat up.

So this was Fifi! A tiny Yorkshire terrier, teacup size, I believe they're called. She jumped off Granny Ufarte's lap, shook herself in a blur of silver and danced after the fairies who were already heading for the woods behind the cemetery.

I once watched a Spanish television show where people in the street were asked which month of the year was their favourite. Most agreed, April, and I wouldn't argue. The sun is warm, but not fierce, and the mountainsides are lush with new grass and wild flowers. As though an artist has flicked paint randomly over the landscape, splashes of crazy colour dot the hillsides. The wild figs unfurl tender leaves, and the olive trees stand knee deep in poppies, providing a stage for every bird to sing for a mate.

April is when the sneaky cuckoo arrives in the valley. The first carpenter bees appear, blundering blindly, noisy as little jet engines as they search for a home. The first swallows arrive from Africa, performing aerobatics against a vivid blue sky. At twilight, foxes and ibex call, their unearthly cries echoing around the valley.

But today I didn't appreciate the beautiful April day. I was far too intent upon catching up with the Ufarte fairies and Fifi, already far ahead.

"I wish you would walk," I said crossly to Snap-On who seemed to get heavier every second. Balancing him, the bucket and spade, the tennis racquet and the walking stick wasn't easy. I glanced across at the little patch of cultivated land where Uncle Felix grew neat lines of baby lettuce. The new green leaves contrasted vividly against the freshly watered black soil.

The fairies' footfalls on the street ahead suddenly softened as the ground beneath their feet changed from hard road to old pine needles. I followed them into the wood.

Exchanging the bright sunlight for the soft dappled shade of the pine trees, I sat down on a fallen log. I inhaled a deep breath of the scented air and little Snap-On aped me, drawing in a big breath and letting it out with an exaggerated sigh. I noticed the needles at the tip of each branch were lime green with new growth.

"*Tía* Veeky, we can't find any Nature!" called a fairy.

"We've looked everywhere, there's no Nature anywhere!"

"Well, keep looking! I've got the meat ready here in case you see the sabre-toothed tiger." I was enjoying the rest too much to follow them farther into the wood. They would be perfectly safe. There were few people in the village, and El Hoyo was the safest place we'd ever lived in.

All too soon, the fairies were weary of tramping through the wood and reappeared, looking bedraggled, leaves and twigs caught in their clothes and wings. I noticed one fairy had torn a hole in her pink tights. Fifi bounded out of a bush and sat panting at my feet, her pink tongue quivering. I scratched her behind the ears, and she rolled onto her back hoping for a tummy tickle.

"Fifi likes you," said Fairy #1.

"And she doesn't like everyone..." said Fairy #2. A tiny alarm bell rang in my head, but why should a comment like that sound like a warning?

"Anyway, we couldn't find the sabre-toothed tiger," went on Fairy #1. "And we looked everywhere!"

"This wood hasn't got any Nature in it," announced Fairy #2, hands on her hips.

"You said we'd find lots of Nature!" said Fairy #1.

"Now, come on, this wood is full of wonderful things," I said, putting on my teacher hat. "You just have to know where to look." I stood up and pointed at a pine branch. "It's spring! Look how green the pine needles are. And all the new buds are opening on this bush." I twisted the branch down. Snap-On seized it and stuffed it into his

Baked Baby Lettuce

This slightly unusual dish is a great side dish or starter.

4 baby lettuces such as Little Gem
Half litre (17 fl oz) chicken or vegetable stock
2 tablespoons extra virgin olive oil
Few sprigs fresh thyme
Few sprigs fresh rosemary
Salt and pepper

Wash the lettuces, trim off the ends and remove any brown outer leaves. Place the lettuces in an oven dish or earthenware cazuela and pour the stock over.
Drizzle the oil over, then pull the needles off the rosemary sprigs and the leaves off the thyme sprigs. Sprinkle over the lettuces, and season with salt and pepper.
Cover with foil or a lid and cook for 20 to 25 minutes until the lettuces are soft and tender.

mouth.

I removed it and tried again. "Listen to the birds singing! They'll be making their nests and laying eggs now."

The fairies looked unimpressed.

"What about the sabre-toothed tiger?" accused Fairy #1.

"What about the sabre-toothed tiger?" echoed Fairy #2, sticking her magic wand into a hole in the fallen log.

"Well, I suppose he must have gone out for the day," I answered, and gave up.

Suddenly, one of the fairies squealed, startling Fifi who jumped to her feet.

"Oh! Oh! Look what I have found!"

"Oh!" sighed Fairy #2 (or was it Fairy #1?) her hands clasped under her chin in rapture.

There was a bush sprouting out from under the log I was sitting on. Creeping across one of the leaves, almost the same colour as the leaf itself, was a caterpillar. It looked suspiciously like a cabbage-white, the kind I declared war on back in England.

"Oh! I found some Nature!" sighed Fairy #1.

"Clever girl," I said. "Now, *that* is the best caterpillar I've ever seen!"

"Is it? Better than *all* the caterpillars you have ever seen?"

"Much better!"

"We will keep him," she said. "His name will be Francisco."

So we picked some leaves and stuffed them into the jam jar, and gently placed Francisco in, too. Then we collected all our equipment and wandered out of the wood. Fifi scampered behind, stopping to snuffle at every rock and tree.

"I do not think Mama will like Francisco," said Fairy #1 sadly.

"Mama does not like things with many legs," agreed Fairy #2.

"We'll worry about that later," I said. "Come on, let's see what *Tío* Joe and your brothers are doing..."

4
Football and Fifi

Before we even reached the square, we could hear the sounds of a game of football in progress. Joe always maintains that soccer is a universal language, transcending all international and generation barriers. And here was proof.

It appeared to be an evenly matched game between Barcelona and Real Madrid. Representing Barcelona were Joe and Jorge Ufarte. Joe was glowing red with exertion, puffing and gasping, trying valiantly to pass the ball to Jorge. The Real Madrid team comprised Geronimo and little Scrap. Geronimo had generously abandoned his beer bottle which was standing in the shade on a bench, awaiting his return. His three dogs lay panting, tongues lolling, guarding the half-empty bottle. Scrap Ufarte pelted after the ball, elbows out, legs pumping, the dummy in his mouth clenched with grim determination.

This game even had spectators. Old Marcia had emerged from her shop and was seated in the shade beside Uncle Felix, fanning herself with a bunch of letters. Uncle Felix sat with folded arms, cloth cap drawn down to shade his eyes. His bony frame took up very little space on the bench. Nearby, his mule was tethered to a lamp-post, resting, head hung low, one large watchful eye on her beloved master.

"Don't you want to get down and play soccer?" I asked little Snap-On. "I'll take that as a 'no' then," I sighed as I felt his arms and legs wrap tighter, and his fingers dig deeper.

Joe had just taken possession of the ball.

"To me! Over here!" yelled Jorge, dancing from foot to foot, anticipating the ball.

Joe glanced up, positioned himself, and swung his leg right back, poised to take an almighty kick at the ball. Then a most unexpected thing happened, causing Joe's foot never to make contact with that ball.

And why did Joe's foot never connect? Because at that moment he came face to foot with what was to become his archenemy.

From behind me, a snarling streak of silver flashed past, hurling herself straight at Joe's raised foot. Small sharp teeth sank into his ankle. Fifi! He never even saw her coming.

"What the..?" he yelled, leaping into the air in surprise. He was ready to do battle, but cunning Fifi had already darted away and was hiding behind Fairy #2.

"Oh! Fifi does not like *Tío* Joe," observed Fairy #1.

"She does not mean to hurt you, *Tío* Joe!" said Fairy #2.

"Stupid mutt has a funny way of showing it..." Joe growled, rubbing his nipped ankle and glaring balefully at Fifi.

Scrap and Jorge were clearly familiar with Fifi's delinquent behaviour. Unconcerned, they chased the football round the square. Geronimo, amused by the Brit versus Manic Mop incident, used the interlude to re-acquaint himself with his beer bottle. Marcia and Uncle Felix sat side by side on the bench, watching, but uninvolved.

Fifi

"What brought that on?" protested Joe. "Look at her, she's going to have another go at me!"

Sure enough, Fifi, snarling softly, was preparing herself for a second attack. As fast as a hairy bullet from a rifle, she shot straight for Joe. Joe backed away, but Fifi was committed. Deaf to the fairies' calls, she nipped at Joe's ankles.

"Stop it!" yelled Joe, twirling and dancing in an effort to escape the determined little dog. "Get her off me!"

Then I had an idea. The sabre-toothed tiger bait! I pulled the beef steak out of my pocket with the hand that was not clasping Snap-On.

"Fifi!" I called, waggling the steak in her direction. "Fifi! Look what I've got!"

I saw a dark beady eye glinting through her fringe, and with one last warning snarl at Joe, she scampered over to me.

"Naughty, *naughty* Fifi," said Fairy #2 fondly, tapping her gently on the head with her magic wand.

"You must not bite *Tío* Joe," said Fairy #1.

Fifi stopped in front of me and sat begging, front paws pedaling the air. What could I do? I gave her the steak, of course.

Joe was still ruefully rubbing his ankle when the minibus drew up. I hadn't even noticed its arrival in the excitement. Geronimo glanced into the car, saw who was sitting in the back, flushed red and retreated.

"Mama! Papa! *Tía* Lola!" chorused the fairies. Snap-On bounced excitedly on my hip and his big brothers abandoned their game and ran over.

Mama Ufarte wound down her window. "Have you been good?" she smiled. "Have you had a lovely time with *Tío* Joe and *Tía* Veeky?" Lola, in the back seat, smiled and twiddled a lock of hair. I caught her looking across at Geronimo, busy with his beer.

"We've been playing soccer,' said Jorge.

Scrap grinned silently around his dummy.

"We have a new pet!" said Fairy #1. "He is a caterpillar and his name is Francisco." She held up the jam jar for her mother to see.

"Very nice, darling, but you cannot bring it into the house."

Both fairies' faces dropped. I stepped forward and took the jam jar. "I'll look after Francisco," I said. "Your Mama has enough little ones to look after. He'll be safe with me."

"And where is my little Fifi?" asked Mama Ufarte. "Has she been a good little doggy while I've been away?"

"Huh!" grunted Joe and quickly turned it into a cough. Fifi had demolished her steak and trotted forward. Mama Ufarte opened the car door, leaned down, scooped her up and made a fuss of her.

"Have you been playing tennis?" Papa Ufarte asked me, leaning across his wife and eyeing the tennis racquet.

"No," I said, but didn't elaborate.

"Well, we must go," said Mama Ufarte. She handed Fifi to Lola behind her and held her arms out for Snap-On. I released him and he coiled himself up on her lap, gurgling happily.

"I hope you've been a good boy," she said, ruffling his hair. "Now, why don't you children run on ahead and tell your *abuela* we're home? Your Papa and I will follow in the minibus."

The children raced away and Papa Ufarte started the engine. "*Hasta luego*," he called. "See you later! It is nice to know there is somebody next door who will look after the children whenever we need."

"Yeah, right..." I heard Joe mutter in English and I kicked him on his already sore ankle, making him yelp.

The minibus accelerated away, and Joe and I collected up the tennis racquet, walking-stick, bucket and spade. We waved to Marcia, Uncle Felix and Geronimo and headed home. Joe put his arm through mine as we walked.

"What a day!" he said. "I'm exhausted. And hungry. By the way, what *were* you doing with the walking-stick and tennis racquet? And the bucket and spade?"

"It's a long story..." I said.

"I think that wretched Fifi would still be stalking and attacking me if you hadn't shown her the meat." Joe went on, then paused and I saw his brow furrow. "Just a minute! That meat... Am I right in guessing that steak's off the menu tonight and it's scrambled eggs for dinner instead?"

I nodded and began a countdown silently, in my head. *Five, four, three, two, one, zero...* Right on cue...

"What? WHAT? Do you mean that bad-tempered, hairy little monster has just eaten my dinner? My steak? I don't bloody believe it!

You gave my steak to that delinquent midget Yorkshire terrier? First they dump their kids on us - without even a 'thank you' - then their dog savages me for no reason! And then, *then* you give my dinner to that malicious little tyke?"

Of course I've sanitised this rant, no reader deserves to be exposed to the full, unexpurgated version. Suffice it to say that Joe was still polluting the air with expletives as we reached our front door.

Much later, after our supper of scrambled eggs, I caught Joe with that faraway look in his eyes again.

"What's bothering you?" I asked. "Is it the Ufarte family?"

Joe shook his head. "The Ufartes? No, of course not."

"Well, what is it? I know something is bothering you. Aren't you happy here in El Hoyo? Are you sorry we decided to stay?"

"No, no! I love our life here. It's just that..."

I waited, but Joe refused to say more.

Spring is the time for new beginnings, and that year it was certainly true in El Hoyo. After Uncle Felix's severe winter pruning, our grapevine sprang into life, juicy green leaves unfolding and reaching for the sun. Day by day, corkscrew tendrils groped for supports until, once again, we had a thick green canopy shading our patio. Sparrows flocked into our chicken coop to steal grain and strands of straw for their nests. Gorgeous bee-eaters arrived from Africa, their feathers a frenzied flash of crazy colours. The valley rang with their incessant chatter and calls as they flew in flocks from tree to telephone wire. Expert excavators, they bored perfectly round nest holes in the cliff-face, as efficient as any workman's drill.

Bee-Eaters
(photo by Kiersten Rowland)

On our kitchen windowsill, Francisco the caterpillar spun himself a silken cocoon and transformed into a chrysalis. Every time I saw the Ufarte twins, they'd ask, "How is Francisco? Can we come in and see him?"

Even in our chicken coop there were new beginnings, although not, as one would expect, of the feathered variety.

Beef in Sherry

This Spanish recipe for beef uses sherry along with various herbs to create a real flavour of Spain. The dish is quite spicy although only fresh herbs are used. It is best served with Spanish rice or on a simple salad. Any leftover beef strips also make unusual but flavoursome Spanish tapas.

1kg (2.25 lb) beef
8 tablespoons Oloroso or sweet sherry
1 red bell pepper, diced
1 small onion, diced
5 leaves of mint, chopped
2 sprigs of rosemary
3 garlic cloves, sliced
6 sprigs broadleaf parsley, chopped
Olive oil
Salt
Cracked black pepper
Cut the beef into inch-wide steaks, then into half-inch wide strips (as if for fajitas)

In a frying pan, heat some olive oil. Add the beef strips and two rosemary sprigs and fry for 5 minutes. Season well with salt and pepper.
When the steak begins to brown all over add the garlic, onion and pepper and stir well, cooking for a further 5 minutes.
When the onion has softened add the Oloroso sherry and cook over maximum heat, tossing for 5 minutes.
Let the juices bubble and throw in the mint leaves and parsley.
When the sherry has evaporated remove the beef.
Serve over fresh salad or rice immediately.

Tip: For tapas, serve any leftover strips of beef on top of tomatoes or peppers, drizzle with olive oil and enjoy with bread.

5
Little Tabs

Cats became part of our lives when we moved to El Hoyo in the summer of 2004. Most were feral and roamed the village, hiding beneath cars or in derelict buildings, away from dogs and humans. Rarely did they venture into the open. But the daily delivery of fish to the village flushed them out in large numbers. When the fish van hooted its horn at the top of the mountain road, as many as 30 cats would magically appear outside Marcia's shop, along with the village ladies, awaiting the arrival of the fish van. El Hoyo was the last on the fish man's itinerary of villages, and the cats were assured of fish scraps which they carried away to eat in private. Sometimes they used our garden as a sanctuary, but bolted if we approached.

However, a few became accustomed to Joe and me and although keeping us at paw's length, were happy to accept any offerings we left in a bowl on our kitchen window sill.

The first was a village cat we named Thief Cat because she stole fish from our barbecue when our backs were turned. She took up residence in our garden for a year or so, before disappearing altogether. Whether she died of old age or strayed away, we never knew.

Then old Marcia gave us Sancho, a kitten born to her own cat. Little Sancho sadly also disappeared, although I never stopped looking for him.

Then another feral cat moved into our garden. We suspected this newcomer was Thief Cat's daughter. A typical tiger tabby with huge green eyes and perfect stripes, she became very tame, although she never allowed us to touch her. She learned to wait on the kitchen window-sill, peering in on our activities until we fed her. We named her Little Tabs.

Little Tabs

Little Tabs soon learned our routine and knew when we were preparing food in the evening. As Joe chopped vegetables and meat, her emerald eyes bored through the glass, watching every move he made. Sometimes she would lightly pat the window glass, as though asking him to hurry up.

"Patience, Little Tabs," he would say. "Dinner's coming. Look, I've already set aside this nice pile of beefy bits for you. I'll be finished in just a minute."

Then he'd open the window and Little Tabs would spring away, always nervous, always shy. He'd set down the dish of treats while Little Tabs watched, focused and alert, but just out of reach.

"There you are, enjoy!" Joe said, withdrawing his hand and pulling the window shut. As soon as the window-latch clicked closed, Little Tabs resumed her position on the sill and devoured his offerings, enthusiastically licking the plate so clean that it clattered. Satisfied, she'd stay to wash, her velvet paw moving over her face in light circular strokes. Fed and washed, she'd sit for a while in what I called the 'tea-cosy position' before melting away into the night.

One night, back in the depths of winter when the frost had scattered a layer of diamonds on all the dead leaves on the ground, we were disturbed in our cosy house by a caterwauling outside. Joe switched on the outside lamp and the garden flooded with light. On every available surface crouched a tomcat. On the garden chairs, the wall, the water tank, the chicken-house, the woodshed roof and on every step of the cast-iron staircase leading up to the roof terrace. There must have been a dozen or more of them.

Tomcats of every shape and size. Black ones, tabbies, tortoiseshells, black and white ones, tomcats with Siamese looks, battered old bruisers, alert youngsters, huge tomcats, skinny tomcats, tomcats everywhere. Green eyes, blue eyes, orange eyes, dozens of pairs of cats' eyes, all smouldering with passion.

Little Tabs's Suitors

And the object of their desire? Little Tabs, of course.

"Get out of our garden!" yelled Joe, grabbing the garden hose. But even with the jet of icy water trained on them, the tomcats slunk just out of range, watching, waiting. Lust had given them courage and they had no intention of abandoning their mission.

"Leave Little Tabs alone!" Joe bawled at the ardent suitors. "She doesn't want you here!"

But he was wrong, of course. Little Tabs was shameless. She arched and mewed and rolled on the ground, inviting her admirers to approach.

"You hussy!" said Joe, frowning at her with disapproval. But he had to admit defeat. Little Tabs didn't want her virtue protected.

The army of tomcats stayed in our garden for nearly three days and nothing deterred them. Gradually, they faded away until only Little Tabs remained. Joe forgave her, peace returned and we forgot all about it.

Then one terrible day in February, I was sweeping off the front doorstep, a job that always made me feel very Spanish, when I noticed a pile of something looking like dirty rags a little further up the street. I investigated, and to my absolute horror, it was Little Tabs. She was hurt, badly hurt. Cars are infrequent in El Hoyo, but there was no doubt that Little Tabs had been hit by a car or tractor, and she was barely alive.

"Joe! Quick! Get the car keys! Little Tabs has been hit by a car, and we need to get her to the vet fast!"

Joe ran out, squatted down and looked at poor Little Tabs. Her green eyes were open, and spoke of shock and pain. There was blood, and one of her legs was bent at an impossible angle.

"Poor little thing," I said, stroking her head, something she'd never allowed me to do before. "I'll get a blanket, we need to get her to the vet as fast as possible."

I scooted inside, grabbed a big towel and rejoined Joe. Very carefully, we wrapped her up and lifted her gently into the car, then sped down the mountain to the vet.

Little Tabs was still breathing, but only just. Thankfully she was unconscious so I hoped she wasn't suffering at all. Blood soaked alarmingly through the towel.

"Stay alive, Little Tabs," I whispered to her. "We're nearly there."

It was the longest trip down the mountain that I ever remember, but finally we arrived and Joe carried Little Tabs inside.

The vet's assistant summed up the situation with a practiced eye, and took the bundle from Joe, jumping the queue of waiting animals and fast-tracking Little Tabs into the vet's operating theatre. The door shut firmly behind her, so Joe and I sat down to wait.

The door opened again, and the assistant beckoned us inside. Little Tabs lay on the table. Apart from her head, a white cloth covered her whole body. The lady vet looked up at us and spoke, sympathy in her eyes.

"I'm sorry," she said, "your cat is very badly hurt. I have given her a sedative so she is comfortable now."

"Can you save her?" I asked, dreading the answer.

"Your cat has extensive injuries. Her head has been hit, and she has many broken ribs and bones. With your permission, I think the kindest thing would be to give her an injection and let her go."

"Put her to sleep?"

"She will not feel a thing. Her injuries are too massive for me to be able to help her."

I looked down at Little Tabs, my heart thumping. Joe squeezed my hand and I heard him sigh deeply.

"It's for the best," he said.

I nodded and stroked Little Tabs's head one last time. I would miss her. I would miss her face at the kitchen window. I would miss her green unblinking stare. I would miss seeing her asleep in the garden. And we would never see her kittens, kittens conceived in our garden but destined never to be born. Hot tears welled in my eyes.

We stood there a little longer looking down at Little Tabs's shape under the white shroud, and her familiar face and ears. Her eyes were closed now, the emerald green lights switched off for ever. Then Joe put his arm around my shoulder and turned me away. He guided me out of the room, through the waiting-room and outside.

"Excuse me! *¿Señor? ¡Señor!*" A voice floated out of the reception area.

Dumbly, we turned back to see the vet's assistant waving at us. Obediently, we went back inside. The assistant had her pen poised over a stack of papers.

"The bill," she said. "That will be 60 euros, please. How would you like to pay?"

"That's a bit steep!" said Joe, scratching his groin. "She's not even our cat, she's a feral cat we feed sometimes."

The assistant looked surprised, and all the waiting pets and owners watched with interest.

"It's okay, we'll pay," I said quickly, giving Joe one of my Looks and opening my purse.

We were silent all the way back up the mountain. I was remembering all the times that Little Tabs had sat on our window-sill waiting to be fed and how she lightly tapped the window pane to get our attention.

Back in our kitchen, I made coffee. We sipped it silently, each lost in our own thoughts.

Suddenly, Joe stiffened and stared past me, over my shoulder. I swung round to see what he was looking at.

"Oh my G..." I whispered. "It's a ghost!"

We both stared at the tabby cat sitting on the kitchen window, its emerald eyes staring back at us. The cat raised a paw and lightly tapped the glass.

"That's no ghost!" said Joe. "That's Little Tabs!"

Joe and I stared at each other, mouths agape, then back at the cat.

"It can't be..."

"I'm telling you, it is! That is Little Tabs."

"Then who was the cat we took down to the vet?" I asked.

"No idea... Must have been another village cat." Then the facts sank in. "I don't believe it! Have we just paid a vet bill for a strange cat? We shelled out 60 euros to have a strange cat put down?"

I didn't care. I was overjoyed to have Little Tabs back and filled her bowl with chunks of our best Serrano ham to celebrate. I felt terribly sorry for that other poor cat, but to have Little Tabs back on our window-sill was wonderful.

"Well, it's good to have Little Tabs back, whatever," admitted Joe eventually, having finally stopped complaining.

In the weeks that followed, Little Tabs continued to visit us, to wait for food on our window-sill, and we watched her grow rounder daily. She looked healthy and glossy, and we knew her kittens would be born soon.

One April day, I was cleaning out the chicken coop when I heard tiny sounds coming from the laying boxes. Puzzled, I put down my broom and went to investigate. A flurry of stripes sprang out of a box and streaked past me. I peeped into the dark laying box and could just make out two tiny newborn kittens nestled on the bed of straw. Little Tabs was a mother.

"Joe! Joe! You'll never guess what I've just discovered in the chicken coop!"

"Eggs?"

But even he was surprised when I told him. Feral cats usually hide their litters well away from human interference. Little Tabs trusted us enough to give birth to her litter in our garden, in our chicken coop. We felt very honoured.

We kept our distance, but made sure Little Tabs had a constant supply of food and saucers of milk. The chickens ignored the new cat family and chose other boxes to lay their eggs in. I took sneaky looks at the kittens when Little Tabs's back was turned, and they were doing well. I could already tell that one was destined to be a beautiful silver tabby, and the other was a replica of her mother.

We were undecided about what to do. Should we try and tame these kittens and attempt to find them homes? Would Little Tabs allow us to handle them? Or should we allow her to raise them alone to join the rest of the village cat community?

It turned out that the decision was taken out of our hands when old Marcia hobbled up to our house to deliver a letter. I knew she liked cats because she had one of her own, and I was excited about our new family.

"Don't show the kittens to anybody," Joe had warned. "You know what the Spanish are like with village cats."

"Marcia! Do come in and see our new kittens!" I should have kept quiet, should have heeded Joe's warning, but I didn't.

"Kittens? There are too many cats in this village already," grumbled Marcia, but she hobbled behind me to see them anyway.

In the chicken coop, the hens crowded round, necks craning to see if we were bringing treats. Little Tabs watched us approach, her body tensing as we drew closer. At the last second, she streaked away in a flurry of stripes and sat high on the garden wall, very still, watching, emerald eyes unblinking. Marcia's gnarled old hand reached into the laying box and scooped up both kittens.

"*¡Qué bonitos!*" she exclaimed. "How beautiful! This little grey one is going to be a real beauty." The kittens' eyes were still closed but they mewled and squirmed in her hands, their tummies round and fat from good mothering. I looked up at the wall. Little Tabs had us locked in her emerald stare.

When Marcia had gone, Joe and I sat in the garden to watch what would happen next. When Little Tabs was absolutely sure that the coast was clear, she crept back into the chicken coop, straight to her babies. Minutes later, she reappeared, one fat, limp kitten dangling from her mouth. Up she leaped onto the garden wall and out of sight. Ten minutes elapsed before she came back. Into the chicken coop she darted, emerging with the second kitten. Then a mighty jump onto the wall before disappearing into the village.

"Well, that's that," said Joe. "I told you not to mention them."

I sighed. My heart was heavy. I knew that we'd probably never see them again and it was my fault. I'd betrayed Little Tabs's secret hiding place and she felt forced to relocate her babies.

Little Tabs returned to us to be fed, but never stayed for long now she had a family to raise. I often wondered how the kittens were coming along and hoped one day she would bring them to see us. Many weeks were to pass before we saw those kittens again, and then it was in bitter-sweet circumstances.

6
The Monstrosity

The cats and wildlife were not the only nest-builders. The Ufarte family next door had begun renovations, and the drilling, mixing and hammering became a constant background noise as they refurbished their little house. Unlike the other villagers who usually came to El Hoyo just for weekends, the Ufarte family arrived randomly, stayed a few days, then vanished again. And they rarely came alone. If the Ufarte minibus drew up, it was usually tailed by several other cars filled with friends, family members, tool boxes, cement mixers and tile cutters.

And the Ufarte noise didn't cease at nightfall. As bats swooped overhead, Papa Ufarte, seated on their doorstep, dreamily strummed his guitar. Sometimes the visitors brought guitars, too, and washed our street with sultry Spanish music and applause. Mama Ufarte would rise to her feet and sway her hips, carried away by the rhythm of the music. If Lola was there, they'd dance side by side. Tossing back their black hair, they entered a kind of trance, feet tapping, hands clapping, bodies sinuous and graceful. Friends and relations joined in, until the street was a mass of whirling, clapping and foot-tapping Flamenco.

Mediterranean Chicken Tapas

Homemade mini chicken bites Mediterranean style, with hints of garlic and lemon, perfect for outdoor summer evenings.

2 chicken breasts
4 cloves garlic
Juice of 2 lemons
4 tablespoons olive oil
Flour

Cut the chicken breasts into bite-sized pieces.
Place the chicken into a bowl, add the olive oil, the juice of two lemons and the garlic, peeled and crushed.
Leave to marinate for 2 to 3 hours in the fridge.
Once marinated, roll the chicken pieces in the flour. Shake off the excess and fry in hot olive oil for about 15 to 20 minutes until golden brown and tender.
Sprinkle with a little salt, serve with alioli (garlic mayonnaise) or tomato salsa.

Sometimes Geronimo joined the party, but I never saw him dance. He would remain seated, staring longingly at Lola, hooded eyes following her every move, one finger lightly stroking the side of his beer bottle.

In the bungalow on the plot of land behind our house, the

newlyweds, Federico and Roberto, were also nest-building. The year before, their plot of land had been our orchard, but, reluctantly, we'd had two bungalows built on it. One of these was purchased by Federico and Roberto: The Boys. They moved in, but before long, we saw architects with clip-boards taking measurements. Soon after, a gang of Romanian workmen arrived and The Boys' bungalow began to grow upwards. In weeks it gained another level and finally a roof terrace. It was a bungalow no more.

One Saturday, we were sitting in Paco and Carmen-Bethina's little kitchen. We'd been invited to sample Paco's latest batch of home-made wine, which, as every year, Paco insisted was unquestionably the best batch yet. Joe complimented Paco on its clarity and fruitiness, then launched into his favourite topic of the moment.

"Building, building!" said Joe. "If it's not the Ufartes on one side of us, then it's The Boys on the other."

"Oh, you do not like the noise?" asked Carmen-Bethina sympathetically.

"It's not the noise that bothers me, it's their new roof terrace," growled Joe, forgetting his manners and irritably scratching himself down below. "Federico and Roberto can see right down into our garden now. We've lost all our privacy."

"Don't worry," I said. "You know the Spanish aren't like us crazy English - they don't sit out in the sun. I bet they'll hardly ever use their roof terrace, especially as they're building a swimming pool in their garden. And the grapevine gives us a lot of privacy in the summer."

Carmen-Bethina nodded.

"Pah!" shouted Paco, thumping the table with his clenched fist and making me jump. "Never mind Federico and Roberto and their roof terrace! What about the new apartments?"

"*¡Claro!*" said Carmen-Bethina. "Yes, what about the new apartments!"

"What new apartments?" we asked.

Paco leaned forward. "You know the olive grove below? Near the dry river bed? Well! The Mayor may give permission for a block of apartments to be built!" Paco leaned back in his chair, enjoying our reaction. "The building will be four floors high, 27 apartments!"

Joe and I gaped.

"An apartment block? Here in the village? What is the Mayor thinking of?" Joe asked. "That wouldn't fit in with the village at all!"

"It will be a monstrosity!" Paco slammed the bottle down hard on the table, making the red wine slosh in our glasses.

"*¡Claro! Una monstruosidad.*" All Carmen-Bethina's chins wobbled in agreement.

"You mark my words," said Paco darkly. "The Mayor will soon

have a fine new house built for himself..." He refilled our glasses as we thought about that. We'd heard rumours of village Mayors receiving favours in exchange for building permits. Was that really happening in El Hoyo?

"I don't think it will really happen," I said. "Who is going to buy an apartment in El Hoyo? The village doesn't even have a proper bar or shop."

"Well, the next time I see the Mayor, I shall give him a piece of my mind. I'll tell him what I think of that crazy idea!" said Joe. "An apartment block in El Hoyo? Whatever next!"

"Now, about your grapevine," said Paco, changing the subject. "You must use this sulphur I have brought for you. It will stop the mildew." He pointed to an evil-looking sack of yellow powder leaning in a corner. "You will need a 'puffer'. Every 12 days you must puff the sulphur up into the new shoots and leaves of the grapevine. Do as I tell you, and in September, your grapes will be good, perhaps nearly as good as mine."

Joe and Paco discussed the 'puffer' at length. Apparently it resembled the bellows we used for our fire, but had a long nose with a bowl on the end. Sulphur was placed into the bowl, and the bellows action puffed doses of sulphur up into the grapevine.

"Be careful," said Paco. "Sulphur is nasty stuff. Don't let it get into your eyes, it will sting."

We took the sack of sulphur with us when we left. Outside, some of the Ufarte children and their cousins were playing in the street. Scrap kicked at an empty can, and the twins, dressed as nurses, were immersed in a game of medical make-believe. Papa Ufarte sat on his doorstep, idly twanging his guitar while Granny Ufarte slept in her arm-chair in the shade, oblivious to the ministrations of the miniature nurses intent on taking her blood pressure. The wicked Fifi sat on Granny Ufarte's lap, watching the nurses from under her fringe.

"*Tía* Veeky! How is Francisco?" called Nurse #1.

"Oh, he's very well," I said. "He's having a good sleep. He's really enjoying being a chrysalis. One day he'll climb out of his chrysalis case, unfold his wings and turn into a beautiful butterfly." Satisfied, the nurses turned back to attending to their comatose grandmother.

"Quick!" hissed Joe. "Get inside before Fifi sees me."

At the sound of Joe's voice, Fifi's head reared up. She leapt to the ground but we bolted into our house and slammed the door before she could reach us.

We were planning to go down the mountain to replenish our pantry that afternoon, so I added 'sulphur puffer' to our shopping list. The shopping trip was uneventful - until our return. In a lay-by on the mountain road, just before the turn-off down to El Hoyo, workmen were putting the finishing touches to a massive new billboard. It was an artist's impression of a new block of apartments.

Joe stopped the jeep so we could study it carefully. A photograph had been taken of the village, upon which the planned apartment block had been superimposed, providing a clear picture of what the village would look like in the future. The apartment block stood, four levels high, as Paco had said, looming malevolently over the ancient white houses like an ugly, evil giant.

"It's *awful*," Joe said at last. "Paco was right. It's a monstrosity."

I agreed wholeheartedly, and from that moment on, whenever we mentioned that building, we referred to it as The Monstrosity.

Apart from the sheer size of it, the architect, in his infinite wisdom, had decided that the building should be painted an unpleasant shade of yellow, making it even more conspicuous against the traditional white-washed cottages. The billboard shocked us to the core and we drove the short distance home in silence.

It was still light when we returned home. The evenings had lengthened and were noticeably warmer. Joe unpacked and assembled our sulphur 'puffer' purchase while I made coffee.

"Might as well give the vine its first dose tonight," said Joe, but I wasn't really listening. I had picked up Francisco's jam jar and was peering into its depths. Francisco the chrysalis, quite frankly, didn't look at all healthy. Where the pupa case had previously looked fat and shiny, now it was dull and powdery. I'm no expert, but I would have pronounced that chrysalis sick. I shook the jar gently, and to my horror, Francisco disintegrated.

"Oh no!" I groaned, turning to Joe. "Look at Francisco... He's fallen to pieces. What on earth am I going to tell the twins? They're going to need all their nursing skills to cure this!" I looked at Joe, expecting him to reply, and nearly dropped the jam jar. Joe was standing beside me, stark naked, brandishing the sulphur 'puffer'.

"What ARE you doing?" I asked in surprise.

"I'm going to puff the grapevine," he said. "Paco said the sulphur is nasty stuff. This way I won't get any on my clothes, and I'll take a shower straight afterwards. And these," he said, fishing out a pair of safety goggles from a drawer and pulling them on, "will protect my eyes."

I roared with laughter. "You look ridiculous!" I said. "Stark naked apart from a pair of goggles!"

Joe shrugged and marched purposefully out of the door into the garden.

I have a theory that life is peppered with 'cringe moments'. Incidents that, when recalled, causes one's face to flush hot with embarrassment as one relives them. I was about to add yet another 'cringe moment' to my list.

But for now, I reluctantly accepted Joe's reasoning and closed the kitchen door behind his naked rump. I wanted to stop the evil sulphur blowing back into the house, and the telephone was ringing.

Mackerel Fillets in Garlic and Paprika

Spanish mackerel recipe using some traditional Spanish ingredients.

2 mackerel fillets
3 cloves of garlic (sliced)
Broadleaf parsley
1 teaspoon smoked paprika
Splash of red wine vinegar
Salt
Cracked black pepper
Extra virgin olive oil

Heat up some olive oil in frying pan, add the mackerel fillets and fry for 2 to 3 minutes, skin side down.
Turn the fish over, season and cook for an additional 60 seconds.
When the fish is cooked, remove from the pan and plate up ready to serve.
Add a splash more olive oil to the frying pan, then throw in the garlic, parsley, vinegar, pepper and paprika. Mix and fry for 1 minute.
Pour the mixture over the mackerel fillets and serve.

Tip: This mackerel dish is great served with summer salad, boiled vegetables or simply with fresh crusty bread.

7
Half a Melon

I picked up the receiver and held it to my ear, only to grimace and quickly pull it away again. The voice was loud, upper-class British and unmistakable, a voice that hardly needed a telephone. I could have heard her shouting from the next village. Judith.

"Vicky? Vicky? Is that you?" Dogs barked excitedly and I imagined the scene. Judith trying vainly to bring her ten dogs to order, cats all over the place, and Mother, complete with face-pack, elegantly gliding around in a transparent negligee, wafting herbal cigarette smoke.

"Yes, it's me," I said. "How are you, Judith? How's Mother?"

"Oh, we're both ticketty-boo, dear gal. Fluffy, stop it! Buster, wait until I get off this ruddy phone - I'll let you out in a minute. Vicky? Oh, there you are... Mother's awfully well, thank you. Hard to believe she's in her 90's. Fluffy, no! For goodness sake, that's an antique! I told you to wait!"

"Oh, glad to hear you're both well. Joe and I haven't been over to your village for a while. Now, how can I help you, or was this just a social call?"

"Ah, yes! It's about Mother, actually, m'dear. She's knocking on a bit now, and she's taken up a new hobby, don't you know. Jolly good for her, I say! It'll keep her young!"

"Oh, that's nice. What hobby has she taken up?" My mind played over the possibilities. Modelling, perhaps? Sky-diving? Rock-climbing? I wouldn't be surprised whatever activity Mother adopted.

"She's suddenly got awfully serious about specialist vegetable gardening."

"Really? Gardening?" That sounded a bit tame for Mother.

"Yes, she's ordered these really expensive tomato seeds from Amsterdam. Cost €5 a seed, don't you know! Anyway, she's got all in fluster about them."

"Why, what's the problem?"

"It's the animals, m'dear." On cue, several of the dogs started barking, drowning out her next words. I waited.

"Sorry, Judith, I didn't quite catch that."

"Dratted dogs! BE QUIET! Right, Vicky, as I was saying... She's planted the wretched seeds, but the cats keep scratching them up and the dogs knock the pots over. She was wondering if you'd have the pots over at your place, until they grow a bit and the animals leave 'em alone. Your garden's nice and safe, isn't it?"

"Well..." I hesitated, thinking of the devastation the Ufarte boys' football had caused. "The only trouble is we have these new neighbours, the Ufartes. Their kids have done quite a bit of damage in our garden with their football."

"The Ufartes? Related to the Fish Man? Lord! I know that family well! I'll bet they're noisy! You don't let those little vandals play football in your garden, do you?"

"Well, yes. I mean, no..." Judith was right - I wouldn't be allowing those boys to play soccer in our garden again.

"So you'll take Mother's tomato plants?"

"Of course, no problem. She'll have to tell me how to take care of them, though, I don't know much about growing tomatoes."

"Jolly good, m'dear, most grateful. I'll tell Mother, and I'll bring the pots round. I'm sure there's nothing difficult about raising tomatoes."

We carried on chatting until the dogs' baying and howling rose in a crescendo and made further conversation impossible. We shouted our goodbyes and hung up. Most phone calls with Judith ended this way.

I wanted to discuss this latest development with Joe and wondered how he was getting on outside. I also wanted to visit the chickens. The chickens adored fruit and I had half an over-ripe melon to give them.

Chickens eating melons

Joe was doing a grand job. His arms worked the bellows, reminding me of those Victorian wind-up monkey toys that clash their cymbals together. His naked body was coated with a fine layer of yellow dust, streaked where sweat had run in rivulets. His face was red from exertion and a film of sulphur had settled on his goggles.

"Paco was right," he grumbled, "this stuff is horrible."

It was the sound of laughter that prompted me to look up. I really wish I hadn't, because what I saw remains carved into my memory to this day.

High above us, on The Boys' roof terrace, silhouetted against the sky, stood a row of people, shoulder to shoulder. Every face was looking down into our garden and in that instant I recognised many of them. I saw The Boys - Federico and his paunchy wife, Roberto, each with a small dog in his arms. I saw Papa Ufarte grinning through his dark beard, and a smiling Mama Ufarte by his side, Snap-On on her hip. I saw all the other Ufarte children, the twins tittering behind their hands. I saw Geronimo, beaming broadly. Even Lola the temptress was there, standing just a little too close to Geronimo, throwing her head back in laughter. And I saw other, unfamiliar faces, undoubtably the Ufartes' friends and relations, each one laughing.

My reaction was instantaneous, unplanned. I clapped the over-ripe half-melon I had in my hands over Joe's manhood. Yes, it must have looked ridiculous and howls of laughter erupted from the spectators above.

Joe jumped in surprise and looked down at the melon I was pressing to him. "What the..? What on *earth* are you doing? Are you *insane*? That's bloody cold!"

"Quick!" I hissed, jerking my head to indicate the audience above. "Get inside!"

Joe wiped the sulphur off his goggles with the back of his hand and glanced up. His appreciative audience were, by now, helpless with laughter.

Joe shrugged. "Well, I've only got a bit left to finish," he said. "Might as well do the last square foot - no point leaving it for another time."

The next two minutes felt like a lifetime. As Joe puffed the bellows, I stayed with him, keeping the half-melon pressed in place, desperately trying to retain his modesty. My face burned as melon pips slithered down his thighs and the gales of laughter from above rang in my ears.

At long last it was done. Joe lowered the 'puffer', turned to his audience and bowed. With as much dignity as is possible with one's wife pressing an over-ripe half-melon to one's privates, he marched back inside the house. Our audience cheered and clapped.

Why were there so many people on The Boys' roof terrace that day? Later we found out that Federico and Roberto were giving the Ufarte clan and Geronimo a guided tour of their house and their latest refurbishments. I regret to report that the story of 'Joe and the Melon' has entered village folklore.

The next day, Judith appeared in her ancient, noisy car. Joe and I helped her bring in the tray of little pots, each one with a bright green seedling thrusting its head out of the soil.

"Thanks awfully for looking after these, m'dears," said Judith, flipping her long plait over her shoulder. "Mother's very grateful. She says to put them in partial shade, and keep them moist but not over-watered. She says they grow very quickly. Anyway, she said she'll be in touch and she'll let you know what to do with them next."

We found a good spot for the pots and I promised to take good care of them. To be honest, I felt a little nervous of the responsibility, knowing the price of each seed.

Spring spilled into summer and the wild flowers gave up their battle, withering away from the sun's fierce embrace. Each day was hotter than the last, and the tomato plants grew fast. Every week, Judith would phone on Mother's behalf to ask after them, and to issue new instructions.

"Mother asks if you can see tiny new shoots in the crook of the side branches?"

"Er, yes, I can..."

"Mother says pinch out the topmost growing tip, it'll make the plants stronger and bushier."

"Okay."

"Mother wants to know if you're turning the plants regularly."

"Yes, I am, every day."

"Mother wants to know if you think the plants need supporting yet."

"I thought this gardening lark was supposed to be Mother's hobby?" Joe complained after yet another of these phone calls. "It seems you're doing all the work. I hope we get some of these tomatoes when they're ready."

"Oh, I don't really mind," I said. "But I can't see any tomatoes forming yet, I hope I haven't done something wrong. Also, I don't know if I'm imagining it, but the plants are beginning to smell really strange. I didn't know tomato plants smell."

"It's probably because they're a special sort," said Joe. "They've got really big now, let's hope she wants them back soon."

Federico and Roberto rarely emerged from their house, but had become firm friends with the Ufarte family. The Boys filled their brand new swimming pool and we could hear the shouts of the Ufarte children as they splashed and played in the water. Fifi's excited yaps united with those of Canelo and Copito, The Boys' two little dogs.

Canelo was Roberto's dog, his pride and joy. A strange mix of Chihuahua and something undefinable - he had short legs, barrel chest, a curly tail and eyeballs that bulged disconcertingly. Roberto lovingly hand-fed Canelo endless tidbits, and the little dog's weight problem matched that of his devoted master. Both shared the same waddling gait, both panted furiously after any exertion.

Copito, or 'little snowflake' was Federico's dog. His long white fur was dotingly brushed, fluffed, puffed, teased and twiddled into a halo of snowiness. Federico always carried a comb in his back pocket, not for himself as he was virtually bald, but for Copito. I was often reminded of my daughter Karly, when she was about seven years old and going through her Barbie stage, constantly playing with and brushing Barbie's hair. As a result, little Copito possessed an aura of arrogance and strutted along with his nose in the air, perfectly aware that he was by far the most beautiful dog in the village.

Copito

Once a day, usually in the cool of the evening, The Boys would 'take' the two little dogs for a walk. Not in the conventional way that we Brits understand, but for a walk - Spanish style. The front door would open and the two dogs were let out into the street, one waddling, the other trotting like a little white show-pony. Ten or fifteen minutes later, two heads would appear on the roof terrace as The Boys called their beloved pets home.

"Canelo!" called Roberto.

"Copito!" called Federico, cupping his hands.

No response.

"CANELO!" yelled Roberto.

"COPITO!" yelled Federico.

No response. This calling would continue for up to half an hour until eventually the two little dogs appeared, trotting side by side. The Boys would vanish from the roof terrace and reappear at the front door to greet the escapees.

"You *naughty* little dog!" Roberto would say fondly to the panting, gasping, overweight Canelo, scooping him up and feeding him pieces of roast chicken, or *tortilla*. "Now come in, you must be hungry after that long walk!"

"Look at you!" Federico would say to Copito with mock severity, picking him up and pulling a comb through the white, ruffled fur. "What a state you have got yourself into! A bath for you, young man!"

Order restored, the front door would close behind them all.

Copito enjoyed having his hair brushed and fussed. Unlike me. I'm unusual I suspect, but I heartily dislike having my hair done. I disliked it in England, and more so in Spain. I'm aware that most women regard a visit to the hairdresser as a relaxing experience, some valuable 'me time', I suppose, but I can't agree.

It's not that I'm a fussy customer - I don't really care how my hair turns out, it'll always grow again. No, I think it's the boredom, being a prisoner, chained to the salon chair until it's all over, that I object to.

But in Spain it was a little different. Allow me to share my pain with you...

Herbed Chicken Wings

This dish is simple and tasty and makes for great summer tapas, a must at any summer function.

Tapas for 4

12 chicken wings, tips removed and cut in half at the joint
3 cloves garlic
Bunch fresh parsley
2 teaspoons dried oregano
Large sprig fresh thyme
Half teaspoon ground black pepper
Salt
Glass dry white wine
Juice of half a lemon
100ml (3.5 fl oz) olive oil

Peel and crush the garlic, finely chop the parsley and thyme.
Mix all of the ingredients except the chicken in a bowl and leave to infuse for half an hour or so.
Place the prepared chicken wings in a resealable freezer bag and add the other ingredients. Close the bag and knead well or shake the bag up to ensure a good covering. Leave in the fridge to marinate for two hours or so, shaking the bag from time to time.
Place the wings onto a greased oven tray, pouring over any left over marinade and cook in a hot oven for 20 to 30 minutes turning halfway until golden brown and beginning to crisp.

8
Hair

When we arrived in Spain, Judith and her ancient but glamourous mother always had advice for us. For more than twenty years they'd lived in the next village and knew their way around. So it was Judith's recommendation that brought me to Tracy the hair stylist's door.

"Mother and I always go to Tracy," said Judith. "She's frightfully good, y'know. Mother's very fussy about her hair, dear, and she'll only trust it with Tracy. Can't be doing with those salon-type places meself, so it suits me to go to Tracy's house, don't you know. She's got a nice dog, too, so it's like home from home." She paused to pat one of her ten dogs as it passed. "Awfully nice gal, Tracy, you'll like her."

Judith was right, I did like Tracy, but I didn't like the experience. It began badly when I rang the doorbell of Tracy's trim little house in the *urbanización*, or housing estate, on the edge of the city. Exactly like Judith's house, the doorbell set off a baying within. But this wasn't the howling of a pack of good-natured dogs, it was the deep, furious bark of one single dog. A big one.

"Now, stop that, Brutus!" said a voice with a strong Birmingham accent, and the door opened to reveal a slight young lady hanging desperately on the collar of a powerful Rottweiler. The Rottweiler filled the hallway and was straining to reach me, drooling and angry.

"Don't mind Brutus," said Tracy, "his bark's worse than his bite." I hoped so.

Eventually Brutus calmed enough to allow me into the house and Tracy set to work on my hair.

"Coffee? Tea?" asked Tracy, already snipping and not waiting for my reply. "Judith told me all about you. How are you liking Spain?"

I opened my mouth to answer but Tracy didn't pause. "We've been here seven years now - very settled, we are," she said. Brutus rested his great head on my knee and dozed, oblivious to the snippets of hair tumbling down on him. "And how are you enjoying living in El Hoyo? Very small village, isn't it?"

"It's..." I began but Tracy cut across me.

"Don't know if I'd like living up there in them mountains meself," she said. "But it suits some I suppose. (*snip, snip*) I had a second cousin in England who lived in a small village. He always said that..." Tracy's voice pressed on, relentless.

I nodded or grunted occasionally but didn't attempt to answer any more of her questions or join the conversation. A wet patch was forming on my skirt from Brutus's drool as he slept, soothed, no doubt, by his mistress's voice. I almost dozed myself, but my thoughts turned to worrying about Joe. I'd been watching him, and I knew for a certainty that he had something on his mind. Something about our life in El Hoyo. Something that he wouldn't speak about. He'd often said how happy he was to be in Spain, but I felt instinctively that he was missing something. Did he miss the UK? Did he want to return? Surely not! Yet again I resolved to ferret out the truth.

"...and it was the best paella I ever tasted! (*snip, snip*) I said to my friend, Debbie, 'Debbie,' I said, 'Debbie, have you ever tasted a paella as good as that?' Anyway, she said, 'no' and we had a good laugh and then..."

The kitchen clock ticked. Brutus snored. The wet patch on my lap grew. The scissors snipped. I wondered if Tracy ever took a breath... But at last the haircut was finished and I was pleased with the result. I paid and thanked Tracy, patted Brutus and left, never to return. Brutus I could cope with, the haircut was a good one, but my ears felt used, bruised and abused. I would need to find another hairdresser. Which was how I came to Antonio's salon in the city.

It was the Union Jack in Antonio's salon window that attracted me. ***'We speak English'*** declared the sign. *Goody,* I thought, *I won't have to revise difficult Spanish words like 'fringe' or 'parting' or 'layered'.*

Confidently, I entered the salon and was greeted by Antonio.

"You speak English?" I asked.

"*Sí*," he replied, his face lighting up. He ushered me to a chair in front of a large mirror. "You seet. How like type today you want?"

Oh dear, I thought. *Perhaps I should have brought my Spanish/ English dictionary after all.* I resigned myself to communicating in Spanish and filling the gaps with sign language when necessary.

I liked Antonio. He was tall, thin and well-groomed, with hair that stood in stiff, waxed spikes. His smile was easy and he listened attentively. Yes, he did speak English, but not well. His English was so heavily accented and jumbled that I didn't understand a word he said. The problem was, in an attempt to be helpful, he *insisted* on speaking English. However, I couldn't understand his English, and he didn't understand my Spanish. The result was a very serious communication breakdown.

For example, someone popped into the salon and handed Antonio a cardboard box. I could hear scuttling coming from inside the box, the scrabbling of claws on cardboard. Antonio seemed delighted, put down his scissors and carried the box over to the other assistants. I watched in the mirror as he carefully opened the box for a look, surrounded by his colleagues. They all exclaimed and admired the contents of the box.

Curiosity consumed me. "What animal is in the box?" I asked in my best Spanish when he resumed work.

Antonio's scissors stopped snipping and his brow furrowed as he tried to understand me. I tried again. This time he leaned forward, concentrating intently, reading my lips in the mirror as I spoke.

I said it again, in English this time. "Is there an animal in that box? What is it?" I tried pointing.

"My sorry. Understand no," said Antonio, shaking his head sadly. I gave up.

But the communication problem was most severe at the end of the session.

"Desire you spritz?" asked Antonio, a giant industrial-size can of hairspray already poised and aimed, ready to fire.

"No, thank you, I'm allerg…" Too late. Phhhhhttt! The air turned heavy and sticky with spray.

I left the salon coughing and wheezing, nose running, eyes streaming, but not before I'd managed to take a peep into the cardboard box. Inside were two young homing pigeons. The pigeons were attractive, but the spray was just too much. I didn't return.

And so my quest for the perfect hairdresser continued. Two months later I found myself knocking on the door of Juanita's salon in the small town of Alhama de Almería, quite some distance from our village.

Alhama is just one of a string of villages in the Andarax Valley, the gateway to the Alpujarras. It is a pretty town, unremarkable in many ways except for one thing. It has natural hot springs that gush continuously, causing it to be a mecca for elderly ladies who believe the water has health-giving properties. There is a pretty cascading waterfall and so much spring water in the area that huge pipes channel it away. I imagine some goes to fill the town swimming pool and the rest is destined for other needs, such as irrigating the vast orange and lemon orchards, a feature of the area.

Alhama public swimming pool

Alhama had a smart new supermarket that Joe and I visited fairly frequently. They had their own bakery on the premises and parking was easy. Being new, this supermarket was forever running promotions. Buy one loaf of bread, get another two free. Buy a case of beer, get a free parasol. If we refused the free gifts, the assistants would be affronted, so we had a freezer full of surplus bread and an ever-growing pile of yellow San Miguel parasols in our garage.

"I'll just wander round the village and wait for you," said Joe. "I'll probably pop into the supermarket, too. Meet you over the street in an hour."

Juanita's beauty salon was in the main street of Alhama. It was fronted by the typically tall Andalucian double wooden doors, painted in heavy brown gloss and opening onto the pavement. This was Juanita's home, but she had allotted two rooms downstairs to run her hair and beauty business.

I liked Juanita. She was friendly, and pictures of her family decorated the walls of her salon. Her kitchen was next door to the salon and delicious aromas wafted through to me as I sat in the chair ready to have my hair cut. She told me all about herself.

In her thirties, Juanita shared her house with her husband, little daughter and her elderly mother. Her husband worked in construction and was seldom home. She had never travelled outside Andalucía, and never wished to, happy living in Alhama in the bosom of her family.

Juanita was clearly a confident business woman, and had a reasonable number of regular clientele. She ran the business by herself, aided only by her burly Lithuanian assistant, Olga. To be frank, I found Olga rather alarming. When she smiled, she revealed a set of teeth capable of crushing concrete, and whereas Juanita's white overalls were crisp and dainty, Olga's barely contained bulging biceps a Russian weightlifter would have envied.

The pair were masters of salesmanship.

"You would like Product?" asked Juanita, pausing with her scissors. "Extra vitamins for your dry hair? You would like Olga to give you an Indian Head Massage?" Olga flexed her fingers and cracked her knuckles hopefully.

"No, thank you, just my hair trimmed…"

Juanita wasn't giving up. She picked up one of my hands and inspected it at close quarters. "Your nails are ragged. You need a manicure." Olga began rearranging the rows of nail polish on a glass shelf. The bottles rattled and looked tiny in her huge hands.

"Thank you, but really I just want my hair cut..."

Juanita lost interest in my hand and dropped it back into my lap, focusing on my feet instead. "Pedicure?" Olga switched allegiance and busied herself with the foot-care tools: scrapers, cutters, clippers and all manner of evil-looking equipment.

"No, really, just a haircut."

But Juanita was made of sterner stuff. "Your eyebrows have grey hairs in them," she observed. "Olga will dye them."

My whimpers of refusal were ignored as Olga parked her trolley firmly by my chair. I was helpless. My head was wrenched back, and I closed my eyes as Olga's huge face loomed close to mine. Half an hour later, while Juanita sat on the front door-step smoking cigarettes, Olga had transformed my eyebrows into black hairy caterpillars.

Juanita returned to finish cutting my hair. "There is a lot of water in the road outside," she commented.

At last the job was finished and I paid them both and departed. As promised, Joe was waiting for me on the other side of the street. I wasn't surprised to see he had yet another yellow San Miguel beach umbrella under one arm and yet more loaves of bread sticking out of a carrier bag clutched in his other hand. He'd evidently visited the supermarket and been showered with the usual mandatory gifts. However, I *was* surprised to see the state of the street.

Juanita spoke the truth because a river coursed down the previously bone-dry road. Cars splashed and drove gingerly through the water. I hitched up my skirts and waded through warm water to join him.

"You should have seen it!" said Joe, wisely not remarking on my duelling raven eyebrows. "The digger up there on the mountainside broke through one of those big water-pipes. Never seen so much water! Absolute torrents! Hot water came rushing down the mountainside and down the road like a mini tsunami!"

I was disappointed. But for my caterpillar eyebrows, I might have seen it too.

Back in El Hoyo, three more things happened. As we parked the car in our garage, Federico walked past. Trotting at his heels was a small, rather ugly little dog. Its hair was very short, coarse and patchy. There was definitely Chihuahua somewhere in its ancestry, but beyond that, I couldn't fathom. Even so, there was something about this dog that seemed familiar.

For some reason, Federico seemed mortified to see us. I left the talking to Joe as I was still very conscious of my coal-black eyebrows.

"*Buenas tardes,* Federico," said Joe. "How are you?"

"*Buenas tardes,*" answered Federico, looking uncomfortable, and standing deliberately between Joe and the dog as if hiding it from Joe's scrutiny.

"I see you have a new dog," said Joe innocently. He looked up and down the street, adding, "And where is your beautiful little dog, Copito?"

Two spots of livid colour appeared on Federico's cheeks. His fists clenched and he could barely contain himself. "I *like* children," he said furiously. "Everybody knows I like children. But today I do *not* like children! Today the Ufarte boys have spoiled my beautiful Copito!"

"You mean *that's* Copito?" asked Joe in surprise, pointing at the ugly little dog behind Federico.

"*¡Sí!* The Ufarte children, they painted my Copito! They opened all their father's tins of paint, and painted my poor Copito! And so, *(dramatic intake of breath)* I have no choice, I shave all poor Copito's hair off!" Federico crammed his knuckles into his mouth, squeezing his eyes tight shut in pain. Copito didn't seem concerned in the slightest and trotted off to cock his leg against a wall.

"Oh dear..." said Joe sympathetically, but Federico was already walking away, wailing and wringing his hands in despair.

"Poor Federico," I said. "He was so proud of Copito's snowy white fur."

"Oh well," said Joe. "No harm done really. It'll grow back in a few months. Like your eyebrows..."

I flinched.

And there were still two more surprises left for us that day. As Joe unlocked our front door, the Ufarte twins, dressed as ballerinas, skipped up behind us.

"*Tía* Veeky! *Tía* Veeky! We saw Francisco today!"

"Er... Francisco the chrysalis? You saw him?" I hadn't confessed that Francisco had crumbled into a pile of dust at the bottom of the jam jar.

"*¡Sí!* He is a beautiful butterfly now! He was flying up the street..." Ballerina #1 fanned her little hands, demonstrating, then pirouetted.

"And then... Oh, then he sat on the wall beside us, watching us play!" said Ballerina #2.

"How lovely!" I said, enjoying their pleasure and heaving an inward sigh of relief. I'd gotten away with it. I wouldn't have to tell them about the real Francisco's demise.

"And you're very sure it was Francisco?" asked Joe, a twinkle in his eye.

"Oh yes!" chorused the ballerinas. "We'd recognise him anywhere!"

But the day was still not over, and the final surprise knocked the wind out of my sails. Being a Friday, Paco's family arrived for the weekend as usual.

"We have good news!" said Carmen-Bethina, the dimples appearing in her plump cheeks as she smiled.

"Pah!" roared Paco, thumping the door frame with his fist. "Don't get excited, woman! You know what Sofía is like! That daughter of ours is too fussy!"

"Sofía has a new boyfriend!" continued Carmen-Bethina. "He is a policeman!"

"Pah!" roared Paco again. "It won't last. Sofía will find something wrong with him. I do not think she will ever get married!"

"They seem very happy," said Carmen-Bethina, ignoring her husband. "Who knows? Perhaps this will be 'The One'. He is coming up to the village tomorrow, Sofía will bring him round to meet you."

Which would have been fine if I hadn't been idly watching the local Spanish news on TV that night, and saw something that made my mouth hang open in astonishment.

Roasted Chickpeas with Thyme

Chickpeas, or "garbanzos" as they are known in Spain, are a regular ingredient in many Spanish recipes, usually served with lamb, pork or as a side dish. One alternative way of cooking chickpeas is to roast them in the oven. You can make a large batch for the guests and serve them up in small tapas bowls or as a replacement to peanuts and other snack food. Tremendously healthy and full of flavour, chickpeas make ideal and unusual tapas at any time.

Chickpeas, soaked or cooked
Sea salt
Dried thyme (or herbs of choice)
Olive oil

Preheat the oven to 180°C (355°F).
Drain and dry the chickpeas.
Place the chickpeas in a bowl and drizzle with olive oil before giving them a good mix by hand, making sure they are covered in oil.
Place on a baking tray, sprinkle with salt and roast in the oven for 25 minutes, giving them a shake halfway through.
Remove from the oven and season well with your chosen herbs (smoked paprika also works well).

Serve hot or cold.

9
A Night Flight, New Faces and Melons

"...Police helicopters have been scouring the area and have successfully spotted several cannabis cultivations. Arrests have been made, and police are confident that the current crackdown on the growing of these illegal plants will result in more..."

The reporter's voice continued, and the camera zoomed in on an individual plant. I froze, gripping the arms of my chair in horror.

"Joe? Joe! Did you see that?"

"Yes, why?"

"Mother's tomato plants! They're not tomato plants at all!"

"Mother's tomato plants? What *are* you talking about?"

"They're not tomatoes! She's given us marijuana plants to look after!"

Joe stared at me, then started laughing. "Are you sure?"

"Quite sure! The TV just zoomed in on a plant, and it's *exactly* the same as Mother's plants!"

"Haha, that wicked old lady!"

But I wasn't amused. "Stop laughing, Joe, this is serious!"

"Don't be ridiculous! Do you think the Spanish police helicopters are going to be spying on our garden? Hovering around checking on us? They're looking for big cultivations, not six plants in somebody's garden!"

"Twelve plants, actually. And I wasn't thinking of the helicopters. Have you forgotten we've got Sofía and her boyfriend coming round tomorrow?"

"So? They won't know what those plants are, don't worry."

"Has it slipped your mind? Sofía's new boyfriend is a policeman!"

"Oh!"

"And even if he didn't spot them, he'd smell them. Those plants stink, and now we know why!"

Joe's hand crept down to his groin for a good scratch. "I guess we'll have to hide them or something," he said at last.

"How can we hide them? They're huge!"

"Hmm... Then we'll have to take them back to Judith and Mother. Get on the phone to Judith."

I hate it when Joe orders me around, but this time I obeyed him without question.

"Judith?" I said, when the barking dogs had quietened sufficiently for her to hear me. "I'm afraid we'll have to bring Mother's tomato plants back."

"Oh, really? Why's that, m'dear?"

"Er, they've grown quite large. Er, *very* large. Too large! We don't have room for them anymore!"

"But I spoke with you yesterday. You didn't say anything about their size being a problem."

"Er, they've suddenly grown very quickly."

"What, overnight? Never mind, of course we'll take them back. I know Mother will be *most* excited about seeing them, she reads books about specialist gardening all the time. Some time next week suit you?"

"No! Can we bring them tonight?"

"But it's already eleven o'clock, dear! Are you quite alright, Vicky? You sound strange."

"I'm fine, thanks, Judith. But we *really* do need to return those plants tonight."

"Haha! Worried they'll grow even more overnight?" guffawed Judith. "They're just little tomato plants, dear thing, not Jack's beanstalk!"

I tried to sound more relaxed. "So, will tonight be okay with you?"

"Well, Mother's already gone to bed, and I was just about to toddle off meself..."

"You could just leave your side-gate open? We'll bring them over later tonight and put them in your garden."

"Vicky, are you sure you're quite well?"

"Yes, I'm fine. Don't worry about a thing, Joe and I will bring them over, don't wait up."

"Righty-ho, m'dear, if you're sure..."

That night was a long one. The Ufartes were singing and dancing in the street until 2.30 a.m. and we couldn't begin our mission until the coast was clear. We dozed fitfully in our armchairs, waiting, waiting. Finally, at 3.30 a.m, we agreed that the village was asleep, and that it was time to begin Operation Evacuate.

Like burglars under cover of darkness, we loaded the jeep as silently as we could. At that time of night, every creak and footstep seemed magnified, and I kept checking that all our neighbours' shutters remained closed. The plants had grown so tall that we needed to fold the car's canvas roof down, and they filled the back like a miniature green Amazonian jungle. The smell was overpowering and the plants were awkward and heavy, but at last we drove away.

All went well until we passed through the village and out the other side. A figure was weaving down the road, bottle in hand, trailed by three dogs.

"Oh no," I breathed, "it's Geronimo..."

The road was too narrow to drive round him, so we were forced to stop.

"Geronimo! *¿Qué tal?*" said Joe, as if this nocturnal encounter was the most normal thing in the world. "How's things?"

"*Mal,*" Geronimo said, shaking his head grimly as usual. (Bad) He rested his beer bottle on the car. "What are you doing?"

"Oh, nothing," said Joe airily. "Just going for a night drive."

"It's such a lovely night," I babbled. "A full moon."

"The back of your car is full of plants," said Geronimo, slurring a little.

"Yes," said Joe brightly, "It is! Well, we must go... See you in the village tomorrow, probably."

Joe revved the car's engine and Geronimo stepped back. We drove off, but not before I noticed a mysterious, shapely figure hiding in the shadows. Was that Lola Ufarte? Geronimo tossed his long hair aside and took another lengthy pull on his beer.

"He won't remember anything in the morning," said Joe as we drove away.

"I don't think he has us on his mind at the moment," I said.

Judith had left her side-gate open as promised, and we saw nobody as we unloaded the plants. By 4.30 a.m. we were back in our bed in our cave bedroom, vastly relieved that our garden was innocent once more.

The next morning, Sofía brought her policeman boyfriend round to meet us. With clear consciences we sat under the vine in the garden, chatting. Only once did she break off and peer into our faces, saying in that blunt way the Spanish have, "You both look tired. Are you sleeping well?"

How could she know that her new boyfriend had cost us a night's sleep?

In summer, the sun seemed to increase in size, hanging longer and longer in the sky, bleaching all the colour from the mountainsides.

During the day, sensible people hid from the fierce rays in the shadowy depths of their cottages. Cats and dogs were rarely seen, skulking in dark hiding places away from the punishing heat. Our chickens tucked themselves away in their hen-house and dozed, not becoming active again until the sun lowered in the sky. But as the sun sank, the villagers spilled out of their cottages and the streets became lively with gossip and the Ufarte's Flamenco guitar. Cats magically reappeared and dogs loped round the village, stopping to sniff and water every corner.

Little Tabs, our semi-wild cat, usually whiled away the days asleep in the shade of our jasmine. Her beautiful stripy coat was a perfect camouflage. The sun could only penetrate the leafy depths of the jasmine in slashes, and Little Tabs's stripes blended perfectly. Only her emerald eyes, unblinking, gave her position away.

She'd never brought her kittens back to see us and we wondered if they had survived. I imagined how big they'd grown, how they would look: one with silver stripes, the other a clone of its mother.

Joe and I had been working on the house and had some rubble to dispose of. The village had several dumpsters, one conveniently parked in our street. Joe raised the lid of the dumpster and I lifted my bucket of rubble, preparing to tip it in. In that split second, my brain registered something strange. I halted and stared into the depths of the dumpster. Stiff and still, Little Tabs lay there, her emerald eyes wide open and lifeless. Her burnished stripes had lost their shine and were already covered in a film of dust.

I was inconsolable. How had she died? Who had thrown her in the dumpster? Had she been shot? Poisoned? Why would anyone do that?

With heavy hearts we trudged back to our house, Joe with his arm around my shaking shoulders. He was upset, but more philosophical than I was. We both knew that village cats were not highly rated by the villagers, and it was not unusual for children to use cats as target practice. True, we couldn't find any wounds on her, but the stark fact was that Little Tabs would no longer sit on our window-sill, peering into the kitchen and gently tapping on the glass.

"I shall miss her so much," I sighed. "She was always in our garden. I can't believe this has happened again. After that other time when we thought she was dead, and now she really is." Miserably, I turned to gaze out of the kitchen window, remembering how Little Tabs used to sit there with her nose pressed to the glass.

Gravy and Sylvia

What happened next was a minor miracle. Instead of Little Tabs's face, two almost-grown kitten faces gazed back at me - one silver, the other a perfect replica of its mother.

We named one Sylvia because of her colour, and the other Gravy, I have no idea why.

By day they slept in the shade of our jasmine, always together, often entwined. And by night they played in the garden or prowled the village. Like their mother before them, they grew quite tame, but never actually allowed us to touch them. And so, through her daughters, Little Tabs lived on.

As the temperatures soared, we, like the Spanish, rarely ventured outside in the middle of the day. Our house, built in the typical Andalucian style, had metre-thick walls and small shuttered windows, perfect for keeping the interior cool even when outdoors was a furnace.

One hot weekend I needed a letter posted urgently, so I sent Joe to the mailbox in the square.

A few minutes later he returned, letter in one hand, a bulging, heavy-looking plastic carrier bag in the other. He looked hot and bothered.

"You're back already?" I said, surprised. "What's in the bag, and why didn't you post my letter?"

"Paco saw me pass by and gave me all these melons," Joe explained. "They're so heavy I thought I'd bring them home first, before posting the letter." He mopped his forehead and once more braved the hot street, letter in hand.

Ten minutes passed and Joe still hadn't returned. I stuck my head out of the window, glanced up and down the street and saw Joe approaching, this time weighed down by a big cardboard box.

"More melons," he panted, sweat dripping off his nose. "Antonio, in the end house, called me in. I told him we already had loads, but he insisted."

"What are we going to do with all these melons?" I asked. "And did you post my letter?"

Joe rolled his eyes ceiling-ward. "No, let me just catch my breath first and have a cold drink, then I'll try again."

I dragged the box of melons into the kitchen, and Joe set off for the third time, this time successfully posting the letter and returning empty-handed.

"Well, the chickens are in for a treat," I said as we sat at the kitchen table, eyeing the melon mountain. "There's no way we can eat all those melons ourselves."

Just then, the phone rang. It was Marcia, from the village store.

"Come to my shop," said Marcia. "I have a surprise for you."

Obediently, in the searing heat, we retraced Joe's steps back

Melons from Marcia

down to the square, to find Marcia waiting for us, hairpins escaping from her silver hair. There was a large plastic crate on the counter. "Melons!" she smiled, patting the crate with a gnarled hand. "Melons for you, from my son. He grew them himself. The English supermarkets are buying all the melons he grows. Imagine! Your friends in England are probably eating my son's melons grown here in El Hoyo!"

We put in an Oscar-deserving performance of thanking her, and, gasping and sweating, lugged the crate home. Then we feasted on melons. The chickens feasted on melons. Judith, Mother and all our English friends in the next village feasted on melons. Even the men who delivered our new fridge went away with melons, and we still had plenty left...

There are many advantages to living in an isolated area. The peace is priceless and soothes the soul. One feels far removed from the turbulence of the town, the traffic and the people. Regrettably, there are disadvantages, too. No shops just around the corner for last minute necessities. No banks to quickly visit for bill-paying. We all loathe receiving bills, but thankfully, direct debits make paying bills easy, although not necessarily pain-free. That hot summer, Joe and I discovered the pitfalls of direct debits and dealing with big companies.

10
Battles

When we first moved to El Hoyo, there were only three telephones in the village. Marcia had one, Paco and Carmen-Bethina another, and we had the third. It was then 2004, before mobile phone signals had reached our village. We felt fortunate even to have a land-line because at least it allowed access to the Internet.

Now it was the summer of 2009. Construction had started on the dreaded new apartment block that we called The Monstrosity. New telephone poles were erected, cables stretching and connecting to each apartment. So, the 21st century was finally going to reach El Hoyo?

Long ago, we'd sorrowfully accepted that living up a remote Spanish mountain meant that broadband, or any kind of speedy Internet access, was an avenue of pleasure denied to us. We implored the mighty Telefonica, but they were very firm, stating that broadband was not an option for us. We had no choice. We could have a painful, grindingly slow dial-up Internet connection, or nothing. Perhaps benefits would come with The Monstrosity after all, like broadband?

Dial-up was annoying but we made the best of it. We couldn't watch anything on YouTube or download much, but it was better than nothing. Joe and I were reliant on the Internet. It enabled us to keep in touch with friends and family, and keep track of our finances.

I'd had a shock a few months earlier, when I was online routinely checking the balance in our bank account.

What? Was the computer screen playing tricks on my eyes? Our telephone bill had leaped from the usual hefty-but-acceptable 90 euros to the totally-ridiculous-astronomical-definitely-not-acceptable sum of 880 euros. So we dialed Telefonica and asked for the English-speaking Helpdesk in order to lodge our complaint.

"We've made hardly any calls," Joe said pleasantly. "Our usual bill is approximately 90 euros. And we've been charged 880 euros! That's enough to buy a small car, haha! There's obviously been a mistake."

"Hmm... I'll just check on our computer... (*long pause*) No. No mistake," said Telefonica. "I can see you changed your Plan. You used to have the 24/7 Internet Plan, and you changed it. Now you are being charged by the minute every time you go online."

"WHAT? Charged by the minute? But we haven't changed anything! We didn't change our Plan!"

Twenty minutes later, Joe and Telefonica were still arguing, and

Joe was getting precisely nowhere. His blood pressure was sky-high.

"As an act of goodwill, I will refund you 100 euros," said Telefonica magnanimously.

Joe gave up but I was furious. Seething, I phoned the Helpdesk again. I was livid, and Telefonica got both barrels. There was a long, long pause, and finally they agreed. We *had* been charged far too much. It *was* a mistake, and we were refunded.

Satisfied, and more than a little smug that we'd won the battle, we forgot all about it until a couple of months later when Joe and I stared at the computer screen in horror and disbelief. They'd done it again! Telefonica had seen fit to help themselves to the funds in our bank account for the *second* time! This time, our usual 90 euro telephone bill had swollen to a whopping 1,011 euros.

After I'd scraped Joe off the ceiling, he dialed the Helpdesk again.

"You've made another mistake," he said between gritted teeth.

"No mistake," said Telefonica breezily. "I can see from the computer what has happened. You changed your Plan. You used to have the 24/7 Internet Plan, and you changed it. Now you are being charged by the minute every time you go online."

"BUT WE HAVEN'T CHANGED ANYTHING! WE DIDN'T CHANGE OUR PLAN!"

It was déjà vu, but eventually we got it sorted. Telefonica refunded our money and issued the normal 90 euro bill. But now we watched our bank balance like neurotic hawks.

The third time was the straw that broke the camel's back. In July, Telefonica helped themselves to 530 euros out of our bank account. By now the Telefonica Helpdesk was on speed-dial and Joe was bellowing down the telephone wire like an enraged wildebeest. The telephone poles in the valley trembled.

"You've done it AGAIN! You've ROBBED our bank account! Our telephone bill cannot possibly be 530 euros! Why do we have to go through this fiasco every time?"

"Please wait one minute and I will check for you. (*Long, long, long pause*) "Ah, now I can see what has happened - it's quite clear. You have changed your Internet Plan. You switched from the 24/7 Plan to the Pay by the Minute Plan."

Joe turned purple and a vein in his forehead throbbed. "I DIDN'T! I've changed NOTHING!" he shouted. "It's YOUR mistake and this is the THIRD time this has happened!"

"But Mr Joe, nothing in this life is free," said Telefonica, affronted. "You changed your Internet Plan."

Many phone-calls later, Telefonica grudgingly agreed we'd been overcharged, refunded our money and issued the normal 90 euro bill.

We phoned our bank and got the direct debit stopped. We researched online and found another company, an alternative to Telefonica, one that *didn't* tell us that we lived in a far too isolated spot to receive broadband. (Amazingly, it was British Telecom, not a company I remember with much affection.)

But, hurrah! BT were offering us unlimited broadband, a router and 400 free minutes calling time to anywhere in Europe for *less* than Telefonica were charging us for dial-up.

The changeover was painless and transformed Joe and me back into happy bunnies. Happy that we finally had broadband instead of the dreadful dial-up, and happy that we'd successfully severed all links with Telefonica.

Result! The telephone poles in the valley relaxed.

Except that later we discovered that Telefonica and BT are one and the same company. Hey-ho. Nevertheless, we had no further trouble.

Unfortunately, that self-satisfied smug feeling Joe and I enjoyed after having conquered the mighty Telefonica didn't last. Soon after, we had another run-in with a huge company that left us feeling rather ashamed.

Living so far from town, we were forced to keep shopping trips to a minimum. Once a month we shopped at the Carrefour Hypermarket and filled several trolleys with industrial-sized quantities of everything we needed, like toilet rolls in packs of 32, gallons of longlife milk and big 500 gram catering drums of instant coffee. Anything overlooked was topped up from shops and smaller supermarkets in neighbouring villages.

One morning I prised off the lid of a recently opened coffee tin and was appalled. The coffee was clearly contaminated. Fluff, bits of dirt and debris mingled with the coffee granules.

"Eww... That's disgusting!" I said, pulling a face and pushing the coffee drum away.

"What's the matter with it?" asked Joe and peered inside. "Eww... That's revolting! We're taking that back. Carrefour can't sell us coffee like that and get away with it!"

I knew he was reliving the Telefonica battle and would not let this incident pass. So we took the drum of coffee back and Joe plonked it down on the Customer Care counter. The Carrefour lady looked faintly surprised and asked how she could help.

"Take the lid off and look inside," said Joe. "Your company should be ashamed of itself selling stuff in that condition!"

The lady used a letter-opener to remove the lid which clattered on the counter. She peeped inside.

"Eww..." she said, recoiling and wrinkled her nose in disgust.

"That's horrible!"

"Exactly!" said Joe, standing tall, triumph in his voice. "It's full of rubbish and all sorts of stuff. It's unusable! And these big tins of coffee are very expensive."

"I'm so sorry," said the lady. "Leave it with me. I will give you a voucher to replace it, and I'll have it sent back to the supplier. They'll carry out tests and find out what is wrong with it. Leave me your name and address, and I'll be in touch."

"Well, that told them!" said Joe as we drove home. "I wasn't going to let them get away with that!" I didn't point out that the lady had been more than helpful, and that she had agreed with everything we had said.

Three weeks later, a large parcel arrived for us on the fish van. True to her word, the nice Carrefour lady had followed up the case of the contaminated coffee and had written us a letter. It was written in perfect English:

Esteemed customers,

I have sent the tin of coffee back to the suppliers and asked them to run tests on it. They have now replied and say that although they cannot exactly identify the cause, they agree that the coffee was severely sub-standard and should not have been on sale. They assure me that they are making massive enquiries to find out how your coffee was contaminated and are double-checking to make sure no other similar batches exist. They are very grateful that you returned the drum of coffee allowing them to research the problem.

On the behalf of Carrefour, we would like to apologise for the inconvenience caused and hope you will accept the gifts enclosed.

We look forward to serving you in our store in the future.

Yours sincerely,

Antonia María García
Customer Care Supervisor

We tore open the parcel. Inside were two more drums of coffee, a tin of Luxury Wholemeal Chocolate cookies, some After Dinner mints and a stack of vouchers to use in the supermarket.

"Well!" said Joe. "That was nice of them. You see, you shouldn't just accept shoddy goods or poor treatment from these big companies. You have to fight for your rights."

That should have been the end of the story, but it wasn't.

A week later, two identical royal princesses were seated at our kitchen table scoffing the last of our Luxury Wholemeal Chocolate cookies washed down by glasses of milk. Tiaras sparkled in their dark hair. I filled the kettle, took the drum of coffee off the shelf and prepared to spoon some into Joe's and my coffee mugs.

"Oh, I would *not* use that!" whispered Princess #1 loudly to her royal sister.

"Eww... No! That is all dirty!" agreed Princess #2, pulling a face.

I froze. The twins knew nothing of our coffee complaint story, so why were they discussing the state of the coffee? I swung round.

"I heard that," I said. "Why? Why shouldn't I use this coffee?"

"Well..." said Princess #1, after a hesitation. "Our brother, Prince Jorge knocked the tin off the shelf with his football."

"And the lid came off..." added Princess #2.

"And the coffee spilled everywhere!"

"But we found your dustpan and brush and we cleaned it all up."

"We brushed everywhere, right into the corners, just like Mama showed us."

"You mean 'The Queen'," Princess #2 corrected her royal twin.

"Yes, we cleaned up really nicely, just like The Queen showed us at home." Princess #1 paused, waiting expectantly for the praise.

"And what happened to the coffee you swept up?" I asked at last, but my heart was filled with dread. I already knew the answer.

"Oh, we put it all back into the tin," chorused the princesses. "Do not worry, *Tía* Veeky, we did not waste a bit!"

El Hoyo is high in the mountains, many kilometres from the nearest big town. One may think it too isolated, or too high for the Spanish passion for sport to affect anyone much, but one would be mistaken.

Whatever the weather, insane, dedicated cyclists pedaled their way up the steep, winding mountain roads. Dressed in stretchy multicoloured Lycra, their muscles screaming with effort, they perspired their way uphill. Joe and I overtook them in our jeep, but on the downward stretch, the bicycles sailed past us with ease.

Our valley was almost perfectly circular, no doubt hollowed out by gargantuan volcanic upheavals eons ago. It behaved like a Roman amphitheatre, trapping sound, echoing and amplifying it. The smallest sounds from the other side of the valley were crystal clear and even conversations could be picked up. A goat's bell, or birdsong, echoed round the mountains, clear and loud.

So imagine the noise in July, when another sporting event took place. The mountain road was closed to general traffic and rally cars raced each other instead. From early morning to evening, car after car roared past, negotiating impossible hairpin bends at speeds that left us sweating.

The valley echoed with engine noise, but we'd noticed a pattern. All too frequently, the roaring stopped, to be replaced by sirens. Joe and I exchanged glances. We could only assume there'd been an accident. However, shortly afterwards, the race continued and the valley reverberated once more with the roaring of racing engines.

In autumn, the olives and almonds were harvested. Nets were spread under the trees and families knocked the branches with sticks to dislodge the fruit and nuts. The sound of wood hitting wood reverberated around the valley. This was soon followed by the sound of almond de-husking machines that stripped the green husk from the hard shell inside. Like an old-fashioned washing mangle, the handle was turned producing a sound not unlike a cement mixer filled with rocks. Most families owned one of these machines, and the noise of almonds being de-husked filled the village. Nothing was wasted. The families ate or sold the almonds, and the husks were fed to the goats. We were always given enough almonds to last us all year.

Weekdays and weekends were easy to tell apart. In the winter there were only about six or eight souls in El Hoyo, including Joe and me. But in

Amoroso Mussels with Almonds

This recipe for mussels uses Spanish Amoroso sherry, a change from white wine, and produces a real depth of flavour to the shellfish. Almonds are also scattered over the mussels whilst steaming. The mussels are then served in bowls and garnished with parsley.

1.5kg (3lb 4oz) fresh mussels
3 garlic cloves, thinly sliced
50g (2 oz) butter
75ml (5 tbs) Amoroso sherry
Juice of half a lemon
30g (1-2 oz) toasted almonds, crushed
Parsley

Melt the butter in a large deep pan.
Cook the garlic for 2 minutes.
Tip your cleaned mussels into the pan, add the sherry and almonds and squeeze over the lemon juice.
Using a wooden spoon, stir the mussels well to mix in the ingredients.
Steam for 4 to 5 minutes until mussels have opened.
Spoon the mussels into bowls adding a tablespoon or two of the mussel liquid from the pan.
Garnish with chopped parsley and serve.

Serves 4

summer, and every weekend, it was a very different matter. All the Spanish families piled into their cars and drove into the mountains to open up their cottages and relax. On Sunday night they reversed the process, leaving the village quiet and empty.

I experimented one weekend in autumn and wrote a list of the sounds I heard.

Almonds we've been given

<u>Weekends</u>

People laughing
People shouting
Babies crying
Papa Ufarte strumming Flamenco guitar music
Dancing and hand-clapping
Cars
Scooters - lots of them (Many are tiny scaled-down versions ridden by little boys.)
Almonds and olives being knocked off trees
The rumble of the almond de-husking machines
Children playing soccer in the square
Dogs barking
Football matches (I mean on the TV, but our neighbours bring the TV out into the street, followed by the 3-piece suite and extra chairs. Then other villagers bring their chairs and join them.)
Hooting delivery vans selling bread, fruit and fish
Joe cracking almonds

I set the list aside and picked it up again at mid-day in the middle of the week. As before, I closed my eyes and listened. As before, I made a list of the sounds I heard.

<u>Weekdays</u>

A very distant tractor
Birds rustling in our vine stealing grapes
Geronimo's donkey singing to his girlfriend in the next village
Cocks crowing
Joe cracking almonds

In September, Joe and I knew the Log Man would appear. Winter approached, and the Log Man was a necessary visitor. His visits always meant a day of hard labour ahead and we awaited his arrival, the first of the season, with some trepidation.

Roast Pumpkin with Chili and Honey

This recipe for roast pumpkin combines the flavour of chili pepper with honey. A great vegetarian side dish or to accompany main meals. Butternut squash can be used instead of pumpkin.

1kg (2.25 lb) pumpkin
4 small onions
Pinch of chili flakes
4 tablespoons of honey
100ml (3.4 fl oz) wine vinegar
Olive oil
Salt

Cut the pumpkin into good-sized wedges, leaving the skin on.
Quarter the onions and arrange on a baking tray with the pumpkin.
Drizzle with olive oil, scatter over with the chili flakes and lightly season with salt. Bake for 40 minutes.
5 minutes before the pumpkin is ready, heat the wine vinegar and the honey in a pan and bring to the boil, then let simmer for 5 minutes.
Serve the roasted pumpkin with a generous drizzle of the honey mixture.

11
The Log Man and the Gin Twins

We never knew *exactly* when the Log Man was coming. Every September he simply turned up, usually early in the morning on a Saturday or Sunday, before we'd woken up properly. He leaned on the doorbell, and when I opened the door, he grunted, "*Leña*". Not as a question, you understand. Just the statement: "Firewood".

It would be tempting to politely say "No, thank you," but we'd regret that. If we didn't accept the load, we'd have to collect it ourselves, in our jeep. That meant a weekly trip just to keep our greedy wood-burning stove happy. No, it made more sense to have it delivered, even if it meant several hours of hard work.

On this particular September Saturday, the sun was particularly warm and the sky particularly cloudless and bright. Wearing our oldest clothes and protective work gloves, we waited in the street. Being the weekend, most of the Spanish families had arrived and the Ufarte twins were playing in the street. Lola Ufarte sat on the doorstep, filing her fingernails, occasionally tossing her hair back and glancing up under her eyelashes at Geronimo, who leaned casually against the wall beside her.

The Log Man reversed awkwardly down the narrow street and parked with a hiss of air-brakes. He let down the side of the truck and stood aside to allow his young helper to climb up and hurl all the logs into the street. All shapes and sizes, the logs piled up into a jumbled, precarious heap of olive wood, almond, fig, some great stumps, ragged timber wedges and perfectly round logs that bounced and rolled.

Joe felt sorry for the lad. "He can't shift those logs all by himself," he muttered and, panting, climbed up onto the lorry to help him.

The Log Man stood back and made no effort to assist, and the two workers soon drew an audience of villagers, children and village dogs. The log pile in the street grew. Papa and Mama Ufarte appeared on their doorstep, Snap-On clamped to Mama Ufarte's hip. Mama Ufarte glowed with health, the rise of her unborn baby clearly visible beneath her loose top. That day, the Ufarte twins were nurses again, each with a stethoscope swinging around her neck.

When the lorry was empty, the lad leaped down. Joe jumped down too, but forgot he was probably 45 years older than the lad. He landed badly, staggered, then stepped back onto one of the round, rolling logs. Poor Joe ended up on his back, legs flailing, like an overturned tortoise.

The spectators gasped, "*¡Madre mía!*" in one voice, and Papa Ufarte and the Log Man's lad sprang forward to pull Joe back onto his feet.

"Silly old fool," Joe chided himself, but his misery was not quite complete.

Joe helping to empty the log truck

From nowhere, out shot Fifi, the Ufarte's spiteful Yorkshire Terrier. Darting through the forest of legs, she headed straight for her archenemy. Before he'd even straightened, or composed himself, Fifi's teeth were sinking into his ankle.

"*¡Madre mía!*" the spectators gasped once more.

"Fifi! No!" shouted Mama and Papa Ufarte in unison.

"Fifi is biting *Tío* Joe again," observed Nurse Ufarte #1, heading toward Joe, stethoscope at the ready.

"Fifi does not like *Tío* Joe," explained Nurse Ufarte #2 to the world in general, plucking a bandage out of her apron pocket.

Joe forgot there were children present and cursed, thankfully in English. "Get off my leg, you stupid mutt!" he hissed, shaking Fifi off his leg. Fifi bounded away, past the onlookers and into the dark sanctuary of the Ufarte house.

The show was over and the Log Man drove away. The crowd dispersed, and Joe checked himself. No real damage done, except to his dignity. We started clearing the road of logs. It took three hours of wheelbarrow load after wheelbarrow load, pushed uphill to our back gate, where each log was individually stacked in the woodshed. As usual, I broke all my nails, developed severe backache and totally lost my sense of humour.

But it was worth it. Despite the humiliation, backache and broken fingernails, by the time the sun set, we had a nearly FULL WOODSHED. Nearly enough beautiful, scented logs to satisfy our voracious little wood-burner for the coming months. One more delivery, and winter would be sorted.

Priceless!

October arrived and the leaves on our vine turned crimson and crisp, twirling and whirling in the breeze before releasing their fragile hold and gyrating to the ground with a dry rustle. The temperature at night dropped and each evening we lit the wood-burner a little earlier.

One unusually warm day, I scrutinised Joe closely. "You need a haircut," I said, "with our new hair clippers."

Joe doesn't have much hair. It grows quite thick at the back and at the sides. But on the top...well, let's be honest, there isn't a lot, mostly shine. When his hair grows too long, it goes all tufty, resembling an insane professor.

Barbers charge full price whether you present only half or a full head of hair. To save money, it seemed like a great idea to buy some hair-clippers and I would take charge of the cutting. After all, how hard could it be to shave a head?

It was midday, and Joe nervously sat on a chair in the garden. I opened the box containing the shiny new clippers and graded clip-ons.

"A Grade 3, I think," I said, attaching the guard over the cutting blades with a confident flourish.

"That sounds quite short," Joe said doubtfully.

"No, it'll be fine." I clicked the 'On' button and the clippers buzzed into life.

All went well for a while. Joe obediently tipped his head this way and that as a gentle breeze stirred the remaining dry leaves on the grapevine. Snippets of hair drifted down to be lifted by the breeze, which wafted them across the ground in lazy circles.

KER-BANG!

A massive blast ripped through the air and Joe and I jumped in fright.

"It's too early for the Fiesta," said Joe, settling back into the chair. "It's probably Geronimo. Maybe Real Madrid won a match and he's celebrating. Why do the Spanish like such loud fireworks?"

Behind Joe, I resumed cutting, then stood very still. To my horror, a bald patch, the width of the hair-clippers, gleamed palely on the back of his head. Somehow the guard had been knocked off the clippers and the naked blades had chomped a track through his hair. I recalled my daughter telling me this was called a 'Runway' or 'Brazilian' or something, but didn't think it a style usually adopted for men's haircuts.

"They'll be letting off more of those bloody fireworks when the Fiesta starts, you mark my words," said Joe. "How's the haircut coming along?"

"Oh, fine..."

It was a blatant lie.

I didn't replace the guard and worked desperately to repair the damage. I tried to even out the remaining hair length, but sadly, my efforts were in vain. The more I clipped, the worse it all looked. Joe's head looked as though a plague of starving moths had descended and feasted.

"I think that's it," I said, brushing off the last hair clumps from his shoulders.

Joe stood and went inside to admire my handiwork in our large living-room mirror. I counted down... Five, four, three, two, one, zero...

On cue, an anguished howl rent the air.

"What have you DONE?" yelled Joe.

"I'm sorry."

"I look like a blasted criminal!"

"Perhaps you could wear a cap for a while?"

Fifi had always made it perfectly clear she detested Joe, but the jaunty baseball cap he now sported absolutely *enraged* her. She redoubled her efforts to sink her wicked little teeth into his ankle whenever an opportunity arose, hairing down the street the moment he left the house. Joe was not pleased with me.

I suppose there is a moral to this story. Perhaps, get your hair cut professionally. Or, never cut your beloved's hair during Spanish fireworks.

El Hoyo's annual fiesta came and went amidst its explosion of fireworks, processions, marching bands and dancing. The same band that always played at our village fiestas poured music into the valley until the small hours of the morning. Joe and I made an appearance and I noticed Lola Ufarte, dressed in a low-cut, skin-tight dress, dancing with every male in the village. Geronimo stood close by, watching, a look of abject misery on his face. I shook my head sadly, I could see no future in that relationship, it was bound to end in tears.

I also saw Sofía wrapped in the arms of her policeman boyfriend. I hoped, for Carmen-Bethina's sake, that Sofía had finally found The One.

When the Log Man returned a month later, his timing was perfect. Our wonderful friends from the UK, the Gin Twins, were due for their annual visit. We suspected that the Log Man might appear that weekend and we were right. I collected the Gin Twins from the airport, and drove them home to El Hoyo to find that the Log Man had just left. Joe was attempting to shift the log mountain single-handed. Despite having travelled all night, the Gin Twins downed a swift gin and threw themselves into the task of stacking logs. That day we cleared and stacked the log pile in record time. Video evidence of this domestic triumph can be found on YouTube: http://youtu.be/nfMurRdX4Zo

Thinking back to that October always makes me a little giddy. Many small things happened, but for me, the big event was the launch of my first book, *Chickens, Mules and Two Old Fools*. One day it appeared on Amazon, and life was never quite the same again.

Suddenly I was being invited onto radio programs. Reviews of

Chickens popped up in strange places and complete strangers wrote to me telling me about their chickens or dreams of moving abroad. My email inbox was never empty.

Of course I received complaints, too, the most common coming from American readers who objected to two of the chickens' names, Bugger and F**k. Many have asked why we chose these names, and the answer is simple. Our two black chickens were very tame and consumed by curiosity. Shoe-laces, every leg hair, mosquito bite, or wrinkle in a sock were investigated as soon as we entered the orchard. Joe was forever falling over those two chickens and cursing. Consequently, the swear words stuck, and the two black chickens were always referred to by those unfortunate names. In Britain, the word F**k is bad, but not shocking. I have since talked to American friends who tell me that the word is much, much worse in the States. So I apologise to you ladies in the USA, I genuinely didn't mean to offend.

The launch of *Chickens* coincided with the Gin Twins' visit, and they arrived laden with wondrous gifts from the UK. It took nearly half an hour to unwrap them all. We sat under the vine, opening gift after gift amidst squeals of delight and gin.

Question:

What do you give a pair of old fools who live in paradise and already have everything they need?

Answer:

The stuff on this table.

The Gin Twins brought:

A HUGE box of Christmas crackers
Bread sauce mix
Chocolate advent calendar for Little Paco next door
Blackboard for counting off the days until Christmas
Reindeer antlers
A Christmas pudding
Extra hot curry powder *(can't find it in Spain)*
Extra hot chili powder *(can't find it in Spain)*
Sag aloo *(can't find it in Spain)*
Box of poppadums *(can't find them in Spain)*
2 vacuum packs of naan bread *(can't find it in Spain)*
A tub of E45 cream
Fancy tin
Tin of chocolate cookies
Another tin of chocolate cookies
A supply of bayonet-type light bulbs *(can't buy them in Spain)*
Anti-bacterial counter spray *(why can't we buy that in Spain?)*
A little book of wine quotations
DVDs for Joe *(Great Escape, Battle of Britain, A Bridge too far)*
A huge bag of books
Magazines from home, like *Sussex Life*
Packs of seeds
A small soft toy chicken
And...a copy of *Chickens, Mules and Two Old Fools.*

I had never seen a copy, or held one in my hands until the Gin Twins brought me that first copy. I couldn't stop sniffing and handling it, flicking through the pages, holding it, stroking the cover.

One of the nicest side-effects of the book launch was my Internet Twitter life. At first I didn't even understand how Twitter worked and the Twitter community was a mystery to me. However, I took to it like a tramp to cider. I soon had a following of several thousand, both as @VictoriaTwead and my other identity, @StephenFrysCat. What fun I had!

@StephenFrysCat

As Victoria, I met and chatted to people all over the world, many who'd read *Chickens*. And as my alter ego, Stephen Fry's Cat (I've never had the honour of meeting Stephen Fry himself, although I'm a huge fan) I chatted and laughed my socks off.

Stephen Fry's Cat developed a character all his own and I chose an avatar that made me laugh every time I looked at it. I named the cat Oscar (after Oscar

Wilde) and Oscar the Cat was a gentleman. His greatest passion was food and I only had to tweet *rumble, rumble* for his followers to respond by the dozen, offering ><(((((((°> and all manner of virtual delicacies to fill his magnificent tum.

Occasionally Stephen Fry would tweet me, too. For instance, once, when he'd just returned from a trip abroad, I tweeted:

***Bliss! Sitting on @StephenFry's knee looking at his holiday snaps* :-)**

Back came the reply from Stephen Fry:

Holiday? Why you silly cat - I was working my botty off to put salmon in your bowl... holiday? Tchah!

As Victoria, I made friends with fellow chicken owners, expats, readers, fellow writers, food-lovers and nice people from every corner of the planet.

I 'met' Paul Hamilton, (Twitter name @HamsteratFrys) the steward of Driffield Golf Club, Yorkshire, who conceals an extraordinary artistic talent and a sense of the ridiculous that I adore. I am grateful to Paul for the wonderful cover he designed for this book and for the many, many hilarious 'photos' he tweeted and posted on Facebook over the months. They include pictures of Her Majesty, William and Kate, politicians, footballers, comedians, celebrities, animals and even a Michelangelo, each one doing something silly with a copy of *Chickens*. One day I think I'll surprise him. I'll saunter up to his bar at Driffield Golf Club, order a nice glass of Spanish wine and introduce myself.

Driffield Golf Club

Squirrel reading 'Chickens'.

I chatted with new Twitterfriends bearing the most exotic names: GreenMousey, HilaryLuke, BigWidu, AnitaPlum, TravelMaus, ChaosGerbil, FarmingFriends, MrsJollyRed, Malloise, Ellnhank, KnittingPuppy and IceEgg22. I compared weather observations and experiences with other Spanish expats: KierstenRowland, Nichick, JoJoNewman, InMalalagaToday, EbroApartments, NickySwain and MolinoCharrara. Some were aware that VictoriaTwead was also StephenFrysCat, others had no idea.

And as Oscar, Stephen Fry's cat, I indulged myself in silly banter... and still do. But at the same time, Joe was also making a new friend.

Stuffed Tomatoes and Prawns

Stuffed tomatoes are a classic tapas recipe and make the tapas table very colourful. A very simple combination stuffed with heaps of Mediterranean flavour.

200g (8 oz) large cooked prawns
4 olives
4 large vine ripened tomatoes
1 stick celery
2 tablespoons mayonnaise
2 mint leaves
Parsley

Roughly chop the prawns and mint leaves, thinly slice the celery, then mix with the mayonnaise.
Cut the tops off the tomatoes and carefully remove the insides (a melon baller works well).
Place 1 olive in the bottom of each tomato, then stuff with the prawn mix.
Drizzle with olive oil and garnish with parsley.

Makes 4 tapas

12
Poinsettias and Underpants

November in the Alpujarra mountains brought air so crisp and cold that sucking it in almost hurts the lungs. By early morning, ice had formed a glassy layer over puddles, and the tarmac of the roads glistened with ice crystals.

Apart from the chickens and Sylvia and Gravy, our two semi-wild cats, we didn't have any pets. I hoped we'd have a dog one day but as we still travelled, it didn't seem a sensible idea yet. However, Joe had befriended something green and about six inches long. As the weather grew colder, Joe's visits to the woodshed became more frequent, and it is was there that his new friend had decided to live.

Bug-Eye

Joe named him Bug-Eye and he probably wasn't the most ideal or attractive of pets. He wasn't furry, or fluffy. He didn't do tricks or obey commands. He didn't answer when spoken to, or ask for walks or food. He just sat there, motionless, whatever the weather.

I would often hear Joe talking to him. "Hello, Bug-Eye, how are you today? Bit chilly, isn't it? No, don't move, I just need this log over here. No, you're not in my way. Sorry to disturb you, mate, this won't take a minute."

Bug-Eye never replied.

That November, I had a Facebook message out of the blue. My old college friend, Andy, contacted me. I'd seen my friend Anna, his wife, briefly before we'd left for Spain, but we were poor correspondents and hadn't caught up with each other's news for a long time.

November 23, 2009
Hi Vicky,

How are you? Been a long time! Well, I finally bought Chickens *as a Christmas present for Anna and I would like to get a flight for Anna to come over and see you as part of her present (and to sign the book). Say a Friday flight returning on Sunday some time in Jan/Feb?*
If you think this is a good idea then please let me know. If this is not a good idea, then again let me know I would understand .
My view was that a visit from Anna may provide material for the next book haha!
All the very best for the book, the future looks great...
Andrew
X

November 24, 2009
Hello Andy,
How nice to hear from you! Of course it would be lovely to have Anna here for a weekend. The only thing that worries me is the weather. Winter in the mountains is very unpredictable, often cold, often wet and windy. If that doesn't matter, then fine, but a little later in the year may be more pleasant. It's totally up to you.
We have niece Becky coming in June for a week, and other friends in May, apart from that any time is great.
love,
Vicky xx

November 25, 2009
Hi Vicky,
Well that's great, I started to read the book and I could not put it down, so I wondered if we could both come? What if Anna and I came out to see the chickens and the mules and two very special people on the 12th of March returning on 14th March?
I thought it would be a special present to send Anna on her own but that was before reading the book. Is this doable? (new word). IF it is I will look out for flights, if not let me know what fits in best for you, re dates...
Your fan, haha
Andrew
X

November 26, 2009
Hello Andy,
Those dates in March are absolutely fine and it would be lovely to see you both. We've got plenty of space and although I can't guarantee the weather, it will be a little warmer than Jan/Feb and the mountain wildflowers will be starting which is always pretty.

Hope you can find flights.
Vicky xx

In Spain, the 8th of December is a public holiday called *Immaculada,* the feast of the Immaculate Conception. Around this time, poinsettias suddenly appear in the shops and are planted on roundabouts and public places in the city. The Spanish have different names for this flaming red plant. Sometimes it is called the 'Christmas Star' or 'Flower of the Holy Night' and we were told they grow wild in the Canary Islands, mainly on the northern slopes. Every December, Carmen-Bethina would knock on our door and hand us one of these festive, colourful plants.

One year, I asked her to explain the significance of the poinsettia. It was such a beautiful story that I listened in awe. I have since heard many different versions, but this is the story that Carmen-Bethina told me:

> 'There were once a very poor orphan brother and sister living in a small village. Their names were Pablo and Pepita and because they wore rags and were forced to beg to survive, they had few friends.
>
> At Christmas time, the village held many parties and festivities, but Pablo and Pepita were never invited. The village set up a beautiful Nativity scene in the church which everyone admired, but Pablo and Pepita had never seen it.
>
> On Christmas Eve, the Midnight Mass would take place and all the village children were encouraged to attend and bring the Baby Jesus a gift.
>
> "How can we go," wept Pepita, "when we have nothing to give?"
>
> Her brother put his arm around her shoulders to comfort her but could think of no reply. What gift could they bring when they had scarcely enough food to keep themselves alive, and no shoes on their feet?
>
> Suddenly an angel in shimmering white appeared before the two children. "Any gift that you give with love will be cherished," said the angel before fading away in front of

their eyes.

Hand in hand, Pablo and Pepita walked down the lane to the church. Pepita, deep in thought, stooped and picked an armful of weeds growing in the hedgerow.

"This is what I'll give the Baby Jesus," she said. "It will make a soft bed for Him."

When they entered the church, it was already full of villagers. Children were placing expensive presents around the crib, and looked up in scorn when they saw Pepita's offering.

"Those are weeds!" they cried. "Is that all you've brought?"

Pepita held back tears of shame and tried to ignore them, gently laying down her gift.

And then a miracle happened. The dull weeds burst forth into glossy green leaves and petals of flaming red appeared. The villagers gasped. They had never seen such marvelous flowers before and were speechless with wonder.

The villagers were ashamed. They now understood that a gift given with love is far more valuable than the most expensive gift money can buy.

From that day on, they invited Pablo and Pepita into their homes, and fed and clothed them. They named the beautiful plant 'The Flower of the Holy Night' and it continues to grow wild, like a weed.'

When Carmen-Bethina gave us the potted poinsettia, it was like the one in the story; glossy of leaf, crimson petals that burst with colour and health. But the second that Carmen-Bethina turned her back, the plant began to wither. One by one, the leaves turned sickly yellow and dropped off. The glorious red petals curled and fell. Before long, I was left with a bare stem, a skeleton.

I tried watering it more, then watering it less. I tried giving it more light, then placing it in shady places. Perhaps temperature was important? So I put it in warmer spots, then tried standing it in cooler locations.

Nothing worked. Those wretched plants never survived and were dead by Christmas. Every year was the same - whenever Carmen-Bethina visited, I had no choice but to push the latest poinsettia into a cupboard to hide it.

ዩዩዩ

When we lived in the UK, we foolishly believed that by moving to southern Spain, we would never again need to endure cold winters and constant rain. Our first winter in El Hoyo was a revelation. We were snowed in for four days with no water or electricity and El Hoyo was cut off from the outside world. That particular winter was unusual, but we often had sprinklings of snow during subsequent winters, and night temperatures frequently fell below freezing point. Our chickens fluffed out their feathers and spent the cold nights huddled together on their perch. Sylvia and Gravy grew thick winter coats.

Sometimes wild winds would arrive, sudden and unexpected, ripping the last stubborn leaves from the vine and howling down the chimney, puffing woodsmoke back into our kitchen.

One particular day I'd pegged out the laundry on the rotating washing-line on our roof terrace, and promptly forgot all about it. Clothes don't take long to dry in Spain and a cool winter breeze spun the dryer briskly. I went back downstairs and inside, not noticing that the wind was strengthening. Gradually, it whipped itself up into a rage and Joe and I could actually see the gusts arriving. The wind bent the trees at the top of the mountain, and like a Mexican wave, it travelled down the mountainside, contorting the trees in its path. Through the valley it roared until it engulfed our house, angrily rattling the shutters before moving on.

Then I remembered the laundry on the line and ran back up the outside staircase to retrieve it. The wind still roared in the valley and whipped at the washing, bunching it together, twisting it round the line and trying to snatch it from my fingers. I filled the laundry basket and retreated back inside. I was dumping the basket onto the kitchen table as someone knocked on the front door.

"I'll go," said Joe, and I listened as he opened the door and spoke briefly to the visitor. I recognised Geronimo's familiar voice.

"Vicky! Come here a minute," Joe called and I joined him at the door.

Geronimo stood hunched on our doorstep, collar up, his Real Madrid scarf wound tightly around his neck, the ends thrashing in the wind. The usual bottle of beer peeped out of his coat pocket. One hand held his coat together at the chest, defending himself from the wind. His other hand clasped a dirty grey rag.

Female readers will relate to the uncomfortable incident that followed. We all have *nice* undergarments that we wear when going out, right? And we all have big, *dreadful* undergarments that should have been thrown away years ago, yes? But we hang onto that grotty underwear because it's just too comfortable to part with. True?

I recognised the rag that Geronimo clutched.

"*Buenas días,*" said Geronimo, smiling, and to my horror, held up my ancient, faded tattered knickers, the size of the Mayflower's mainsail as it set off for the Americas. "I believe these are yours?" My knickers dangled from his fingers, flailing in the wind.

"No, no, they're not mine!" I said, recoiling, withdrawing as far as possible from the humiliating garment.

"Are you sure?" asked Joe, helpfully leaning forward to examine them more closely. "I think they *are* yours."

"They're *not* mine," I said, willing Joe to stop...

"Come on, Vicky, I recognise them! They're definitely yours! Geronimo found them in the village square, wasn't that lucky? He noticed you'd hung the washing on the line this morning. And you and Marcia are the only ladies in the village at the moment. They're hardly going to belong to Marcia, are they? She's tiny - they'd be much too big for her!"

I wanted to kill him. Slowly. Painfully.

"They got rather dirty, I'm afraid," said Geronimo apologetically, dropping the dreadful knickers into my reluctant hand. "But another wash will make them clean. Just do not hang your laundry up in winds like these, or you will lose it again."

"Thank you," I said through gritted teeth, pocketed the shameful knickers and turned on my heel, my face the colour of a poinsettia. I resolved never to speak to Joe again. Ever.

Joe carried on chatting with Geronimo. I heard them discussing *El Gordo* (the fat one), the biggest lottery in the world. All over Spain people buy Christmas lottery tickets in the hope of winning *El Gordo*. *El Gordo* prizes are massive, and it is not unusual for a good number of people from the same village to become a lot richer overnight.

"We were just discussing the lottery," said Joe later. "Lots of our villagers have clubbed together to buy a ticket. It'd be good if they won, wouldn't it? By the way, you were a bit rude to Geronimo, saying those knickers weren't yours, and walking away like that."

I didn't bother to reply.

Joe looked for Bug-Eye that evening, but he had disappeared, probably swept away by the ferocious wind. Joe missed him, saying that he had lost a good friend, one that never answered back, unlike some people he could name.

When the wind finally blew itself out of the valley we heaved a sigh of relief, but we were not prepared for what Mother Nature was going to hurl at us next.

Spicy Broad Bean and Serrano Ham Fritters

If you like your Spanish tapas hot and spicy, then this Serrano ham and broad bean recipe will certainly get the taste buds tingling. Serrano ham and broad beans are often enjoyed together in tapas bars all over Spain. In certain bars you can see the locals shelling the beans and dipping them in a little salt before accompanying them with a wafer-thin slice of ham, washed down with a glass of ice-cold Fino sherry.

For this recipe these simple fritters combine the same flavour combination but with the added kick of chili and a hint of hot smoked paprika.

250g (9 oz) fresh broad beans
100g (3-4 oz) diced Serrano ham
A quarter teaspoon hot smoked paprika
1 small red chili pepper (diced)
1 tablespoon plain flour
Half a lemon
Salt
Olive oil
Cracked black pepper

Shell the broad beans and place into a food processor.
Add the diced ham along with the smoked paprika and chili pepper. Squeeze the juice of half the lemon into the mix.
Blend for a few seconds until the ingredients become the texture of breadcrumbs.
Remove the mixture and tip into a bowl. Season with salt and pepper and add the flour, mixing together using a fork.
Meanwhile, heat a good inch (3cm) of olive oil in a frying pan.
Using two tablespoons, shape your fritters by rolling between the two and add to the oil, fry until deep golden brown on the outside.

Serve with a cool yogurt mint dip.

13
Rain

In Andalucía, winter is the wet season. Farmers relax, no longer needing to water their thirsty olive, almond and citrus trees. So when it began to rain heavily that December, nobody was surprised. But that year, it started well before Christmas and didn't stop. The sky turned black and poured torrents down to earth, hour after hour, day after day. It rained so hard that decades-dry river beds transformed into raging rapids. Rain bounced off the corrugated asbestos roofs, producing a drumming sound that continued indefinitely. Gutters poured into streets below, creating fast-flowing streams coursing past people's front doors. Even the builders working on The Monstrosity gave up, laid down their tools and went home.

But the wet weather didn't dampen the Ufarte twins' excitement about the coming Christmas celebrations, even though Christmas was a couple of weeks away. One day, when the rain had temporarily eased, we had a visit from two identical fluffy pink bunnies. They sat in our kitchen, paws wrapped around mugs of hot chocolate.

Castilian Hot Chocolate

(with thanks to David Sutton-Rowe)
The Spanish dip small sponge cakes into this drink for a quick breakfast.

55g (2 oz) unsweetened cocoa powder
180g (6 oz) sugar
7 tsp cornflour
140 ml (7 fl oz) water
1 litre (2.2 pints) milk

Mix the cocoa powder and sugar together.

Dissolve the cornflour in the water and combine with the cocoa powder and sugar mixture in a medium-sized saucepan.
Stir to a smooth paste.
Heat this mixture on a medium hob, continuously stirring it with a whisk. Gradually pour in the milk, stirring as you bring it to a simmer. Simmer for 10 minutes, stirring continuously, until the cocoa is thick, smooth and glossy.

Serve warm in mugs or glasses.

"We are going to be in the Christmas Procession!" said Pink Bunny #1, dark eyes huge over her mug of chocolate.

"Our *abuela* is making our costumes now!" said Bunny #2, her long ears flopping in excitement.

"How lovely!" I said. "What are you going to dress up as?"

The bunnies looked at each other conspiratorially, then, "It's a secret!" they chorused.

"And are your brothers going to be in the Procession

too?" asked Joe, amused.

"Oh yes," said Pink Bunny #1.

"*Everybody* is going to be in it. The priest will be in the front, then everybody behind," explained Pink Bunny #2.

"Except our *abuela*," said Pink Bunny #1.

"But she'll be watching," said Pink Bunny #2.

"Our brothers are going to be shepherds..."

"...with *real* sheep!"

This was clearly a Christmas Procession not to be missed. I tried to imagine a flock of sheep processing with the villagers on Christmas Eve. I hoped it wouldn't rain on their parade.

"You can be in the Procession if you like," said Pink Bunny #1 generously.

"Well, perhaps we'll just watch," I said, "like your *abuela*. But we'll make very sure we don't miss it." I spoke the truth. "Now, tell me, have you decorated your house ready for Christmas?"

'Nativity' by Twin #2

"Oh yes! Come and see our *Belén*!" the pink bunnies squealed. "It's beautiful!"

Christmas was celebrated very differently in Spain. It was certainly not the huge commercial event that we saw in the UK, where Christmas decorations appeared as soon as Halloween was over, if not before. Decorations in the Spanish home consisted mainly of a *Belén*, or miniature nativity scene. These tiny, intricate displays were carefully constructed and depicted the baby Jesus surrounded by Mary, Joseph, shepherds and cattle.

"Well, we'd like to," I said, looking down at the excited upturned bunny faces. "But we don't want to disturb your family."

"Papa has gone down the mountain," said Pink Bunny #1.

"And Mama is taking a siesta with Sergio," said Pink Bunny #2.

"And your other brothers?"

"Jorge and Carlos are playing soccer somewhere," said Pink Bunny #2 rolling her eyes.

"And where is Fifi?" asked Joe casually.

"Fifi is in the bedroom with Mama and Sergio. Will you come and see our *Belén*? Pleeease?"

"Of course we will, we'd love to see it," I answered.

The little pink rabbits hopped off their chairs and dragged us by the hands down the street to their house. I looked up at the sky, willing those black rain clouds to go away and leave our village alone.

In the Ufarte cottage, the kitchen and living room were one room. Now it was empty, apart from Granny Ufarte snoring in her chair beside the fire. Her mouth had fallen open, revealing pink, toothless gums. On her knees was a heap of sewing; yards of shiny white fabric and pieces of tinsel that twinkled in the firelight. It didn't take the Brain of Spain to guess that the Ufarte twins would be dressing up as angels for the forthcoming Christmas procession.

The *Belén* was charming, as we knew it would be. The Ufartes had sprinkled sand into a tray and set up a tiny cardboard stable surrounded by a fence made of twigs. There was a Mary, a Joseph, a tiny baby Jesus asleep in a thimble, three kings, some shepherds with cotton-ball sheep and an angel. Little plastic townsfolk stood in a cluster. Tethered to the twig fence were a couple of donkeys, a camel, two cows and a dinosaur.

"Carlos put *that* there," said Pink Bunny #1 crossly, wrinkling her nose in disgust, pointing an accusing finger at the dinosaur.

"And Jorge put *him* there," pouted Pink Bunny #2, pointing at one little figure. I leaned over to inspect the townsfolk more closely. Amongst them stood a little plastic soccer player in full Barcelona colours.

"We don't like them at all - but Papa said we should leave them."

"Well, we think your *Belén* is beautiful," said Joe, smiling.

At the sound of Joe's voice, there was a low growl from behind the closed bedroom door, followed by sharp, furious barks.

"Time to go, I think," said Joe uneasily as claws scrabbled frantically at the door.

I looked out of the Ufarte's window. "It's starting to rain again," I sighed. "Better get home before it gets too bad." I looked back at Joe, but he'd already wisely slipped away, avoiding a confrontation with Fifi. I said goodbye to the twins and followed him out, leaving Fifi to hurl herself at the bedroom door.

I ran into the house as the rain began to pelt down. "Joe! Batten down the hatches, we're in for another really wet night, I think."

It rained all that night, and the next day, and the next. It rained so hard that Joe and I made a worrying discovery.

I noticed it first. A small but determined trickle of water meandering down our dining-room wall. Our roof leaked.

"Well, it's not too bad," I said. "We can easily mop that up."

But it got worse. Much worse. The trickle turned into a stream, which turned into a minor river that developed tributaries. More leaks appeared in different places in the ceiling. Water dripped and plopped all around us and was collecting in large puddles on the floor. There was nothing we could do except move the furniture aside and keep mopping.

And still it rained. We set out pots, pans and buckets to catch the water, and still it rained. We mopped and laid out every towel we owned, and still it rained. The sky was black with no breaks and the raindrops hammered down. I couldn't help silently scolding Spike Milligan. One of his *Silly Verse for Kids* runs like this:

'There are holes in the sky.
Where the rain gets in.
But they're ever so small.
That's why rain is thin.'

Rain is thin? No. Absolutely not. Our raindrops were huge fat affairs that splatted and soaked as they landed.

"If this rain doesn't stop, I'm seriously going to have to think about building an ark," said Joe, gloomily scratching himself down below.

"It could be worse. Imagine what it must be like in the Ufarte household. All those kids cooped up inside - the boys not able to go out and play football. The twins underfoot all the time."

Joe nodded. "If they've got any sense, they'll all go back down the mountain to their town house. I'm sure they'll leave tomorrow. The forecast is rain for the foreseeable future."

But the Ufartes stayed put. We didn't see them because it was too wet to venture outside, but I knew they were there. From our window I could just make out the smoke curling from the Ufarte chimney.

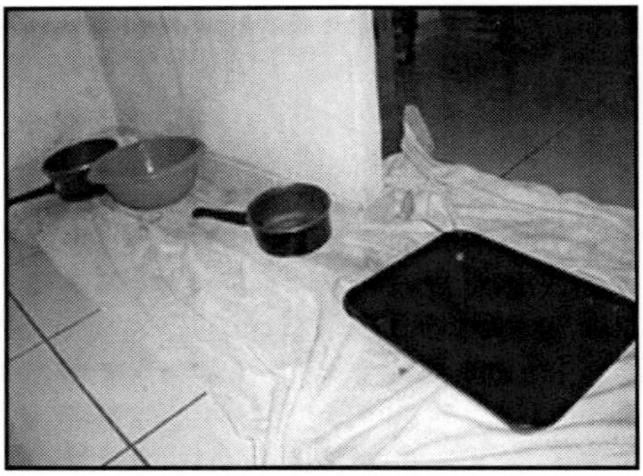

Catching drips

Apart from the constant mopping up, the rain affected not only our mood, but also our British television reception. We had a huge dish on our roof to receive satellite TV but when it rained heavily, the picture fragmented, then dissolved. We could still watch Spanish TV channels, but that didn't cheer us up either. Especially when they showed the drawing of the Christmas lottery. Joe flicked from channel to channel but the drawing of *El Gordo* seemed the only option. We hadn't bought tickets and were not interested, so found other things to divert ourselves instead.

I noticed that Joe didn't always concentrate on the book he was reading, sometimes he withdrew into that private world of his, the one he wouldn't share with me.

"Joe, what's worrying you?"

"Wretched rain! No TV!"

"No, it's not that, and you know it. Why won't you tell me what's really bothering you?"

"Oh, it's nothing, I'm just being stupid. It isn't even worth talking about." And that was all he would say.

Paco came up from the city and Joe grimly told him about our leaky roof. Paco shrugged and showed no sympathy at all.

"Pah!" Paco said, slapping the wall with his hand. "All Spanish roofs leak!"

They do? We didn't know that.

"I have come to check my house, but I am not staying, it is too wet. All the family will come back on Christmas Eve, of course, but we will not stay in the village now, not in this rain."

Apart from the Ufartes, it looked as though the village would remain empty until Christmas Eve. Joe's mood did not improve.

"I'm tired and I'm fed up," he said. "There's nothing on the TV and this rain is never going to stop. I'm sick of staying inside. I wish something would happen, but I know it's just going to be another day of rain-bloody-rain tomorrow. I'm going to bed." And he stamped off, leaving me to check the water leaks, lock up, turn the lights off and follow him. I wondered whether it was really just the weather depressing Joe, or something more serious.

At three o'clock in the morning, we woke in a fright. Somebody was pounding on our front door, ringing the doorbell and shouting, all at the same time. I knew it was three o'clock because I squinted at the bedside clock, and I knew it was still raining because I could hear it hammering on the roof.

"What the...?"

"Who on earth is that?"

"I'd better go and see. It sounds like Juan Ufarte." Joe threw back the covers and staggered out of bed. He pulled on some clothes and made his way to the front door. The wet weather had made the wooden door swell and I heard him wrench it open. I heard brief words exchanged, then Joe returned.

"It's Papa Ufarte, the baby is on its way. Maribel has gone into labour and they need to go down the mountain straight away. They want me to go round and watch the children."

"I'll go with you."

"No need. Doesn't need two of us - the kids'll be asleep anyway. Granny will wake up in the morning and she can take over then."

"Okay, if you're sure."

"I'm sure."

I heard the front door slam behind him and remember thinking,

Well, Joe, you wanted something to happen. Be careful what you wish for... Then, *Oh dear, what about Fifi?* before I fell asleep again.

Mediterranean Roast Chicken

A lovely Mediterranean-style roast chicken, with lots of herbs and seasonal vegetables. The best thing about this dish is that it just goes into the oven and cooks itself!

1 whole medium fresh chicken
2 green or red peppers
2 medium onions
1 medium courgette
3 tomatoes
150g (5-6 oz) mushrooms
Oregano
Thyme
Olive oil
Salt and pepper

Wash the chicken inside and out, removing any giblets, and pat dry. Place in a large oiled roasting tin.

Rub the outside of the chicken with olive oil, season with a little salt and pepper and sprinkle generously with oregano and thyme.

Cook in a high oven for about 20 minutes, basting with the juices.

Prepare the vegetables by washing and/or peeling and chopping into chunks.

Add the vegetables to the pan and lower the heat on the oven to medium, then cook for an hour to an hour and a half, depending on the size of the chicken.

Check the chicken is done by inserting a thin knife between the leg and breast. If the juices run clear, then the chicken is cooked. If not, then leave for another 20 minutes.

Serve immediately with boiled potatoes or lots of fresh bread to mop up the juices.

14
Lollipops

When I got up the next morning, Joe still hadn't returned, so I amused myself by checking emails and Facebook messages. My old friend Andy had written again about his surprise Christmas gift to his wife Anna.

December 23, 2009
Vicky,
I thought I had sent you another message, but it appears to have disappeared in the ether. March looks good for us.
Hoping that's possible for you? Anna will be so surprised.
Merry Christmas
Andrew
X

I looked at my watch. Nine o'clock and still Joe hadn't returned from the Ufartes. I made myself a coffee and quickly answered Andy's message.

December 23, 2009
Hello Andy,
Can't promise good weather as the mountains are very unpredictable, but March is usually nice. The village will be very quiet as the villagers usually only come up at weekends, but I'm sure we'll be able to amuse ourselves... It'll be fabulous to see you both.
Vicky xx

By ten o'clock I began to feel a little anxious. The rain had eased to a drizzle as I walked down the street to the Ufarte house. I could hear their television blaring on some cartoon channel and the shouts of children's voices at play. Crouched on the doorstep looking damp and miserable, was Fifi. The door wasn't locked so I knocked and entered. Fifi slunk in behind me.

The Ufarte home was a mess. Toys littered the floor and there was scarcely a place to step without treading on something. All the children were still in their pyjamas and, judging by the spilt milk and trail of sugar and cornflakes, somebody had attempted to make breakfast.

Jorge was bouncing his football against the living-room wall, making the pictures rattle and only just missing the china crucifix.

Scrap was sitting inches away from the television screen, absorbed in watching Jerry strap dynamite to Tom's tail. He stopped sucking on his dummy in anticipation, waiting for the big explosion. KerrrrBANG! The dynamite exploded, leaving poor Tom hairless yet again. "*¡Olé!*" Scrap shouted, falling over backwards and kicking his legs in the air with glee. Sitting up again, he popped his dummy back into his mouth and resumed sucking, no doubt waiting for Jerry to punish poor Tom again.

The twins were playing with their Barbie dolls. The entire couch and floor in front of it was set out with all their Barbie accessories. Apart from all the Barbie clothes draped over the cushions and arms of the couch, there was a Barbie car, Barbie pony, Barbie jacuzzi - an entire Barbie world.

"*Tía* Veeky!" said Twin #1. "Mama and Papa have gone to the hospital to get our new baby. *Tío* Joe is looking after us."

"Fifi tried to bite *Tío* Joe again. *Tío* Joe put Fifi out in the street," said Twin #2.

"Poor Fifi," said Twin #1, sighing. "She has been out in the rain. Mama would *never* put Fifi out in the rain."

The fire had burned low but still flickered. Fifi was huddled in front of it, steaming slightly, drying off. She sneezed, probably seeking sympathy, aware she was being discussed.

"Poor Fifi, she has caught a very nasty cold. That is because bad *Tío* Joe shut her out in the rain," said Twin #2.

On cue, Fifi sneezed again. It was then that I noticed the armchairs either side of the fire. In one, snored Granny Ufarte, head back, mouth open. In the other, snored Joe, a mirror image of Granny Ufarte: head back, mouth open, both oblivious to the chaos surrounding them. The only difference was that Snap-On was asleep on Joe's lap, his curly head tucked under Joe's chin, dribble darkening the front of Joe's sweater.

"Joe! Wake up!" I said, shaking his shoulder.

"Wh...what? I wasn't asleep," slurred Joe, opening his eyes and sitting up straight.

To my surprise, Fifi ignored him. She looked miserable and bedraggled, her coat damp and dull. She'd evidently had a bad night, leaving her with no energy to battle her archenemy.

"The Ufartes might be back at any minute," I said. "I think we should tidy up a little before they get here."

Joe surveyed the scene. "You're right," he said. "It *is* a bit of a mess. I've been up all night. That dratted Fifi went for me as soon as I arrived and made such a bloody noise that all the kids woke up. I tried shutting her in the bedroom, but the kids kept feeling sorry for her and letting her out again. So I threw her out in the street."

"Oh dear..."

"And Snap-On wouldn't let me put him down. And Jorge's been throwing that football at the wall for hours. And Scrap's been watching that same Tom and Jerry DVD all night."

"Oh dear," I said again. "Listen, you stay there and I'll tidy up. Snap-On won't let you put him down anyway. It won't take me long, and I'll make a coffee when I've straightened things up a bit. Looks like you've had a hard night."

The first thing I did was confiscate Jorge's football. "I'm sure your Mama doesn't let you play soccer in the house," I told him. His sulky silence told me I'd guessed right. I passed him a soccer annual, and he occupied himself by flicking through the pages of that.

I turned the volume of the TV down, and Scrap didn't even notice. Jerry was hitting Tom on the head repeatedly with a hammer and Scrap's head jerked in sympathy with every blow. *Dong, dong, dong...*

I confined Barbie World to the couch, resisting the urge to re-live my childhood and play with the twins.

Finally, I addressed myself to the discarded toys and remaining mess. It took a while to de-cornflake and sweep up, but eventually the place was reasonably tidy.

"There!" I said to Joe. "That'll do. I'll make us a coffee now."

But I never made that coffee, because at that moment the Ufarte car screeched to a halt outside. As the engine switched off and the car door slammed, all the Ufarte children rushed to the door. Granny Ufarte stirred in her chair. In front of the fire, Fifi sneezed, but didn't lift her chin from her paws or open her eyes. Joe stood up, a waking Snap-On in his arms. We watched.

"Mama! Papa!" squealed the twins.

The front door opened and Papa Ufarte entered, alone. He looked tired but happy, his face aglow with good news.

"Where is Mama?" asked Twin #1 hanging onto her father's sleeve.

Papa Ufarte put down the shopping bag he was carrying and hugged his daughters, burying his beard in their shiny hair. "Your Mama is fine. She is having a little rest at the hospital. And I have the *best* news for you all - you have a brand new baby brother!"

"We have?" asked Twin #2. "Is he in that bag?"

"No, silly!" answered her father. "In this bag I have treats for you all!"

Now the boys were more interested and surged round their father, curious to see what he had brought. Papa Ufarte dug into the bag.

"First, soft-centred chocolates for you, *abuela*." Granny Ufarte had woken up and was smiling gummily. "Now, do not get chocolate on those angel costumes you are sewing!" he teased. Then, in a stage whisper, "They are those liqueurs you like so much. You know, the chocolates with the zing in the centre... We are celebrating!"

Granny Ufarte smiled proudly at her son-in-law, and accepted the box of chocolates with a nod.

"What about us! What about us!" yelled all the children, jumping up and down. Even Snap-On jigged in Joe's arms.

"Have you been good?" he asked, eyebrows raised, eyes twinkling.

"We have been good! We have been good!" yelled the children.

"Ah, well then... for the rest of you, I have... (*rummage, rummage*) LOLLIPOPS!" He grabbed a handful of lollipops and threw them into the air. The children scrambled for them and retreated, licking busily. Joe unwrapped one for Snap-On, who clutched it in his fat little fist. Within seconds, his pink tongue had turned blue.

"And this is for us," said Papa Ufarte, delving into the bag for the last time and pulling out a bottle of best brandy.

"Congratulations," said Joe, "but you must be tired. We'll go and leave you in peace."

"No, no, I insist!" said Papa Ufarte, pouring a generous measure of brandy into three glasses. Somebody knocked on the door. "Ah, that will be Geronimo! Pass me another glass. I saw him in the square a moment ago and invited him to join us for a little celebratory drink."

And so we celebrated the new baby Ufarte's entrance into the world that wet, pre-Christmas morning. The more I sipped, the more blurred and surreal our surroundings became. I stopped caring that Jorge had found his football and was bouncing it off the wall again. I stopped caring that Barbie World had spread back all over the floor. I didn't care about the blue stains from Snap-On's lollipop smeared all over Joe's sweater. I didn't hear Jerry pummeling Tom, or Fifi sneezing, or Granny Ufarte chomping on her liqueurs. I was just glad to be alive, in Spain and in the bosom of this warm, wonderful family.

Much later, Joe and I stumbled home and fell straight back into bed. Mopping up the puddles in the dining room could wait.

Christmas Eve dawned and the skies remained dark and dismal. Heavy clouds hung low above the mountains, poised to empty their load - but it didn't actually rain. Sometimes there were breaks between the clouds where the sun tried hard to penetrate. Joe and I took the opportunity to take a walk around the village.

Everything was wet. The channels at the sides of the road coursed water, the olive and almond trees dripped and the soil was black and soaked. Only the coloured banner proclaiming '*Feliz Navidad*' strung across the village entrance and the white fairy lights on the trees in the square provided any brightness.

In spite of the weather, cars packed with villagers were beginning to arrive from the city. Christmas Eve, or *Nochebuena,* is the most important family gathering of the year. Shops, businesses and restaurants all over Spain shut their doors for *Nochebuena* allowing families to enjoy the day together. Two important events take place on *Nochebuena:* the all-important family meal, and Midnight Mass.

The Christmas Eve meal is never rushed, and consists of many courses. Typically, starters may be shellfish or prawns in mayonnaise with cold cuts of meat. There may also be soup and another fish dish, perhaps baked bream, lobster, salmon, sea bass or trout. Then comes the traditional roast: either lamb, suckling pig, duck or turkey with truffles.

Prawns with Garlic Mayonnaise

A common Christmas meal starter. Use shelled, frozen prawns if you prefer, although fresh ones are more flavoursome.

50g (2oz) mayonnaise
50g (2oz) large prawns
1 large clove of garlic, crushed
Sea salt

Mix the mayonnaise and crushed garlic in a bowl and set aside.
Shell the prawns and place on a baking tray.
Sprinkle with a little sea salt and olive oil, then place under a medium grill.
Turn the prawns several times so that they are thoroughly cooked on both sides.
When the prawns are golden, place on a serving dish with the garlic mayonnaise to one side.

Finally, the meal is rounded off with a selection of sweets and cakes, such as marzipan, *polvorónes* and *turrón*, a nougat made from sweet almonds. Often the meal doesn't start until after Midnight Mass. '*Esta noche es Nochebuena, y no es de dormir*' so the Spanish saying goes, meaning 'This night is the Good Night, and is not meant for sleeping'.

Paco and Carmen-Bethina arrived with the whole family, the car stuffed with bags of food. We popped next door briefly to wish them *Feliz Navidad,* deliver our Christmas presents, and to relay the Ufarte news. Paco was sitting on the doorstep cracking almonds with a hammer, using an old tree stump as an anvil.

"Pah!" he said, his hammer whacking an unsuspecting almond with such force that the shell splintered and shot in all directions. "The women have banished me from the house. They are preparing for tonight."

Nougat
Turrón

Turrón is a very traditional Christmas treat. This recipe is for the original variety that the Moors brought with them when they occupied Spain, and very much nicer than the pink or white sticky nougat we are familiar with.

1 kg (2lb 4oz) of honey
500g (18oz) sugar
2 egg whites
1½ kg (3½lb) ground almonds
1 lemon

Heat the honey in a pan over a low heat.

Slowly add the sugar to the pan while stirring with a wooden spoon. Beat the egg white until stiff and add to the honey and sugar mixture in the pan.

Remove from the heat and stir for 8 to 12 minutes before placing the pan once again over a low heat. Continue stirring until the mixture begins to caramelize (it will turn brown).

Add the ground almonds together with the zest of the lemon. Mix everything together and then set aside to cool for a few minutes. Put the mixture into a metal tin lined with grease-proof paper. Allow to cool for at least 2 hours.

15
The Procession

While Paco pounded the living daylights out of the almonds outside, Carmen-Bethina was rushed off her feet preparing the special evening feast inside. She and Sofía were surrounded by bags, utensils, pans, ingredients and all the paraphernalia necessary for the perfect Spanish *Nochebuena* meal. Saucepans steamed on the hob and a cauldron bubbled on the tripod over the open fire. The kitchen was as hot as Hades and suffused with a million different cooking aromas. Bianca, their over-fed spaniel, sat panting under the kitchen table, poised to gobble up any scrap that was thrown in her direction.

After the usual rounds of kisses, Carmen-Bethina cleared a small space on the kitchen table, just enough to open their gifts. Little Paco was watching the TV but jumped up when he saw our Christmas parcels. Carmen-Bethina's plump face was wreathed with smiles as she unwrapped her necklace and other bits and pieces. Sofía liked her necklace too, and Little Paco lost no time finding a dead fly to examine with his new microscope.

Little Paco examining a dead fly

Apart from the wrapped parcels, we also gave them the box of Christmas crackers that the Gin Twins had kindly brought from the UK last October.

"What is it?" asked Carmen-Bethina, turning the box over and over.

"Christmas crackers. You know, you pull them," I said.

"I do not understand. Pull them?" Carmen-Bethina had no idea what I was talking about.

I took the box from her, opened it and took out a gaudy green cracker, complete with tinsel and Rudolf the Red-Nosed Reindeer sticker.

"*Madre Mía*, what is it for?" she asked.

"It's just an English tradition," I said. To demonstrate, I put one end in Sofía's hand, and the other in Carmen-Bethina's hand. "Now, pull hard!" I instructed.

Mother and daughter pulled. CRACK! The cracker split apart and the contents tumbled to the floor. Bianca shot out from under the table, hoping it was food, but retreated when she was satisfied that it was nothing edible.

"*¡Madre mía!* That gave me a fright!" said Carmen-Bethina, dabbing her plump red face with a teacloth.

"*¡Madre mía!*" laughed Sofía.

"Whoever is holding the big end of the cracker is the winner," explained Joe, picking up the trinkets from the floor.

"That is me! I am the winner!" beamed Carmen-Bethina. "What have I won?"

"Hmm..." said Joe. "As you're the winner, you're allowed a Christmas wish."

"Oh, I know what Mama will wish for," said Sofía, rolling her eyes in mock exasperation. "Mama always makes the same wish. She will wish that I find a husband soon."

"*¡Claro!*" said Carmen-Bethina severely. "You are thirty years old now. It is time you had a husband."

"Now, stop that, Mama! You do not want me to be like Lola Ufarte, do you? What else did Mama win?" asked Sofía, neatly changing the subject.

"First of all, this joke..." Joe read, translating it into Spanish.

'Question: What is white and goes up?'

Sofía and Carmen-Bethina thought hard, brows furrowed.

"I do not know," said Carmen-Bethina. "Perhaps a house? No, I know! A sheep walking up the mountain?"

"No," said Joe, reading from the slip of paper again.

'Answer: A confused snowflake.'

"Hee hee!" laughed Carmen-Bethina, throwing her head back, double chins wobbling with mirth. "A confused snowflake! Hee hee! That is a good one!"

"Then there's this," said Joe, passing her the little packet containing the novelty. "I think it's one of those puzzles that you have to work out how to untangle."

Carmen-Bethina was fascinated. She examined the little shiny metal links, then tried solving it, her chubby fingers pulling and twisting this way and that.

"This is impossible!" she muttered, head low in concentration.

"And finally... We mustn't forget the Christmas hat!" said Joe, unfolding the yellow paper hat and placing it on Carmen-Bethina's bent head.

"Beautiful!" said Sofía, laughing.

And so we left them to cook their Christmas meal and work out the puzzle.

I have a piece of advice for any business-minded readers. Start selling Christmas crackers in Spain - there is a fortune to be made.

Back in our house, Joe and I looked at the clock. It was only a few hours until the Christmas Procession. Mercifully, the rain still held off, although the omnipresent black clouds loomed overhead. The village was quiet apart from muffled revelry behind closed doors.

Then, a little before midnight, the church bells began to peal, the sound filling the valley. Shortly after, dozens of footsteps could be heard shuffling outside in the street. The Christmas Procession was approaching.

Village processions always passed our front door, so we were guaranteed an unobstructed view. Joe and I stood in our doorway to watch.

The priest led the way, walking slowly and solemnly. The lamplight caught the rich gold embroidery of his robes making it glitter.

Then came two identical, very serious, small angels complete with tinsel halos nodding above their heads. Neither twin looked up at us, each concentrating hard on the big church candle she carried, the flames flickering slightly. Granny Ufarte had sewn tinsel around the hems and sleeves of the twins' white robes, and gold sequins sparkled on their ballet shoes.

Behind the angels walked Joseph and Mary, carrying the Baby Jesus. Joseph was bearded and dressed in long brown robes. One hand held a walking stick, and with the other he led a donkey. The donkey trotted obediently beside the couple, occasionally shaking his ears.

Joe gave me a sharp nudge. "Do you recognise him?" he hissed.

"Of course!" I hissed back, "That's Geronimo's donkey!"

"No! Not the donkey! Look at Joseph!"

I stared. It was Papa Ufarte. And of course the blue-robed Mary beside him was Mama Ufarte, proudly cradling her newborn. Mary gazed down at the baby she held, the tip of his little nose just visible between the folds of the white shawl. Madonna and child. It was absolutely perfect.

Joseph and Mary wore quiet smiles, but looked neither left or right, immersed in their roles. Behind them walked the Two Kings, resplendent in ornate royal, flowing robes, with crowns and gifts that glittered with jewels. They walked with their heads held high, haughtily, enjoying their finery and the characters they played. There was no mistaking who they were - Roberto and Federico: The Boys.

Two Kings? But where was the third King? Joe looked at me and raised his eyebrows in question. I shook my head, I didn't know.

Following the Kings was a throng of townsfolk, all dressed in costume but far more hastily put together than the leading performers. Some wore old curtains or tablecloths, with the obligatory checked teacloths on their heads. Lola Ufarte managed to look devastating even though she wore what looked suspiciously like a bedspread. Snap-On was balanced on her hip. Paco winked at us as he passed by.

Then came the shepherds with their sheep. There were several shepherds and they came in all sizes. The smallest one was unquestionably Scrap Ufarte and I recognised his bigger brother Jorge, Little Paco and several other village boys. But my eyes were drawn more to the sheep than the shepherds. I clapped my hand over my mouth, trying to stifle my giggles.

There were three 'sheep', all on leashes. Each wore a coat that buttoned underneath. Sewn or stuck onto these coats were white cotton balls. One sheep trotted with an air of arrogance, nose in the air. Another sheep waddled, its jacket straining against its sizable stomach. And the third sheep was tiny, resembling a floor-mop wearing a pompom jacket. But there was no disguising these sheep - they were unquestionably Copito, Canelo and Fifi.

Joe stepped back into the shadows of our porch. I knew exactly what he was thinking. This would not be a good time for Fifi to resume their hostilities. But the shepherds and their sheep passed safely by and I sighed with relief.

Behind the shepherds walked the remainder of the villagers, their friends and relations. It was a large crowd and the procession stretched back as far as I could see.

I'd noticed that the church bells had stopped ringing a minute or so earlier but I wasn't prepared for what happened next. From our elevated viewpoint on our doorstep, we could see something was happening right at the back of the procession. Someone was jostling and elbowing his way through the crowd, almost knocking people over in his haste to reach the front. By the time he reached our level, I could see who it was.

It was the third King, Geronimo. His crown was all askew and his robes were hitched up, revealing far too much hairy bare leg. In one hand he held his gift for Baby Jesus, and in the other, of all things - a hammer.

"Quick, quick, out of my way, please!" he urged, battling his way forward.

And then I understood. Of course! Geronimo had been ringing the church bell. On special occasions, and for maximum effect, he would climb the bell tower and hammer on the bell. That was why he was late for the procession.

"He's been ringing the church bell," I said. "That's why he's got that hammer. And that's why there were only two Kings!"

Joe nodded and laughed out loud, a big mistake.

Slightly ahead in the procession, the smallest sheep pricked up her ears and growled. Ignoring the efforts of her shepherd master, the sheep turned and strained on her leash, desperate to confront her enemy. The shepherd boy tried valiantly to restrain her, the leash tight as a tripwire. King #3, still trying to work his way to the front, reached the shepherds. In his hurry, he tripped over the stretched leash and fell to the ground, his gift to Baby Jesus still clutched in his hand. He sat there, cursing in a most unroyal and unholy way and took a surreptitious swig from a flask secreted in his robe.

The orderliness of the procession was destroyed and confusion reigned. People stumbled over Geronimo, fell over Fifi and bumped into each other and the shepherd boy. However, this sheep was not to be distracted. Straining at her leash, she growled and barked at her quarry, cowering in our porch: Joe. I know some villagers were annoyed, others laughed, but eventually somebody hauled Fifi away and we quietly slipped into our house for a large Christmas brandy to soothe our fraught nerves. We never saw the end of the procession.

As I write, Joe has the dubious honour of being the only person I know who can claim he's nearly been savaged by a sheep.

Unlike in Britain, the 25th of December is not a particularly special day in Spain. We couldn't find turkey or brussels sprouts in our supermarket, standard fare on a British Christmas table, so we had roast chicken and as many trimmings as we could find. The sage and onion stuffing, Christmas pudding and brandy butter the Gin Twins had kindly provided were welcome additions and we wore our reindeer antlers in support of this festive time. Sylvia and Gravy feasted on meat leftovers and the chickens guzzled vegetable scraps and fruit. It was a nice day, apart from the fact that the rain had started once more. We were stuck indoors, and the TV reception had died again. I turned to the Internet for entertainment. First, I opened this email from the Gin Twins:

Hi Vicky and Joe,
Sorry we haven't written for ages but you know how it is at school this time of year. We've been concentrating on the Xmas nativity and stuff and loads of staff have been off sick -loads of the kids too. Thank goodness it's the hols now. Weather's been awful, snow and slush and it's freezing. How are you? Bet you're sitting in the sun over Christmas, not like us, lucky things. Did next door like the Christmas crackers, btw?
Anyway, this is just a quick note to say that all your bookmarks arrived, and we had a bit of a 'Book Launch' party thing at school. Those cake

topper things are great, but I did it the night before in a rush and I didn't read the instructions properly and I didn't have any icing sugar so I'm afraid the cake topper thingy was a bit of a disaster but it was funny - we couldn't stop laughing, haha! Those are bits of the cake topper hanging off my knife in both pics, haha!!
Have a great Xmas, I'll write a proper email in the New Year,

Luff to you both and the chickens
Juliet & Sue xxx

Nobody seeing the picture that appeared in the local Observer newspaper later that week would have guessed that the cake topper was a complete disaster. Good job, Gin Twins!

The picture in 'The Observer'.

Having checked my emails, I sauntered over to Facebook to see how my English friends were enjoying Christmas.

Garlic and Pepper Chicken

A hot and spicy chicken recipe using chicken pieces, this recipe is great with thighs, drumsticks, or chicken breast and packs a real fiery punch as a result of cracked black pepper and hot smoked paprika. Ideal for the oven or barbecue. Can be eaten hot or cold.

8 chicken pieces (skinned)
10 garlic cloves (crushed)
1 large sprig fresh thyme
1 pinch rosemary
1 tablespoon hot smoked paprika
1 tablespoon cracked black peppercorns
Splash of fino sherry
Olive oil

Clean and skin the chicken pieces and place on a baking tray.
In a pestle and mortar add a generous drizzle of olive oil and the garlic, herbs, pepper, paprika and sherry.
Crush and mix well, adding more olive oil if required to create a paste.
Spoon the mixture over the chicken pieces.
Cook in the oven on a medium heat for 35 - 40 minutes.
Serve with chips, fritters or salad.

Tip: For an even hotter alternative try adding chili flakes. This mixture can also be used as a very hot marinade.

16
Chickens

Gin Twins

Sue and Juliet, or the 'Gin Twins' as we called them, were not twins at all. In fact they were not similar in any way except that they shared a love for gin and hilarity. Joe and I always looked forward to their visits and spent our time with them in fun, silly games and laughter.

Juliet was a vegetarian and animal lover. Her own children were always allowed pets and she believed that a house is not a home without a few guinea pigs, cats, or even a degus or two. (Yes, I had to Google that, too.) On the other hand, Sue declared she wasn't keen on animals. She had been known to pat a dog or acknowledge wildlife, but she remained firm: no pets allowed, ever.

When Joe and I first acquired chickens, we knew nothing about poultry-care. However, we quickly learned, and soon became charmed and fascinated by these endearing creatures. We were impatient to show them off to the Gin Twins. Juliet loved them immediately and was happy to pick them up or allow them to perch on her lap. Sue, although interested, kept her distance.

So we were greatly surprised and amused when we found out what Sue had received for Christmas. I looked at my Facebook page and stared, before hooting with laughter.

"Joe!"

"What?"

"You will *never* guess what Sue's just written on my Facebook page!"

"Which Sue?" We knew many 'Sues' but I knew Joe wasn't really listening.

"Gin Twin Sue. You have to hear this! Guess what her doting husband got her for Christmas?" I couldn't believe what I was reading.

"Gin?"

"Well, of course gin, but what else?"

"I give up."
"Well, come over here and have a look, then!"
Joe read Sue's Facebook entry over my shoulder.

Gin Twin Sue
Vicky! OMG!!!! Mark got me CHICKENS for Christmas!!! Help! I don't know anything about chickens!!!!
December 25, 2009 at 7.15pm· Unlike · Comment

We both laughed out loud. Sue? Gin Twin Sue with animals? Chickens of her own? Surely not! We couldn't quite believe it. And neither could any of our friends as they gradually came online and read Sue's news.

Victoria Twead
Real chickens?????????????
December 25, 2009 at 7:43pm · Like

Gin Twin Sue
Yes! I'm still in shock.......!
December 25, 2009 at 7:47pm · Like

Eve A
Yes, Pete & I were there. Sue opened wot she thought was a fish tank first, then...a chicken cuddly toy from Ruth.....then a book about chickens.... then a chicken coop...bless...haha!
December 25, 2009 at 8:24pm · Like

Victoria Twead
hahahahaahahaha!!!!!!!! Funniest thing I've heard for ages!!! Anti-Pet Gin Twin Sue with pets?!!!
December 25, 2009 at 8:40pm · Like

Gin Twin Sue
I have now calmed down a bit- Mark gave me a hutch, the actual chickens are coming later...
December 25, 2009 at 8:50pm · Like

Eileen G
Hahahaha really?? Mark got you a chicken hutch? That is so funny LOL x 1000000000000000000 xxx
December 25, 2009 at 11:14pm · Like

Rosemary S
What???????
December 26, 2009 at 11:48pm · Like

Eileen G
I just can't imagine her with them, I can't stop chuckling!
December 25, 2009 at 11:52pm · Like

Eve A
chuckling or clucking ha ha ha
December 25, 2009 at 11:54pm · Like

Gin Twin Juliet
OMG!! Just seen this!

Gin Twin Sue
Haven't got the livestock yet - you are going to have to help me, seriously!
December 26, 2009 at 9:44am · Like

Gin Twin Juliet
I will help you!! Are you thinking of names yet. Wot about Curry and Kiev.... how many you getting!!!
December 26, 2009 at 9:49am · Like

Gin Twin Sue
Tikka Masala and Why Did You Cross the Road?!
December 26, 2009 at 9:53am · Like

Debbie C
Ha,Ha Congratulations Sue, thats soooooo funny!xx
December 26, 2009 at 12:28pm · Like

Mark H
Sue is already getting paranoid about foxes and we haven't got the chickens yet!
December 26, 2009 at 1:29pm · Like

Eileen G
Is that her get out excuse ? Just imagine the fresh eggs!! Yummy!!
December 26, 2009 at 1:50pm · Like

Eve A
No apparently they dont like human hair or the smell from empty wine bottles, well there's hundreds of them in her garden already lol and perphaps she could shave her head and lay her hair down to save her chickens lol, wot u say Sue? ha ha ha ha
December 26, 2009 at 3:30pm · Like

Eileen G
Foxes are put off by the smell of male pee! Keep drinking those pints Mark!!
December 26, 2009 at 5:11pm · Like

And so on and so forth. I'm sure you've got the drift... Sue's husband Mark and daughter Ruth had accomplished the impossible: introducing pets into Gin Twin Sue's life, whether she wanted them or not.

Later, Ruth wrote me an email that further verified events and brought that Christmas day incident to life:

Hi Vicky and Joe,

...In answer to your question - Dad was the one who thought to get mum the chickens - you know she's never liked pets but ever since she saw your chooks, she has had a bit of a thing about the feathery ones!

Part of giving her the present had to involve winding her up somehow - something we like to do every year :) We weren't going to be able to 'hide' the chickens before Christmas so decided to delay getting them and get her the coop and random bits like the feeder and water tray. So Christmas day she unwraps the feeder first...having had a glass of wine (or 3) she is a bit confused by this large piece of plastic. Still none the wiser when she unwraps the cuddly embroidered chicken I bought her. Dad and brother Joe and Eve's husband Pete then say they have something for her outside...In they come with the coop (in bits) - and we ask her what might go in a coop and need a feeder...et voila she realises she is going to be a mummy to chooks! Cue much squealing and running around!...

Next thing is sorting out collecting the ex-batts from the Hen Welfare Trust when the weather gets better...

Ruth

P.S. My Nan (Dad's mother) has knitted a chicken jumper in case one gets chilly! And in the Blue, Black and White colours of Bath rugby team! How cool is that?

Rescuing ex-battery hens is a subject dear to my heart, so I was delighted to hear that they'd contacted the British Hen Welfare Trust. This excellent organisation describes itself thus:

'The British Hen Welfare Trust is a small, national charity that re-homes commercial laying hens, educates the public about how they can make a difference to hen welfare, and encourages support for the British egg industry.'

Now it was just a case of completing the paperwork before Gin Twin Sue could collect the new members of her family. The rescue mission, already code-named 'Operation Sage & Onion' was under way. Joe and I waited with bated breath to hear the next instalment, the arrival of the chickens, next summer.

For the rest of December, it continued to pour with rain. Every day the chores were the same:

1) Mop up the lake in the dining-room
2) Empty the pots, pans, bowls and buckets of water
3) Lay down fresh straw in the chicken run so that the girls don't wade in mud
4) Check for new roof leaks
5) Fiddle with the TV in the vain hope of getting a picture

The whole of Andalucía was being battered by the nonstop rain, so the 28th December, the Day of the Holy Innocents, came as a welcome break to lighten the general mood.

The origins of the *Día de los Santos Inocentes* are somewhat macabre. It is the day commemorating the slaughter of babes, at the time of Jesus's birth, by order of King Herod.

However, in Spain, far from being a depressing time, this day is much like our April Fools day, a day for pranks and tricks. Even the TV and radio stations get in on the act, rather like in Britain. Few people our age will ever forget the TV documentary, years ago, that fooled the British viewing public into believing that spaghetti grew on trees.

Children and adults alike delight in tricking each other and some Spanish bakeries do a roaring trade selling cakes made with salt instead of sugar. When the prankster is ready to reveal his joke, he chants, "*¡Inocente, inocente!*" much like we call "April Fool!" when the prank is over.

Carmen-Bethina popped round to give us a bag of tomatoes from her son Diego's greenhouse empire. From her we heard that the Ufarte children had enjoyed themselves that day. They substituted salt for sugar in the sugar bowl. They removed Papa Ufarte's guitar from its case and replaced it with Scrap's Jack-in-the-box. Jorge Ufarte hung a 'No Parking' sign above Granny Ufarte's chair by the fire and hid his little brother's Tom and Jerry DVD.

Joe and I thought nobody had played a prank on us until Joe went down the garden to feed the chickens.

Devilled Kidney and Wild Mushroom Tostada

The tostada is a typical Spanish breakfast enjoyed in bars all over Spain, and you will see workers eating "tostada de tomate" most mornings. The humble tostada lends itself well to a whole variety of toppings. In this recipe there are pigs' kidneys (although lambs' kidneys work equally well) and mixed wild mushrooms. Together with a little smoked paprika, this hearty tostada will keep you going until lunchtime!

Half a stick of French bread
200g (8oz) mixed mushrooms, quartered
1 pig's kidney (or 4 lambs' kidneys)
50g (2oz) butter
1 tablespoon plain flour
1/4 teaspoon hot smoked paprika
Salt
Cracked black pepper
Parsley

Slice the French stick horizontally and toast on both sides. Leave to cool.

Melt half the butter in a frying pan and fry the mushrooms. When done, set aside and keep warm.

Meanwhile, slice the kidney lengthways, but not all the way through. Open like a book then cut into strips.

Add the paprika to the flour and season with salt and pepper, dust the sliced kidney ensuring a good covering.

Melt the remaining butter in the frying pan and fry the kidney for 2 minutes turning regularly.

Reintroduce the mushrooms for 30 seconds and mix with the kidney.

Butter the toast, then spoon over the ingredients.

Garnish with torn parsley before serving.

Serves 2

17
Mysteries and Midnight

Joe trudged down to the bottom of the garden, head down, bucket of grain in one hand, plastic box full of kitchen scraps in the other. We called the blue plastic box the Chicken Treat Box and one glimpse of it was guaranteed to drive our chickens into a frenzy of anticipation. With head low, and the hood of his coat up to shelter from the drizzle, Joe didn't notice anything amiss until he reached the chicken coop gate.

Not a chicken to be seen. No excited cluckings and flappings and eager leaps at the gate from the other side.

Cursing, he checked and double-checked. No chickens hiding. The chicken run and hen-house were empty. It was most definitely a chicken-free zone. Joe thoughtfully scratched his nethers and pondered.

No visible escape holes. So, none had escaped. A fox? Not possible. If the chickens couldn't get out, then a fox couldn't get in. No sign of a struggle, no feathers strewn around as evidence. Stolen, perhaps? Unlikely. Who'd steal six elderly chickens who rarely laid eggs? And taking our chickens' age into account, any chef attempting to cook them would be presented with a testing culinary challenge.

Hmm... and anyway, there's no crime in El Hoyo. (*deep thought*) Aha! The date! 28th December, the *Día de los Santos Inocentes* when pranks are played... The Ufarte children? But how would they get into the garden without a key for the back gate? So who *did* have a key to get into the garden? Next door, of course. Sherlock Joe turned back to the house, satisfied he had solved the mystery of the disappearing hens.

"That naughty Little Paco has hidden our chickens," Joe announced. "A *Santos Inocentes* prank, no doubt. I'd better pop next door and find out where he's put them."

Out he went again, and knocked on their door, entering when he heard the familiar "Come in!" call from Carmen-Bethina. Little Paco was stretched out on the couch, watching TV. He looked up and greeted Joe briefly, his mind occupied with the TV show he was watching.

"Now then," said Joe, smiling, wagging his finger at Little Paco with mock severity. "Where are our chickens?"

Little Paco looked up in surprise, the TV show forgotten. He frowned and sat up straight, the picture of innocence. "Pardon?"

"Our chickens!" said Joe, still smiling. "Where are they?"

Little Paco stared, his mouth open, then he shook his head vehemently. "I do not know anything about any chickens..."

Sherlock Joe gave a hollow laugh, he wasn't going to be thrown off the trail that easily.

"Now come on! Today is the *Día de los Santos Inocentes,* and you hid our chickens somewhere, didn't you?"

"*¿Qué pasa?"* asked Carmen-Bethina, appearing from the kitchen, drying her hands on her apron. "What is the matter?"

"Oh, I was just asking Little Paco about our chickens. I think he took them for a *Día de los Santos Inocentes* joke."

"I did not!" said Little Paco.

"He did not," echoed his mother. "Little Paco has not been out all day. He has a cold and I would not let him go out in the rain."

"Oh," said Sherlock Joe, deflated. He looked from mother to son and reluctantly accepted that they were telling the truth. "I'm very sorry, I thought it was you."

"You say your chickens are missing?" asked Carmen-Bethina, relaxing a little now that her son had been cleared of the charge. "When did you last see them?"

"Last night, when I went to feed them."

"Hmm..." Carmen-Bethina said thoughtfully, but said no more. But Joe could tell her mind was working overtime.

Back in our kitchen, Joe was relaying the details of his investigation to me. We were still puzzling over the mystery when we heard a familiar pounding on the front door.

"English! English!"

Joe jumped up and let Paco in.

"*¡Inocente, inocente!*" bellowed Paco, following Joe inside and thumping him on the back so hard that Joe jerked forward a step. "*¡Inocente, inocente!*" And he roared with laughter.

"It was you?" Joe asked, astonished.

"Hehe! Of course! Who else has a key? I took your chickens! It was me! *¡Inocente, inocente!*"

"Well!" said Joe, recovering. "And I blamed poor Little Paco..."

"You know how I always get up very early, even when I am not going to work? Today, very early, I unlocked your gate, and I tiptoed-tiptoed-tiptoed to the chicken enclosure." Paco's pantomime re-enactment of the scene, tiptoeing in his work boots made us all laugh. "It was still dark, and the chickens were very easy to catch." Paco mimed how he plucked each chicken off her perch. "And I put them in my box! One, two, three, four, five and six! Then I shut the enclosure, tiptoed-tiptoed-tiptoed out, and locked your back gate again!" He turned the imaginary key with a flourish.

"Well..." said Joe, exhaling.

"*¡Inocente, inocente!*" crowed Paco. "Pah! And you English, you never noticed a thing!" More gales of laughter.

"No, we didn't," said Joe rather lamely. "Um, and where exactly are they now?"

"Your chickens? They are very safe, follow me."

So Joe followed Paco back out into the street and to Paco's store-room, next to his garage. Paco pushed the door open, and there, blinking in the sudden light, perched on an upturned wheelbarrow, were our six chickens.

Chickens can't see at all in the dark, and our chickens were very tame, so it was an easy matter to catch them and transport them home. I set out the brandy bottle and glasses on the kitchen table, ready for Paco the Prankster and Sherlock Joe's return. As Paco banged the table with his fist and retold the chicknapping story for the twentieth time, I was thankful that *Día de los Santos Inocentes* came but once a year. As for Joe, I think he was happy to hang up his metaphorical deer-stalker hat for good.

And still it rained. Low, charcoal-grey cloud slumped permanently in our valley and sprawled over the mountaintops. Beneath the olive and almond trees, murky pools collected, reflecting the dark clouds above. The water sat on the surface, the soil too saturated to soak up any more.

Most of the time the rain was steady, insistent, unrelenting. Occasionally it would turn to drizzle and even seem to stop, but so much moisture hung in the air that stepping outside meant getting soaked, even when it didn't appear to be raining.

We were heartily sick of the water that ran down our walls, and heartily sick of emptying the pots and buckets under our leaky roof. We yearned for a decent TV picture, but sadly, that wasn't going to happen in the near future.

December 31st arrived: the end of the old year and beginning of the new. The Spanish have two curious New Year traditions although it is difficult to guess how many adhere to the first, as it requires the wearing of red underwear. Apparently this will bring luck to the wearer in the coming year. Some declare that this only applies if someone else has purchased the items for you.

The second tradition requires some skill. At the stroke of midnight, one grape must be swallowed with each chime of the clock, each chime representing one month of the year. This feat sounds easy, but believe me it is not. The best chance of success is to prepare your twelve grapes carefully. Peel them, de-seed them, and even then it is difficult to keep pace with the chimes.

This grape-swallowing custom was even more difficult to accomplish in El Hoyo as the church clock was so unpredictable. Sometimes it didn't chime at all, but more often the chimes were duplicated. For example, at one o'clock it chimed twice, and at eight o'clock it chimed sixteen times. Of course at twelve o'clock, the village was subjected to twenty-four chimes, and with the echoes in the valley, seemed to last for ever.

Most Spanish families enjoy a big meal together on New Year's Eve, then congregate outside the church at midnight to eat their grapes and wish each other a happy new year. Joe and I wrapped ourselves up against the rain and cold and walked down to the church just before midnight, our twelve (seedless) grapes at the ready.

"Are you wearing red underwear?" asked Joe.

"Mind your own business."

"I was just wondering..."

"Well, don't."

"Do you think we should have brought twenty-four grapes each, in case the clock chimes twice, as usual?"

"Probably."

There was already quite a crowd outside the church, despite the inclement weather. The lamplight threw crazy shadows against the church walls and the wet street shone. People milled around greeting each other, clutching their handful of grapes in readiness, all waiting for the stroke of midnight. Paco's family were there in force. Carmen-Bethina shared an umbrella with Little Paco, and Sofía and her policeman boyfriend stood a little apart, deep in conversation.

Geronimo stood in a group of villagers, his Real Madrid scarf around his neck, beer bottle peeping coyly from his coat pocket.

Apart from Granny, all the Ufartes were there. Mama Ufarte stood in the centre of a cluster of ladies who were cooing over her new baby. Lola Ufarte was in the centre of another group, mainly male. I could hear her vivacious laughter and I saw Geronimo's eyes repeatedly drawn to her. The Ufarte twins, dressed in identical raincoats and polka-dot Wellington boots, held their Father's hands. A few steps away, Jorge practiced fancy footwork, bouncing his football off his toe, and catching it in midair. Scrap, head down, occupied himself by kicking an empty juice carton, occasionally missing and kicking someone's shins instead. Snap-On slept in a pushchair swathed with plastic against the drizzle.

Even old Marcia was there, dwarfed by her grownup sons and their families.

I wondered idly how many folk were wearing red underwear that night, then glanced at my watch for the tenth time. Twenty seconds to midnight, ten seconds to midnight, MIDNIGHT!

Nothing. No church bells, no chiming, just the chatter of many Spanish voices. Perhaps my watch was wrong?

At five minutes past twelve, Paco shouted, "Pah! Geronimo! It is now past twelve o'clock! That confounded clock has stopped chiming again!"

"Give it a few minutes," said somebody. "The damp may have affected the mechanism."

Nobody seemed to mind, and the clock still hadn't chimed by seventeen minutes past twelve.

"Pah! Geronimo!" shouted Paco again, banging the church wall with his fist. "We are going to be here until next year if we wait for that clock to chime!"

Everybody laughed and Geronimo detached himself from the crowd and entered the church, disappearing from view.

"There he is!" somebody said, and pointed.

In spite of the drizzle, we all looked up. In the church tower high above us, Geronimo had reappeared, climbing the rickety ladder to the bell. Higher and higher he climbed, the village ladies ooohing and aaahing as his feet slid a little on the slippery rungs. I began to worry about how much alcohol he might already have consumed that night.

"Come on, Geronimo! You can do it!" called Lola Ufarte, her hands cupped to form a megaphone.

Geronimo hesitated and looked down at the object of his desire. Spurred on by her voice, he renewed his efforts. When he could climb no higher and was level with the bell, he stopped and drew out a hammer from his coat pocket. Hanging on to the ladder with one hand, he whacked the bell hard. Some terrified pigeons, disturbed in their roost, flapped out of the tower into the night. Down below, everyone cheered and swallowed their first grape. Geronimo hit the bell eleven more times in a reasonably regular fashion, while we all concentrated on swallowing our grapes. I choked on grape #6 and had to be slapped on the back by Paco. Joe got off to a flying start but only managed ten.

After the usual round of cheers, kisses, hugs and 'Happy New Year!' we strolled back home.

"I would have managed all twelve grapes if Geronimo hadn't rung the chimes so fast," grumbled Joe.

"Well, we'll peel the grapes next year, that's supposed to make it easier," I said. "You did well with your ten."

"By the way, *are* you wearing red underwear?" Joe asked. "You never said."

"No, you're quite right - I never said."

Looking back over our shoulders, we could still see Geronimo, lit up by the street light below, high in church tower, head tipped back as he swigged from his bottle.

I made just one New Year's resolution that night. I promised myself to find out what was on Joe's mind. Find out why his eyes sometimes took on that faraway look. Find out if he was tiring of our life in El Hoyo. I clenched my fists in my pockets and prayed that I'd made a mistake, misread him. I never wanted to leave El Hoyo and wished that Joe was as content as I was.

And so began 2010, apart from just one more noteworthy family event.

Baked Mackerel

A very popular Spanish recipe for baked mackerel, which is cooked in the oven with ripe tomatoes and potatoes. Full of herbs and spices, this dish makes a lovely healthy lunch or supper.

4 large mackerel fish cleaned and cut into thirds
3 potatoes, peeled and cut into bite-sized chunks
4 large ripe tomatoes quartered
4 cloves garlic peeled and cut in half
3 large glasses white wine
Olive oil
Handful of fresh parsley, roughly chopped
Salt and pepper

Place the mackerel, tomatoes, potatoes and garlic in a large oven-proof dish and drizzle with a little olive oil. Pour the wine over and sprinkle with the parsley. Season with salt and pepper.
Cook in a moderate oven for 40 to 50 minutes until the mackerel is cooked through but still moist.

18
Expensive Cake

Joe was already asleep when the telephone rang and I answered it.

"Mum? Mum? It's *me*! Happy New Year!"

"Karly! Happy New Year! How are you?"

"Brilliant! Everything's *amazing* here!"

"How's Cam?"

"He's great, everything is just *amazing*!"

"What time is it in Sydney?"

"Nine o'clock in the morning, we've been up *all* night. I thought I'd probably catch you. It's one in the morning in Spain, isn't it? Did you go with everybody to the church and eat grapes? Haha, bet you didn't manage all twelve! Remember a couple of years ago when I nearly choked? But, Mum, you'll *never* guess what's just happened!"

"No, neither of us managed all twelve. What's just happened?"

"Well, we've just had the most *brilliant* night - that's why we're still partying. We were watching the New Year come in at Sydney Harbour - they have the most *amazing* fireworks, it's fabulous with the Opera House all lit up - and the fireworks over the harbour are just *beautiful*, and there were *loads* of people there - and we'd just had a *fantastic* meal - and Cam's parents were there, and *everything*... Then, guess what happened!"

Karly and Cam

"Karly, I have no idea..."

"Guess!"

"I can't!"

"Cam went down on his bended knee and *proposed*!" Excited squeals, chatting and laughter in the background.

" Oh my word! How wonderful! Congratulations!"

"Mum, it was *amazing*! I couldn't believe what was happening!"

"And Cam asked you right there in front of everybody?"

"Yep! It was so *romantic*! And *everybody* stopped to watch, and it all went *really* quiet, and I just *stared* at him, and then when I said 'yes' everybody clapped and cheered - and you should *see* my engagement ring! I'm going to take a photo of it and email it to you. It's just *gorgeous*!"

"Congratulations! That's fantastic news!"

"I *know*! I'm going to be a married woman! Can you *believe* it? I'm *so* excited!"

Karly carried on filling in the details for a further hour. By the time I put the receiver down and went to the bedroom, my ear was sore and Joe was deeply asleep. I hugged the information to myself, looking forward to Joe's reaction when I told him in the morning. We both agreed, it was an excellent start to the New Year.

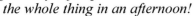

The start to 2010 stayed wet. We scarcely glimpsed our mountains under their permanent shroud of clouds and we rarely ventured outdoors. There was little to do apart from mopping up leaks and catching up on emails. I enjoyed receiving this email from my friends Gayle and Iain of *OrceSerranoHams.com*, whose wonderful recipes I stole for both this book and *Chickens*.

From: *info@orceserranohams.com*
Subject: *Happy New Year*
1 attachment(s): Nico.jpg

Hi Vicky!
Just a quick mail to say Happy New Year! The books we gave as presents were very well received, thank you for signing them, it made the gift very special. How are things with you?
I have read a good few chapters of 'Chickens' today and I am really enjoying it. I took it with me this morning while I went to get residency, thinking I would be in the queue for hours but I got seen straight away which was a very pleasant surprise, so I read a bit on the bus and am having to be strict and force myself to put it down as i could easily read the whole thing in an afternoon!

Anyway, not enjoying the weather too much, it's wet and miserable here although it did snow yesterday which Joshua enjoyed - it's all gone now though. How was your Christmas? We had a really nice time with family here and then on new years eve we went to our neighbours house and did the 12 grapes with them. I am getting better and only had 3 left at the end and Iain managed them all. Nico was so good and slept the whole time.
Anyway, I just wanted to catch up. I have attached a photo of Nico

which we took on Christmas day, he is such a gem and is doing really well.
Take care and lots of love,
Gayle

♀♀♀

Ask any Spanish child which are his favourite days of the festive season, and the answer will always be the same: the 5th and 6th of January. In Spain, children everywhere have only one thing on their minds: *Los Reyes Magos*, or The Three Kings as we would call them.

Back in England, Joe and I were accustomed to thinking that Christmas was over when the New Year had been welcomed in. We'd be tiring of the Christmas decorations, eaten the last shreds of turkey and crumbs of Christmas cake, and we'd be returning to work. But in Spain the best is yet to come. Santa Claus is not the one who brings presents for the children on Christmas Eve, it is the Three Kings in January.

On the 5th of January, there are processions all over Spain that herald the approach of the Three Kings to Bethlehem. The Kings are often on highly decorated floats, and throw streamers and sweets to the children in the crowd. In the Sierra Nevada, the Three Kings arrive on skis. Each town and village has slightly different traditions, but it is common for the parade to end in a gathering at the local church or school. Then each child's name is called out and they are handed a small gift. That night, when the excited children return home, they will leave their shoes out for the Three Kings to fill with yet more gifts.

The 6th of January marks the Feast of the Epiphany when the Three Kings, or Wise Men, arrived in Bethlehem. Spanish children will wake up to find their gifts, and this day is the last holiday before normality returns and school and work begin again.

Another highlight of the day is the *Roscón de Reyes*, that delicious, highly decorated bread-like cake baked to look like a king's crown. We were invited next door for a slice of cake and mug of hot chocolate.

"Lovely cake," said Joe as he munched his way through the slice of Roscón handed to him by Carmen-Bethina. He took another big bite.

Nobody warned Joe. Nobody told Joe to be careful. Nobody told Joe that the cake hid little Christmas figurines. Whoever finds the Christ Child figure is crowned King or Queen for the meal, while the one who finds the dried bean must pay for next year's *Roscón de Reyes*. Guess who broke a tooth as he bit on the Baby Jesus?

Joe clapped a hand to his mouth and spat the Baby Jesus and a piece of tooth into his paper napkin.

"What the..?" he spluttered. Luckily, Joe's horrified grimace was misread by Carmen-Bethina and Paco, who took it to be rapture at finding the Baby Jesus.

"Ahh!" beamed Carmen-Bethina, "you have found the Baby Jesus! I hoped you would be the one to get Him!"

"English!" shouted Paco, giving Joe's back a hearty congratulatory whack, causing him to eject another shard of tooth. "You are King for the meal!" He thrust the golden cardboard crown on Joe's bald head and everybody applauded, Bianca barking with excitement.

Paco whisked Joe's hot chocolate mug away and replaced it with a brandy glass, sloshing a generous measure into it. An hour later, Joe had forgotten all about the tooth.

"That's the most expensive piece of cake I've ever had," he moaned, much later. "I'd much rather have got the dried broad bean and had to pay for next year's cake, than have to go to the dentist and get my blasted tooth fixed."

I sighed and wrote myself a reminder on our kitchen calendar to make an appointment.

January 9, 2010
Vicky,
As you know, we are in the grip of very cold weather here in West Sussex, skiing gear is the order of the day.
I have booked every thing we have a hire car and a european TomTom so we are up and running ready for our visit in March.
Andrew
X

January10, 2010
Hello Andy,
*Yes, we've been watching the UK news with interest! Unusual for England to get so much snow! It's still raining here, never seen anything like it. They say it's the wettest winter in living memory but hopefully it'll have stopped by March... *fingers crossed**
Very much looking forward to seeing you both. Was Anna surprised by the present?
You are very organised - car, flights, everything. Our place is very easy to find, but bring your mobile phone just in case. I can easily draw you a map with main landmarks. We're about 40 mins away from airport (based on Joe's driving, normal driving probably 25 mins). Half the journey is easy motorway, then winding road into the mountains.
Vicky xx

January 12, 2010
Vicky,
We are really looking forward to seeing you as well. Anna was really surprised by your book and flight tickets on Christmas day.
Polly has my TomTom so unable to check whether it will lead us to your house, will do this later.
Take care, see you soon,
Andrew X

It would be nice to write that the weather improved with the start of the new year, but it didn't. It was the second week of January and we were still housebound. I looked out of the kitchen window at the steady drizzle. Would it ever stop? I yearned to see clear blue skies again, but the heavens had other plans. There was plenty more rain destined to fall on Andalucía. Four times the average rainfall for an entire year fell in just two months.

Our home felt permanently damp. Green and white patches of mould decorated our cave bedroom in furry clumps. The faster I scoured them away with bleach, the faster they grew back. Water still poured into our dining room, and in El Hoyo it was gushing in other unexpected places.

Three Kings Cake

Roscón de Reyes

This delicious cake is eaten with hot chocolate on the night of Epiphany when the Three Kings arrive and leave gifts for children. Whoever finds the Christ Child figure in the cake is crowned and becomes the 'king' or 'queen' of the banquet. Whoever finds the bean has to pay for next year's roscón.

400g (14oz) flour
3 eggs
100g (3-4oz) butter
100g (3-4oz) sugar
1 tsp baking powder
1/4 litre (half pint) milk
Zest of 1 lemon
Dried mixed peel or jelly sweets for decorating (the jewels)
Salt

To insert just before baking: A few Christmas figurines and a dried broad bean or similar.

Pour 4 tbsp of the milk into a glass and stir in the baking powder. Add this to a quarter of the flour and mix together until it forms a dough-like consistency.
Cover with a clean tea towel and set aside until it doubles in size.
Place the remainder of the flour in a bowl. Add the eggs, sugar and a pinch of salt. Add the remainder of the milk and zest of the lemon. Mix well. Add the butter and continue mixing for a further 2 minutes.
Add the dough mixture and combine. As soon as a smooth dough has been achieved, cover and set aside for 2 hours.
Take up the dough again and knead the mixture a little. Now shape it into a ring. Wrap some little Christmas figures in foil and also a dried broad bean and push them into the dough. Place onto a greased baking tray.
Brush with milk and decorate using the mixed peel. (Figs, quinces, cherries can also be used.)
Lightly sprinkle with sugar and place in a pre-heated oven (160°C or 320°F) for 15 to 20 mins. Cool on a wire rack before slicing.

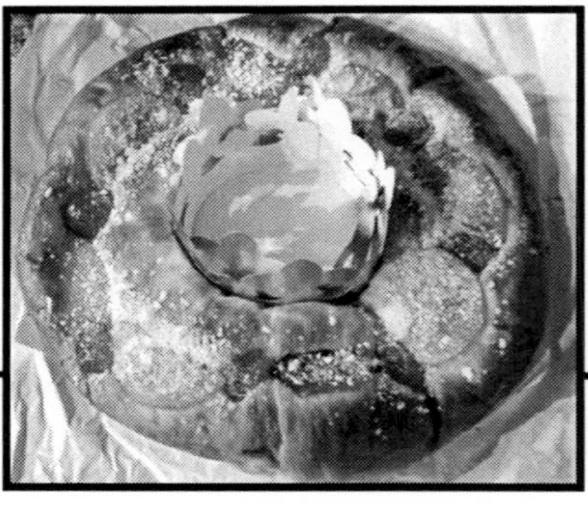

19
The Rain in Spain and a Donkey

Our part of Andalucía was already blessed with numerous underground springs that permanently poured from cracks and fissures in the mountains and valleys. Every village boasted of having at least one natural mountain spring and El Hoyo was no exception.

At the top of the valley was a spring that trickled into a rectangular cement catching-tank about the size of a small swimming pool. The mountain water was clear and sweet and the locals took their empty water bottles there to refill for drinking water. We had never seen the tank even half full until this January. Not only was it filled to capacity, but it overflowed like a giant's bathtub might if the tap were left running. Sheets of water poured over the rim and onto the road where it lay in great ponds.

Brand new watercourses now burst from the mountainside, a result of the prolonged torrential rain. Pretty waterfalls splashed where none had previously existed, all heading toward our village set in the lowest part of the valley.

At the entrance to El Hoyo was a little stone bridge spanning a deep dry gully. Previously, if one leaned over and looked down, one would see grass and weeds clinging to the sides, and trees growing at the bottom. During the past six years, we'd never seen a single drop of water flowing in that gully.

But following the deluge, water flowed. A stream was born that quickly developed into a small river. The river swelled and gathered strength, the level rising daily. Trees fought with the current to remain standing, their roots clinging desperately to the fast-disappearing soil. Water swirled around them and the weaker trees tilted, lost their foothold, and were swept downstream.

All around the valley, the slopes were being reshaped. Water worked into cracks in the ground and turned them into gaping fractures. Saturated, the soil broke away in massive wedges and slid downhill. Boulders, some the size of garden sheds, hung precariously, ready to let go their fragile hold and career down, gathering momentum and crushing all in their path. Landslides were becoming a common occurrence.

Driving anywhere was hazardous. Once over the little bridge with its newborn river gushing beneath, the road became a slalom course. Mud and rocks slid from above, piling up and obstructing the road. The soggy ground beneath the tarmac grew saturated, and in many places

Rocks on the road into El Hoyo

the road had entirely fallen away.

Around the countryside, many ancient and abandoned cottages flattened overnight, the dry, powdery mud and cement holding them together washed away. Walls that had withstood hundreds of years of blistering summers and freezing winters gave up their fight and were reduced to a pile of rubble. One day, the derelict house next to old Marcia's shop surrendered and collapsed into a mound of debris.

We were not alone. Everyone was suffering, most far more than we were. All over the region, homes were flooded as rivers burst their banks. In Jerez alone, 2,000 houses lost their battle with river water. In the village of Valderubbio, 600 of its 800 homes were flooded. Homes were devastated, agricultural land decimated, crops ruined, roads and bridges swept away and buildings collapsed on a scale that no Spaniard could remember. The TV newcasters told us that during three weeks of torrential rainfall, the Andalucían emergency services received 37,000 calls for help.

But it was the personal, heartrending tragedies that shocked us to the core and even stopped Joe complaining about our own situation. We heard countless agonising stories.

A pensioner perished in her own home as a flash flood swept her into the basement.

When the Guadalhorce river burst its banks, 26 horses drowned, their corpses floating onto nearby roads and fields.

We heard the tragic story of a British couple. They were visiting close friends who lived in a house in the country, near Granada. As they sat watching television, a landslide swept through the house, crushing the visitors but leaving host and hostess unhurt. The funeral was attended by hundreds, both Spanish and expats, and as the coffins were carried outside, the congregation clapped, a Spanish gesture to pay their final respects.

And then at last, after nearly ten weeks of continuous rain, the skies cleared and the sun came out - and stayed! We knew it would take a very long time for Andalucía to repair itself, but the future looked bright once more.

The council did its best, clearing and rebuilding the roads as fast as they were able. Work began again on the new apartment block, The

Monstrosity, as the builders returned, took up their tools and switched on their cement mixers.

Old Marcia's grown-up sons and grandsons arrived and donned space-suits. Marcia's roof leaked even more seriously than ours had. Water had poured in, and yet she never complained. The sons sprayed the whole of Marcia's roof with foam, insulating it and making it rain-proof.

I cannot describe the joy in my heart as I resumed simple tasks again, like hanging the laundry outside. The mud in the chicken enclosure turned back to powdery soil. Joe repaired the leaky roof, our rooms dried out, and we applied fresh white paint. It was still midwinter and the days were short, but the sun warmed our skin and lifted our spirits.

Granny Ufarte's chair reappeared in the street, the old lady's head nodding as she dozed, a pile of sewing or knitting heaped on her lap, Fifi at her feet. Sometimes the new baby's stroller would be parked beside her and the twins would be chattering and playing not far away. Of course the good weather allowed Jorge to take up his street soccer practice again, but we didn't mind.

Joe and I felt fat and unfit following the Christmas festivities and the rain-enforced house arrest. Now that the skies were clear, we set ourselves the target of walking up the winding path to the village shrine every day. The path was so steep as to be almost vertical, and the walk made the backs of my legs cramp and my chest heave with the effort. But it was worth it. The view around the valley and back down to the village was glorious. The rain had made the vegetation lush and the white-blossomed almond trees were a stunning contrast. I am aware that many writers, far more talented than I, have successfully described the winter almond blossom, and I understand what inspires them. Those perfect pinky-white waxy flowers against an achingly blue sky is, for me, one of the most beautiful sights in the world.

Almond blossom

If the Ufarte twins were about, they sometimes joined us on our hikes, putting us to shame as they skipped ahead with the energy of youth while we heaved and gasped behind. More often, we set off alone, beginning with a brisk walk that faded to a laborious trudge as

Quails in domed cages

the slope steepened. We stopped frequently, not just to rest and catch our breaths, but to look and listen.

There was a new sound in the village at this time of year. It was an urgent clicking noise, repeated many times and filling the hills. The source was the lady quail, advertising herself to attract a mate. As we passed through the village, we passed rows of domed cages pegged to house walls, each poor occupant clicking insistently. Paco and the villagers would leave at sunrise, find a likely spot to set their cages down, then hide and wait. The lady quail, with only romance on her mind, would click loudly, unaware that she was luring her suitors to an untimely death. The hapless male quails appeared, and BANG! their destiny was sealed. Instead of roaming the hills, they would be served up on plates. At weekends we frequently saw the village men triumphantly returning, rifles slung over their shoulders, cage in one hand, several lifeless quails swinging from the other.

Then, as we laboured up the hill and left the village behind, the clicking continued, but this time, it echoed from the mountains. Luckier, unconfined birds were calling, and we hoped their ardent admirers would remain safe from the village guns.

One cloudless February day, we puffed up the hill, glad of the excuse to stop and chat with Burro, Geronimo's donkey, who was often tethered at the side of the path. Burro was looking sleek and fat, stuffed full of lush grass. But his appetite was only his second priority because Burro was in love: he had a girlfriend. Each daybreak he sang to his lady-love in the next village, adding more verses at regular intervals during the day. His eyes would mist over, he'd lift his handsome head skyward, stretch his

Geronimo's donkey

neck, pull his lips back to display long yellow teeth, and bray long and loud to the mountains. Then he'd whicker, give his head a violent shake that made his ears rattle, and resume grazing. We never heard his lady-love reply but assumed she enjoyed his serenade.

On this particular day, we noticed that Burro's tether was wound tightly round the tree he was tied to. He must have walked round the tree numerous times, the rope shortening with each circuit.

"Poor old boy," said Joe, and seized Burro's halter. "I'll untangle you. All you have to do is walk back round this tree a few times. Come on..."

Would Burro walk? He would not. Apart from a rattle of his ears, he ignored Joe and studiously carried on chomping the grass and wildflowers.

"Now, come on, Burro," Joe urged. "It's for your own sake." He tugged and coaxed and pulled on Burro's harness. Burro stopped grazing but moved not an inch, his four hooves planted firmly in the soil.

"Oh well, please yourself," said Joe. "I was only trying to help you out." He shrugged, let go of the halter, turned and walked away. Instantly, Burro lifted his head and walked behind him.

"Don't look round," I said. "He's following you now."

Joe walked round and round the tree until the rope was unwound. Success! Pleased with himself, Joe stopped, and that was his mistake. Burro nudged him, then gave him a friendly but meaningful nip on the backside.

"OW!" yelped Joe, rubbing his rump. And that was the moment Joe acquired a second bruise on his delicate derriere. Readers of *Chickens* may remember how the Rainbow Man, or Indalo, inflicted damage to Joe's tender posterior, and now Geronimo's donkey had succeeded in doing the same.

It was on the walk up the mountain that we encountered other creatures, potentially far more deadly than Geronimo's donkey. In fact, these creatures are probably the most dangerous in Spain and have been known to take lives.

Huffing and puffing, we reached the bench at the shrine. As always, as soon as we regained our breath, we admired the view. Being February, the mountainsides were dotted with almond trees in full blossom and although the breeze had a sharp edge to it, the sky was clear blue and the sun warm.

Before the walk, I'd made up my mind to ask Joe outright what was worrying him, and I planned to wait until we were rested. We sat side by side on the bench, Joe with his arm around my shoulders. I looked at him sideways. Most of the time he seemed happy enough, but sometimes his eyes would glaze over and he would disappear into his own head. What was eating away at him? What was the matter? Why wouldn't he tell me?

Having gained sufficient breath to form words again, I opened my mouth to question him. My planned words were never uttered because I happened to look down at the ground a few feet in front of us and the moment was lost.

"What's that?" I asked, pointing.

Joe stood up and walked over, crouching down to examine the curious spectacle I'd spotted.

"Oh my gracious aunt!" said Joe. "What on earth..."

Sweet Potato Mash

This rich, creamy potato dish is a lovely vegetarian dish and also a really nice accompaniment to roasted meats.

1 large orange sweet potato
3 potatoes
25g (1oz) butter
125ml (4 fl oz) cream
Olive oil
Nutmeg, grated
100g (3-4oz) cheese, grated

Rub the sweet potato with a little olive oil and bake in a medium oven for 25 minutes until cooked.
Peel and wash the potatoes. Cook in a pan of salted boiling water until tender, drain and mash well and place into a large bowl or pan.
Remove the sweet potato from the oven and scoop out the flesh.
Mix with the mashed potato, add the butter and cream and beat well together. It should now almost resemble a smooth purée.
Season with salt and pepper, and then transfer to a gratin or shallow dish. Sprinkle with grated cheese and dust with a little nutmeg.
Place under the grill until the cheese begins to bubble, and serve.

20
Killer Caterpillars and a Dentist

The shrine stood in the centre of a clearing at the top of the mountain. It was freshly painted and flowerbeds had been planted all around. Several benches stood beneath waving pine trees and glorious views stretched out over the mountains in all directions.

But it wasn't the view that attracted my attention that February day, it was the area directly in front of my shoes. Writhing along the ground was a long, brown, sinuous worm-like thing. Except it wasn't a worm, or even a snake. It was a six-foot-long line of caterpillars, marching nose to tail.

Caterpillars walking in a line

We were enchanted. Each caterpillar was brown with yellow stripes and soft downy hairs. Each caterpillar followed the one in front, never deviating from the line, never being left behind. We stayed awhile, fascinated, watching the determined little procession.

"I wonder what type of caterpillar they are?" said Joe. "And I wonder where they're heading?"

The answer to these questions was to come as a bit of a shock...

We took some photos, headed back down the hill, pausing briefly to chat with Geronimo's donkey, then went home. I switched on the laptop and described our caterpillar encounter on Twitter. And what a response I got!

'@VictoriaTwead They're KILLERS! Don't go near them!'
'@VictoriaTwead Hate them, hate them, hate them!'
'@VictoriaTwead What is the point of those evil things?'
'@VictoriaTwead Those caterpillars are DEADLY, avoid at all costs!'

I was a little taken aback... Killers? Deadly? How could those cute little fluffy caterpillars be anything but charming? My Internet research took me to the Grazalema Guide which has an excellent article on these sinister little creatures.

I read the article. The caterpillars we had encountered were Pine

Processionary caterpillars, destined to morph into unremarkable moths. The female moth lays her tiny eggs in a pine tree. The eggs hatch and the caterpillars grow quickly, feeding voraciously on pine needles at night. To protect and house their community, they spin a white fluffy bundle in the tree and in February or March the entire colony abandons the tree in a long line searching for soft soil to bury themselves and pupate. This procession was what we'd observed on our walk.

So why the horror? Well, if disturbed, the caterpillar sheds its hairs. The hairs cause painful rashes, or much worse. If inhaled, the tiny hairs can be lethal. An inquisitive dog unfortunate enough to inhale them needs to be rushed to the vet within 40 minutes. Children and adults can also suffer severe reactions, including anaphylactic shock. Even walking under trees housing the bundles can be dangerous as the hairs are often airborne.

Clearly these critters are not to be messed with. I read with horror and huge sympathy the comments people had left:

written by John Evans
My Yorkshire has just come in contact with the Caterpillars and it's not looking good as her tongue is inflamed and she is passing blood. We had her in the vet and they said the next 48 hours will decide if she is to survive.

written by Anne Cliford-Banks
My five month old labrador puppy has lost nearly half his tongue which dropped off and is now suffering the effects of all the drugs he has taken. He has devloped two large lumps on his side. He is ok but don't under estimate the effect of theese caterpilars.

written by Raquel
Thank you for this info. I live in the Algarve Portugal and work at a local vet. Unfortunatly we have to treat many dogs and occasionally cats that have been affected by the caterpillar. Their tongues go neucrotic and sometimes the end may drop off. We have to wait a few days to check that the animal can still eat and drink with the remaining part of the tongue.

The last comment on the website made me smile simply because it seemed to me that this particular guy had had a very lucky escape.

written by vox
I came across thousands (and I'm not exaggerating) of these in Menorca last week. Walking up the sand, on the handrails, on the wooden walk-way and squashed underfoot in their thousands. There

were the nests in the nearby pine trees as you described and, looking at the photos above they appear to be the same. However if they are the same then I've been remarkably lucky. I spent ages picking them up and arranging them to get a good photo. I also was curious to know what they did when you moved them from their chosen trail etc.

As if these horror stories weren't enough, the pine trees themselves are devastated by these furry fiends and often die. The next time we hiked up the mountain, I examined the area much more carefully. The caterpillars had gone, but sure enough, we could see the white bundles dangling from the trees, just as the article described. And amongst the clump of pine trees stood dead ones, already stripped by the caterpillars. We resolved to warn the villagers and keep the Ufarte twins away from the area.

White bundles in a dead pine tree

Many men are complete babies when it comes to sickness or visits to the dentist, and Joe is no exception. His tooth was still jagged from biting the Baby Jesus on January 5th, and it took all my nagging to propel him to the dentist. I made the appointment and we drove down the mountain, Joe complaining the whole time.

"Fancy putting plastic figures into a cake! I bet Spanish dentists depend on after-Christmas business. I bet people break their teeth on those figures all the time."

"Probably."

"You know I hate going to the dentist, but still you're making me go. I've got used to that tooth now, I don't mind if it's broken."

"We're here now."

The waiting-room was half full: people sat staring into space or idly flicking magazines. A small boy tapped on the glass of an aquarium, trying to attract the fishes' attention. We found a seat and sat down, Joe still complaining.

"I don't need that tooth anyway, it's right at the back. I don't know why you're making such a fuss."

"The dentist is just looking at it today, then he'll decide what's best to be done."

"Humph! I hate going to the dentist. I hate it when he gets up all close, and peers into your mouth. And those drills..."

"Nobody likes going to the dentist. It's just one of those things..."

I could sense even the other patients were getting irritated by Joe's constant moaning. The small boy tore his eyes away from the fish-tank and stared at Joe, round-eyed. Perhaps he couldn't believe an adult could behave so badly, so much like an annoying child. Joe was speaking English, but the language of whinge is universally understood.

At last the surgery door opened and the dental assistant stood there with a clip-board. She was young and attractive, dressed in a white uniform and checking her list. We could see past her into the surgery where the dentist was busy preparing for the next patient. Both Joe and I saw at a glance that the dentist was female, blonde, good-looking and probably twenty-five years younger than Joe.

"Señor Twead? The dentist will see you now," said the assistant.

Joe stopped moaning, looked at me, then at the assistant, then at the dentist beyond. He rose from his seat and trotted into the surgery like an obedient pony. I heaved a sigh of relief. The little boy's eyes and mine met across the room and I sensed we'd both been expecting Joe to put up more of a fight.

Fifteen minutes later, the door opened. Joe backed out.

"I can't apologise enough!" he was saying, waving his arms. "I honestly didn't know!"

"Please do not worry, señor Twead, you are forgiven already," said the attractive dentist, laughing.

"Please believe me, I had no idea what I was doing."

"Señor Twead, it really doesn't matter, it was a genuine mistake." The dentist was still smiling and her assistant nodded in agreement.

Once again, I locked eyes with the little boy. His jaw had dropped open, and so had mine. His name was called next and his mother dragged him away, but even as he walked, the little boy's head looked over his shoulder, still staring at Joe, open-mouthed.

"What have you done?" I said furiously as soon as Joe and I were alone.

"It wasn't my fault, honestly." Joe snapped the seat-belt together and avoided my eyes.

"What did you do?"

"It was a simple mistake..."

"Get on with it!"

"Well, you know how I hate going to the dentist and I was all in a fluster. Then the dentist turns out to be a gorgeous creature. It all made me a bit, you know, anxious."

"So what did you do?"

"Well, I sat in the chair with the assistant on one side of me and the dentist on the other. She starts poking about in my mouth - you know how I hate all that..."

"Go on."

"So whenever the dentist hurt me or I felt uncomfortable, I'd just squeeze the arms of the chair. (*pause*) Except I was too nervous to notice that my chair had no arms. I was resting my arms on their legs and squeezing their knees."

"Didn't they say anything?"

"No, the dentist said she knew from my record card that I was a difficult patient and she just wanted to finish with as little stress as possible."

"What, all that time? You squeezed their knees for the whole check-up?"

"Pretty much. I just rested my whole arm along their thighs and squeezed their knees when the going got rough. I squeezed very hard."

I was laughing by now. "I can't believe they didn't say anything! When are you going back to get the tooth fixed?"

"Next week, but I'm going to see a different dentist. I can't face her again. I *have* to see a different dentist."

Joe did get his tooth fixed the next week, but by the same lady dentist, because no others were available. He apologised again, lay back in the chair and clasped his hands very firmly together in his lap.

⚲⚲⚲

It was during February that a new Spanish word entered our vocabulary. The word was *grua*, meaning a crane. Not the large long-necked wading bird with long thin legs, but the mechanical sort - the machine used for lifting heavy objects.

The foundations of The Monstrosity were now complete, to our relief. Mechanical diggers had tunnelled into the mountainside for weeks, vibrating the ground and making the plates clatter on my kitchen shelf. The Monstrosity began to rise until one day, a massive *grua* was brought into the village. This was no mean feat, as the road into El Hoyo is narrow with tight bends. I remembered our own removal van arriving five years before, and how it had reversed into the village fountain and destroyed it.

The erection and positioning of the crane took a whole day and required the expertise of two dozen men. I was full of admiration. Constructing it reminded me of the Meccano kit my younger brother used to play with back in the 60's. For those too young to remember,

Wikipedia describes it perfectly: *"Meccano is a model construction system comprising re-usable metal strips, plates, angle girders, wheels, axles and gears, with nuts and bolts to connect the pieces. It enables the building of working models and mechanical devices."*

The crane towered over the village

Except our *grua* was gigantic and towered over the village. Soon it was swinging concrete blocks and bricks from place to place, high over our heads. Sometimes we'd be sitting in the garden and a great shadow would hover above us, blotting out the sun, another great load dangling in an arc over us. It was most unnerving, and set Joe off on another moaning fest, but not for long.

Lamb Cochifrito

Lamb Cochifrito originally came from Northern Spain but is a very popular dish in Andalucía today. You will find this dish as a main meal on many restaurant menus and it is occasionally served up as hot tapas.

1 kg (2lb 4oz) lamb steaks
1 onion (chopped)
1 green pepper (chopped)
2 garlic cloves (crushed)
1 teaspoon smoked paprika
Juice of half a lemon
Salt and pepper
Broadleaf parsley

First, take the lamb steaks and remove the bone from the centre, then slice the meat into strips.

Heat a little olive oil in a large cazuela or frying pan and add the lamb. Cook until browned then add the onion and fry for a further 2 minutes.

Add the garlic, green pepper, smoked paprika and lemon juice, reduce heat and cook for 15 - 20 minutes.

Season with salt and pepper.

Serve and garnish with roughly chopped parsley.

Tip: Adding a splash of cream works very well with the paprika.

21
Cranes

"For goodness sake! I'm sick of that blasted crane! Can't a man sit in his own garden without that thing swinging about above him every two minutes?" Joe gave his groin a vigorous scratch, a sure sign of his irritation.

I tried to placate him, "It won't be for long. The Monstrosity is growing really fast."

I had other things on my mind and was not thinking about the crane or listening to Joe's complaints. My old college friends, Anna and Andy, were coming to stay for a week. I hadn't seen them for years, and was really looking forward to their visit. I only hoped the weather would stay fine, as the mountains had still not recovered from the weeks of rain.

How the time had flown since Andy first made contact before Christmas! We'd been exchanging messages on Facebook and I'd just received another from him.

February 24, 2010
Vicky,
When is a good time to call you , time is flying by...Are you still expecting us on the 22nd March? Can we bring you anything from the UK etc etc.
Life is very hectic at the moment...we would both just like to get off the roundabout and just relax..
Hope all is well will phone soon.
Love
Andrew and Anna XX

February 25, 2010
Hi Andy and Anna,
Of course we're still expecting you! Looking forward to it. We've been rained on for 10 solid weeks now. (So glad you didn't come in earlier in the year!) There were terrible floods and mudslides, and houses have collapsed, even in our village. All Spanish roofs leak, including ours, we've discovered.
Can't think of anything for you to bring for us, apart from yourselves, but will give it thought.
Don't bring anything posh to wear, there are no posh places to go. Recommend jeans. Nights will be cold, but hopefully it'll be hot during

the day.
Rest assured, life is very slow here, so hopefully you'll get a chance to unwind and chill...
love,
Vicky and Joe xx

"Come on," I said to Joe, after sending the email. "Let's take a walk round the village. Blow the cobwebs away."

So we walked down our street, past the square, past the construction work, and out of the other side of the village. Marcia waved from her shop doorway, and Geronimo and Uncle Felix nodded from their bench in the shade. The construction workers greeted us politely, and I hoped Joe wasn't going to take the opportunity to complain about the crane. Of course he couldn't resist it.

"I wish you'd stop dangling that crane over our garden," Joe grumbled to the workers in general. They looked faintly surprised. I smiled apologetically and hurried him away by the elbow before they could reply.

We stopped on the bridge that spanned the gully at the entrance to the village and looked down. As a result of the continuous weeks of rain, water coursed at the bottom of the gully, but the level had noticeably dropped.

"Not so much water down there now," said Joe, leaning over the hand-rail and looking down the steep sides. "It'll be dry by May. I think I'll take a photo. Remind us of the time there was actually a river down there."

"Mind you don't drop the..."

Too late. The camera slipped out of his hand and tumbled down the gully, bouncing off tussocks of grass and vegetation on its perilous journey.

"Oh noooo..." Joe groaned. Miserably, we watched the camera plummet before finally settling on a ledge, about two feet above the water level.

"Well, that's done it!" I was really annoyed. Joe was always lecturing *me* to use the camera wrist-strap, but he hadn't bothered to practice what he preached, and now the camera was lost for ever.

"I'll climb down and get it," said Joe.

"Don't be ridiculous! Those sides are far too steep. We'll just have to claim off the insurance."

We were still staring down glumly when we heard a call behind us.

"*¡Señor! Señor?* You have dropped something?" It was the foreman of the construction team.

"Yes, we stupidly dropped our camera down the gully."

"*We?* You dropped it, I didn't!" I muttered.

The foreman joined us at the hand-rail and peered down. "Ah yes, I see it. You are lucky it did not land in the water."

By now, Marcia, Uncle Felix, Geronimo and his three dogs had joined our party and were also staring down into the gully.

"*¡Madre mía!*" said Marcia, gripping the hand-rail with her ancient claw-like hands. "That is a long way down."

"You'll never get that back," said Geronimo.

"I agree," I said. "It's too far down to reach."

"No," said the foreman, "I think we can get that for you." He looked over his shoulder and called, "Nicolas! Over here! Do you think we could get that camera down there?"

Nicolas, the crane operator, walked over and looked down. "*¡Sin problema!* No problem!" he said. The silver camera, resting on its bed of grass, sparkled in the sunlight. "No problem!"

"You're not going to lower the bucket down there, are you?" asked Joe, astonished.

"Yes, it will be easy." Nicolas was already twiddling with the knobs and levers on the giant remote control in his hands. The crane, as though it had a life of its own, swung its arm round, the massive bucket swaying to a halt and resting on the ground a few feet from where we were standing. "One of the men will go down and get it for you."

"Oh, I don't want to put anyone to any trouble..."

"No problem," said Nicolas again. "Unless you want to go down yourself?" His eyes were twinkling.

"In the crane bucket?"

"Yes. I'll lower you until you can reach the camera."

"Joe..." I eyed the bucket, the chain hanging slack. I wasn't convinced this was such a good idea.

"Me go down? Crikey! I'd love to! What do I have to do?"

"You must stand in the bucket with your knees slightly bent. Hold onto the centre chain. Don't worry, I will move it very slowly."

"This is going to be great!" said Joe to me. "Take photos!"

"I can't."

"Oh, no, of course you can't..." Joe was already heading for the bucket. He stepped in and held the chain, grinning excitedly. "Okay! Up, up and away! I'm ready to go!"

"*¡Madre mía!*" said Marcia.

Uncle Felix narrowed his eyes and shook his head. Geronimo took a quick gulp from his bottle of beer. Nicolas fiddled with the controls, and slowly the chain tightened until the bucket lifted gently off the ground. The crane's arm swung round, carrying the bucket with Joe in it and sweeping them in an arc to hover over the gully.

"*¡Madre mía!*" said Marcia, clutching her heart with one hand.

"Okay! Down now, down, down. A little to the left, down slightly..." The foreman had taken charge. "A bit more to the right - down a little more...and...STOP!"

The bucket stopped, swaying slightly but perfectly poised alongside the camera. It was an easy matter for Joe to reach out and seize the camera.

"I've got it!" came the triumphant crow from the depths of the gully.

I turned to the foreman and spoke quietly. "Um... Could you, perhaps, just kind of...sort of...um...accidentally dip the bucket into the water? Just a tiny bit? I think Joe deserves to be taught a lesson." I should have been ashamed of myself.

The foreman glanced at me briefly, understanding and amusement in his eyes.

"I think that could be arranged..." he said. Then, "Nicolas! Swing forward two metres, then lower three metres."

"Are you sure?"

"Quite sure!" said the foreman and I in unison.

"Oy!" said the voice from the gully. "Pull me up! I've got my feet wet!"

"*¡Madre mía!*" said Marcia.

"Oh dear!" I said softly to the foreman.

The foreman, smiling now, issued instructions to Nicolas until Joe was safely back on terra firma beside us.

"That was great!" said Joe. "I really enjoyed that!"

"I am sorry you got your feet wet," said the foreman. Nicolas gave him a sideways glance.

"That's okay," said Joe cheerfully. "Accidents happen. At least we got our camera back, I thought we'd lost it for ever."

We thanked the foreman and Nicolas and walked home. Joe didn't complain about his soaked feet at all, and we were delighted to find that the camera was undamaged. I made coffee and we sat in the garden, watching the crane at work, arcing over us.

"Bloody marvelous things, those cranes," said Joe, leaning back on his garden chair with his hands clasped behind his head, staring up. "Remarkable inventions, I've always said so."

March 7, 2010
Vicky,
Slow reply, sorry but things here are pretty hectic. Anna and I have dinner suits and cocktail dresses at the ready.... seriously though, we are so sorry that the weather has been so bad, it must have been terrible

for the villages that were badly affected.
We are really looking forward to seeing you both in situ so to speak, it has been a long time since we saw you both in the UK.
Anna will bring a couple of hot water bottles (joking), hot during the day sounds good, the weather here has been bitter, we have just come back from a walk on the Downs and my face is frozen! I should be able to blink and frown again in the next couple of hours.
As I now have a Blackberry I can pick up emails on the go although it still takes ages to reply.
If you need anything at all from the UK just shout, we are both really looking forward to walking the hills and enjoying a few bottles of Rioja with you both.
Take care
Andrew
X

On the 22nd of March, around midday, the telephone rang.

"They must have landed!" I said to Joe, and picked up the phone. "Hello? Andy? Anna? Are you at the airport?"

"Hi! No, El Hoyo was easy to find with our TomTom. We're standing beside your church. There's a very old man with no teeth and a donkey here, trying to help, but we don't understand each other."

"Oh! That'll be Uncle Felix and his mule. Stay where you are, we'll come and get you." I replaced the receiver.

"They're already here?" asked Joe.

"Yep! Come on, they're waiting at the church."

A minute later we were reunited, and what a pleasure it was to see them after so many years. It's a strange thing, but even when you haven't seen good friends for a long time, and you finally get together again, it's as though there has never been a gap. We'd all grown greyer and more wrinkled, yet we were still the same, and very easy and comfortable in each other's company.

For the first day, we just caught up with each other's news, gossip and what our kids were doing. We demolished plenty of food and wine and watched our visitors visibly relax as they shrugged off their hectic life in England. We walked up to the shrine and gave them a guided tour of the village, which didn't take long. We passed the Ufarte house with its litter of bicycles and prams outside, laundry and pillows drying on the wall. Granny Ufarte wasn't snoring in her customary armchair outside, but we could hear plenty of activity from within. Andy and Anna had both read *Chickens* but I don't think they'd grasped quite how small, isolated and purely Spanish our village is.

"It's beautiful," said Andy. "But perhaps a little, er, third-world?"

"No shops?" Anna asked. "And what happens if you need to see a doctor?"

We explained that delivery vans came almost daily with bread, fish and local produce, and that the doctor came once a week and held a surgery in one of the villager's living rooms. Anna looked dubious.

"We'll take you to see Europe's one and only desert tomorrow," said Joe. "They've got a permanent movie set there. All the spaghetti westerns like *The Good, the Bad and the Ugly* and *A Fistful of Dollars* were filmed there. The terrain is similar to the Colorado desert with rocky outcrops and prickly pear cacti. Honestly, you'd think you were in an American desert, not Spain."

"That sounds like fun," said Anna.

Lemon Swordfish with Roasted Tomatoes

Swordfish steaks go very well with salads and potatoes; here it's served with roasted tomatoes. Buy the biggest, ripest tomatoes you can get, as they'll roast slightly quicker. Served with lashings of extra virgin olive oil and fresh bread, you can't get much more Mediterranean than this!

2 swordfish steaks
2 large tomatoes
A squeeze of lemon juice
Parsley
Ground black pepper
Extra virgin olive oil

Quarter each tomato, place on a baking tray and oven roast on a high heat 220°C (420°F) for 30 minutes.
Ten minutes before the tomatoes are ready, heat some olive oil in a pan, add the swordfish steaks and squeeze over with lemon juice.
Lightly fry for 4 minutes each side.
Arrange the swordfish on a plate with the roast tomato segments.
Season with black pepper and add a generous splash of good olive oil.
Garnish with parsley and serve with fresh crusty bread.

Serves 2

22
Cowboys and Getting Plastered

The second day of Andy's and Anna's visit was overcast. Nevertheless, we piled into their hired car and drove to the little town of Tabernas where Fort Bravo is situated. An entire cowboy town has been recreated there, complete with gallows, funeral director, blacksmith, church and school. Visitors can wander round, enjoy a drink in the saloon, watch filming and generally imagine being in the Wild West.

"I thought you said it was a desert?" said Andy, pointing out the lush terrain. Instead of the expected dry, dusty crags, the whole area was green and sprinkled with brilliant wild flowers. It seemed even Europe's only desert hadn't escaped the recent deluge.

The town seemed deserted apart from some rangy-looking dogs loping around, a few horses tethered to a fence, and a corral with some rather moth-eaten bison watching us suspiciously. Normally the place is packed with tourists, but it was March and no filming was taking place.

"We're going to have a nice quiet time," Joe said cheerfully. "We've got the whole place to ourselves."

Of course he was wrong.

We entered the saloon and ordered drinks from the buxom wench behind the bar. The staff at Fort Bravo always dress in authentic costumes, and the wench's low-cut dress left little to the imagination. Joe was mesmerised and needed my elbow in his ribs to focus his attention on reality.

The serving wench

"Behave yourself! Your eyes are out on stalks," I hissed.

"I think her dumplings are boiling over," muttered Joe.

We carried our drinks to a table near the door but not before we noticed the barmaid turn her back and make a furtive call on a very un-Wild West iPhone. We soon discovered why. Our little party was probably a welcome diversion for the staff of Fort Bravo, because it was her colleagues the wench was alerting.

First some cowboys burst into the saloon and held up our party, pistols aimed at our heads. Poor Anna suffered the most. Two cowboys in particular amused themselves by scaring the living daylights out of her at every opportunity. Perhaps her naturally nervous disposition made her an easy target because, as we strolled around, they popped up from behind buildings or furniture, pistols drawn. At one point she was forcibly put in jail at gun point. So much for 'a nice quiet time'.

Anna in jail

We finished the visit with several tours of the town, viewed from a mule cart, rattling along at breakneck speed. The driver, a cowboy, decked in a Stetson and toting six-guns, flicked a whip over the rumps of the mules, urging them on through the muddy streets. He drove us to a huge palisaded fort and Red Indian teepee village before returning to the Saloon. Being the only visitors, we were forced to keep repeating the tour, the driver not allowing us to get down.

Riding in the mule cart

"Today you are my only customers," he said. "I need something to do." So around we went for the umpteenth time.

The day was huge fun, but with gunshots still ringing in our ears, it was a relief to return to the quiet of El Hoyo.

By the time Andy and Anna left for England, the weather was really starting to improve. Tiny nubs began to appear on the branches of our grapevine, and before long, the leaves unfurled. The days grew longer and the sun was more generous with her rays. The Ufarte baby was now nearly four months old and gurgling happily in his stroller.

They say things come in threes, and on one particular day that spring, this was true.

Joe and I avoided going down to the city whenever possible,

preferring the peace and quiet of the village. However, sometimes it was necessary, and especially when we had to visit our bank in person.

Parking in Spain could be described as 'chaotic'. People tend to abandon their vehicles rather than park them. Double-parking outside shops, in the middle of a road, in front of the Police Station, on pedestrian crossings, it's all the same to the Spanish driver.

"Good lord!" said Joe as we reached the bank. "Where am I supposed to park? Look at these cars just dumped all over the place. There are plenty of No Parking signs, but everybody seems to be ignoring them. Oh well, I'll do the same."

"Are you sure? I don't want to get a parking ticket."

"Stop panicking, you know everybody does this in Spain. Anyway, we won't be long." Joe switched off the engine and we walked across the street and round the corner to the bank.

Ten minutes later we emerged and stood in the bank's porch to use the ATM. Traffic hurried past, the Spanish drivers liberally leaning on their horns. A car alarm was wailing.

"If I didn't know better, I'd say that was *our* car alarm," Joe commented.

"No, it can't be, it's getting louder. It does sound very much like ours though."

As I spoke, the alarm's wail dramatically increased in volume, and simultaneously we looked up the street to identify the source. A big, blue, flatbed truck rounded the corner. Loaded on the back of it was our car, the alarm howling.

Joe and I stood side by side, shocked, watching it sail past in the stream of traffic.

"Hey!" shouted Joe, waving his arms, and galloped after it in hot pursuit. "That's our car! Stop! Stop! That's our car!"

He caught up with the truck at the next traffic lights, red-faced and panting, and knocked on the startled driver's window.

"My car!" he gasped. "You've got my car!"

The driver rolled his eyes and indicated that he'd make a U-turn and park in the lay-by on the other side of the street. Half an hour later, we'd signed numerous forms and listened to a lecture on 'correct parking' delivered by the policeman. We knew the 'but everybody does it' argument would not wash, so we listened politely. Our wallet ended up considerably lighter, but at least we'd reclaimed our car. We raided the ATM yet again to replenish our funds and set off for home.

During the drive back, that distant look returned to Joe's eyes. That look that told me all was not well, that something was playing on his mind. What was troubling him? Surely not the silly parking incident? Instinctively I knew it was something much bigger.

But the scene that greeted us outside our house in the village succeeded in wiping all nagging worries from my mind and set us both laughing.

When we'd left that morning, our garage door was a pleasing shade of dark blue. As we'd driven away, I'd noticed that the builders of The Monstrosity had carelessly left a bag of white plaster next to our garage, but I didn't comment. While we were away, the Ufarte children had discovered the bag, and the urge to throw powder at the door and each other was evidently irresistible. Our garage door was now mostly white, and so were the kids.

Our laughter alerted Mama Ufarte, who appeared on the scene, Snap-On on her hip, Fifi at her heels. Fifi growled and headed for Joe's ankles, but Scrap was too fast for her. He hurled the handful of powder he'd been clutching at Fifi. It was a direct hit and instantly turned Fifi into a skewbald. She forgot about Joe's ankles as she shook herself in a flurry of dust.

"*¡Madre mía! ¿Qué pasa?*" said Mama Ufarte. Then to us, "I am very sorry!"

"Oh, we know what kids are like," said Joe. "I'll get the hosepipe out and wash the door and the street down. No harm done."

"Children! You are not coming back into the house like that! *Tío* Joe will wash you down, then it's bathtime and clean clothes for all of you. What will your father say when he hears about this?"

An empty threat, and we all knew it. Papa Ufarte would laugh at his children's antics, or join in. I'd never once heard him raise his voice or be angry with the children.

I had things to do, so I went into the house while Joe got the hosepipe out. Luckily it was a very warm day and I could hear the kids shrieking and laughing, and Fifi yapping as Joe hosed them all down. Then I heard Papa Ufarte returning home and joining in the fun.

Joe came back into the house grinning. He was soaking wet with white trails of gluey plaster all over his clothes.

"I'm going to take a shower and change," he said. "Papa Ufarte has invited me in for a drink with him to apologise for the kids' behaviour."

"Did you tell him there was nothing to apologise for? It was just a bit messy, no damage done."

"Yes, I did, but he insisted. I'll just go over for a couple to be polite. It's too early in the day for a drinking session."

Joe showered and reappeared in a change of clothes. He has appalling taste in clothes and had chosen a dreadful psychedelic shirt with orange and red swirls that were painful to the eyes.

"Is there a volume control on that shirt?" I asked.

"I *like* this shirt," Joe protested as he walked out of the door. "Anyway, I'm only going next door. I'll see you in half an hour or so."

Four hours later, I heard a scratching at the front door. I opened it, and Joe fell in. I looked from the crumpled heap at my feet to the twins who were standing on the doorstep behind him.

"We've just brought *Tío* Joe home," said Twin #1.

"Mama says Papa and *Tío* Joe have had quite enough," said Twin #2 primly.

"Jusht had a couple of drinksh," said Joe, laughing, trying to get back on his feet.

With difficulty, I pulled him up and leaned him against the wall. It was a wasted effort. In slow motion, he slithered down the wall and ended up in a giggling pile on the floor again. I gave up.

"Shall we help you get *Tío* Joe up?" asked Twin #2.

"Thank you, but I'll manage," I said. "Thank you for bringing him home."

"Okay," chorused the twins, and pattered off back down the street.

"I think you'd better take a nap," I said to the untidy heap on the floor.

Manipulating him into a standing position was impossible, so I just let him crawl, herding him in the direction of the bedroom with an occasional tap on the rump with a rolled-up newspaper. I helped him disrobe and left him snoring on the bed.

Next morning, Joe woke up with a throbbing head and very little memory of the night before. Luckily he didn't remember the dreadful shirt either. I'd whisked that away and hidden it, promising myself and the world it would never again see the light of day.

Sylvia and Gravy, the two village cats who'd adopted us, were always in our garden, snoozing or waiting hopefully to be fed. They were both tabbies, like their mother, with gorgeous stripes and that characteristic 'M' on their foreheads, just like their wildcat ancestors.

There were numerous cats in the village, some more noticeable than others. The ruling tomcat of the moment was an enormous battered bruiser of Siamese descent. His head was almost as wide as his body and his ears were flat and tattered. I don't find any animals ugly, but this cat certainly wouldn't win any beauty contests.

The lady cats of the village evidently didn't agree, and found him irresistible, and in the space of a few years many new kittens were born with varying degrees of Siamese markings.

One particular cat that we'd often noticed was very Siamese in appearance, with chocolate ears, paws, and tail and a creamy body. She had the most remarkable blue eyes, as stunning as the Spanish summer sky.

We believed this blue-eyed cat had been domesticated in the past, then abandoned, because she was very affectionate and sweet-natured, far more confident than the other village cats. However, even without an owner she seemed to survive well enough, scrounging fish scraps from the fish van, hunting sparrows and lizards, and raiding whenever the opportunity arose.

One morning, the 13th of April to be precise, Joe stepped out into the street and discovered something that was to completely change the pattern of our lives.

Fried Chorizo with Apple and Cider

An easy and quick tapas recipe with a very big flavour indeed. Sweet caramelised apple slices cooked in the chorizo juices go deliciously well with the spicy sausage. Can be served hot or cold and is sure to get the guests guessing.

3 chorizo sausages
1 apple (sweet)
300ml (half a pint) Asturian cider
1 bay leaf
Olive oil

Slice the chorizo sausages into half-inch segments.
Pour a little olive oil into a frying pan and heat.
Add the chorizo segments and cook for 1 minute each side over a low heat.
Meanwhile, slice the apple into 12 segments.
Add the apple, bay leaf and cider to the chorizo, turn up the heat and cook until the cider begins to thicken.
Serve hot with cocktail sticks.

6 servings

23
Three New Faces

It was the strange throaty meow of a cat that had drawn Joe outside into the street. Curious, he looked around, but didn't need to look far.

"Vicky! VICKY! Come out here! Quickly, and bring the camera!"

I dropped everything, grabbed the camera, and shot outside. Joe pointed to the ground. There, just beside our doorstep, was the blue-eyed cat nosing something resembling a skinned pink mouse. I crouched down for a closer look. It was a tiny newborn kitten.

Born in the street

"Oh my..." I breathed. This kitten was brand new, just minutes old. "Why here?" I whispered. "Why on the street? Why hasn't she made a nest somewhere and hidden it?"

"I have no idea," said Joe. "See if you can find a box, she can't stay here on the street with it. The village dogs will attack it."

I ran back inside and searched frantically for a suitable box, but all I could find was a square blue bowl we sometimes used for mixing small quantities of cement. I grabbed some straw from the chicken coop and lined the bowl. All this only took a few minutes, but by the time I got outside again, a second kitten had been born in the street.

"She just kind of sighed," said Joe in wonder. "And another one popped out."

"I found this bowl," I said. "It should do the job."

"Do you think Mum will let me pick up her babies?" asked Joe. "I'll have to put them in the box."

"We've got no choice, you'll have to try. We can't leave them here."

Very carefully, Joe picked up the first kitten and placed it on the bed of straw. MumCat didn't seem to object. He picked up the second and laid it with the first. Both kittens began to mewl and squirm and MumCat didn't hesitate. She hopped straight into the bowl with them and gave her babies a good wash.

"Now what?" Joe asked, giving his crotch a good scratch. "Where are we going to put them?"

"Can't we..."

"No. You know we can't keep them. What if we want to pop over to Australia again, or somewhere else? Who'd look after them?"

"But if we..."

"We can't keep them. We already feed Sylvia and Gravy, and you want to take on three more cats? No."

"Well, what shall we do?" I was disappointed, but I knew Joe was right.

"I don't know." Joe shook his head. "First we need to find somewhere quiet where the dogs can't get them. When we've done that, we can decide what to do."

I wracked my brain trying to think of a quiet, safe place where MumCat and her babies would be undisturbed.

"How about the cemetery? It's got walls all round, and a gate you have to untie. They'd be fine in there."

Joe thought about it. "The cemetery? Good idea. You're right, dogs can't get in and the village kids don't play in there. Okay, we'd better get them moved then."

He leaned down and carefully lifted the bowl. I expected MumCat to leap out, but she didn't. As slow as a funeral march, Joe carried the family up the street to the cemetery gates. By the time we reached the cemetery and I had untied the frayed rope holding the gates together, MumCat had given birth to a third kitten, much smaller than the first two.

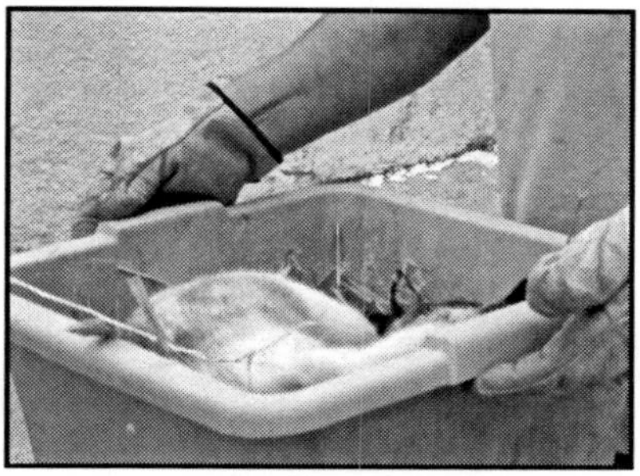

Joe carrying MumCat

I like graveyards, but I've always found English ones rather depressing. Headstones are often vandalised and graves lie untended, with withered bouquets left to rot and fake flowers fading in overturned pots. Spanish cemeteries are much more cheerful places, particularly El Hoyo's. White walls encircle neat gravestones and vases of fresh flowers provide plenty of colour. Plaques with smiling photographs of the deceased can be seen on every wall, glinting in the sunshine. Birds settle in the ancient tree and sing to the dear departed.

The cemetery has a little ante-room with sinks and running water and a table made of flagstones. The table is big, designed to rest coffins on, I suspect, not just for flower arranging. But having never, as yet, attended a village funeral, I'm not sure.

Outside was unsheltered and hot, so we decided to place the box under the huge table in the ante-room. I ran home and gathered together catfood, milk and bowls. By the time I returned, all three kittens had latched on to MumCat and were feeding eagerly.

The cemetery

"Well, that's that," said Joe. "They'll be okay now."

But that night I couldn't sleep. Today was a weekday and El Hoyo was quiet, but the weekend was looming. Although we loved the villagers, we were realistic. We knew that most Spanish people consider village cats to be vermin. If the kittens were discovered their destiny would hang in the balance. At best they would be tormented, at worst, destroyed. And what if a funeral took place in the near future? Their situation was precarious indeed. I tossed and turned.

"Go to sleep," Joe growled, but I couldn't.

At last morning arrived, and I broached the subject to Joe.

"Joe, I don't think MumCat and her kittens are safe in the cemetery. I think somebody will find them and hurt them. You know the village is already awash with feral cats, and three more aren't going to be welcome." I expected Joe to argue, but he didn't.

"No, you're right, I was thinking that myself. Too many people go into the cemetery and somebody's going to find them. But where else can we put them?"

"We could put them in our woodshed."

"Yes, we could... But what about Sylvia and Gravy?"

"They may all be related, you never know, perhaps they'll get on well together."

"Okay Vicky, but we are *not* keeping them, you know that, don't you? It's just a temporary measure. We can't take on four more cats."

We walked back to the cemetery where all was quiet and well. MumCat jumped out of the box to welcome us and the kittens looked fine, even the little runt, the last born. Their fur had fluffed out a little during the night, and we could see that all three were white.

Moving the family again was easy, thanks to MumCat's trusting nature and hearty appetite. I called her and let her sniff the cat-food, then walked down the street, showing her the food at regular intervals. She followed without a fuss. Joe brought up the rear carrying the bowl with the three kittens squirming and wriggling on the straw. MumCat looked over her shoulder a few times to check on her babies but appeared otherwise unconcerned.

Our woodshed is not really a shed at all. It's a brick-built structure with walls on three sides and a tiled, sloping roof. Being April, there wasn't much wood stacked in there, so Joe placed the bowl in a corner. MumCat glanced up, but was too busy eating to fret.

All went well and we didn't really need to do a thing: MumCat had it all in paw. She fed those kittens until their tummies were round and tight, and washed them all day long.

Poor Sylvia and Gravy made an appearance but were chased out of the garden by MumCat. We were concerned, but found a way round the problem by feeding them on the roof terrace, out of MumCat's line of vision.

But the nagging worry remained. Suddenly we were responsible for three new little lives, and their mother. What were we going to do with all these cats? We knew we'd never find homes for them as we seldom mixed in expat circles, and no locals would want them. So I turned to the Internet and posted our problem on some expat forums, including *AlmerimarLife.com,* asking for advice.

2010-04-19 13:02:10
Like most places in Spain, there are dozens of feral cats in our village. Joe and I are familiar with this particular cat because of her china blue eyes and Siamese looks, and she is much tamer than most. We'd noticed she was pregnant, but we certainly didn't expect her to give birth in the street right outside our front door.
This is the YouTube video of what happened next:
(Turn volume on) http://youtu.be/pceTSk00Fjc
Anyway, we had to move them again, and now they are in our woodshed, safe from dogs and human interference.
The problem is, we can't keep them as we already care for and feed two other wild cats.
So, is there anyone who could offer a home to any of them when they're weaned? Their eyes aren't open yet, but if they are anything like Mum, they are going to be beautiful with extraordinary blue eyes and Siamese markings. We'll carry on looking after Mum and get her spayed, but we can't keep the kittens, too.
Can anyone in the Almeria area help? (Keeping my fingers crossed.)
Victoria

The only person to respond was Sandra Marshall, co-owner of

AlmerimarLife.com. She was in the UK at the time, unable to return home because of the Icelandic volcanic dust cloud that was grounding all flights.

2010-04-19 21:35:52
Hi Victoria. Yes I will try and help. I am Chris's wife and I and friends rescue stray animals and re-home them. Check out my blog Alstrays.com.
I am currently stranded in the UK but if you send telephone numbers and email I will contact you when I get home.
I'm assuming we are looking at 4-6 weeks from now anyway?
Where exactly are you?
If the mother is sweet we may be able to help her too. She is very beautiful.
Sandra

What a relief! I got in touch with Sandra and she hatched a plan. Joe and I would foster the family and bring them to the vet for routine vaccinations. Meanwhile, Sandra and *Alstrays* would search out homes for them. Surprisingly, the new homes would be in Germany. Every few months, *Alstrays* packed a truck crammed with cats and dogs and drove them to waiting German owners.

I liked the idea. I liked the thought of watching the kittens grow up in the safety of our garden, knowing they had homes awaiting them. I also liked the fact that they weren't going to join the feral cat community in the village, forced to scrounge food, uncared for. I wasn't sure if Joe would agree as he'd made it clear we weren't keeping them, and Sandra's plan meant we'd have them with us for a couple of months. I broke the news gently to Joe and was greatly relieved when he didn't seem to object to this temporary arrangement.

"Okay," he said, "if it's just for two months. But they're not coming into the house because we'll just get too attached to them."

11 days old

I promised. I thoroughly enjoyed watching MumCat nurturing her little family, even if it was only in the garden.

Very soon, the two first-born kittens' eyes opened, followed by the little runt. They looked blue, and I hoped they'd all inherit that unusual, azure colour their mother was blessed with. All three grew stronger daily, the two big kittens vigorously wriggling around the box, often flattening their weaker, smaller sibling. I could see other differences, too. Their colouring was changing; the ears and tails were becoming darker on all three.

At the moment they were nameless and I had no idea of their gender. Being no expert, I consulted the Internet, and, armed with my new-found knowledge, approached their box.

"They're so tiny!" I said to Joe. "I'm almost scared to pick them up in case I hurt them."

"Oh, they're stronger than they look."

MumCat didn't complain when I picked each kitten up and turned it over for a careful examination. The two big ones protested noisily and tried to squirm out of my hand. The little kitten was much more placid, and didn't object at all to the handling and undignified close scrutiny.

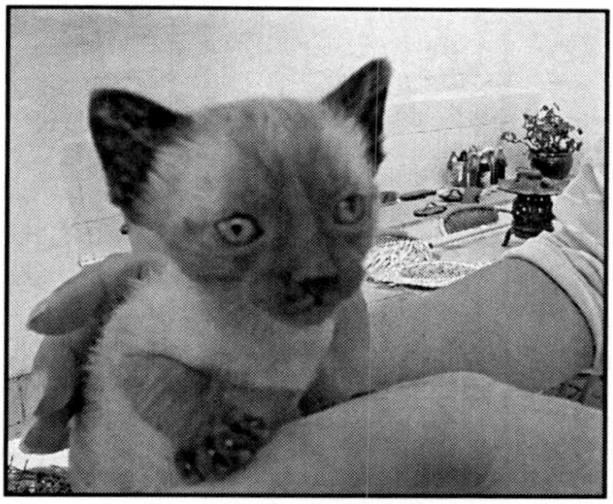

The runt of the litter

Two big girls and a little boy! Even knowing that, we made no effort to name them for fear of becoming too attached. But already they were developing personalities and their markings were changing daily.

Every morning, before I'd even had a coffee or dressed, I'd saunter down the garden to see how they were all faring and fill MumCat's saucers with food and milk. But one morning, I was confronted with an empty box of straw. There was not a cat or kitten in sight.

Slow-Cooked Brandy Chicken

4 chicken legs, separated into thighs and drumsticks
1 and a half bulbs of garlic
Reasonable size glass brandy
1 bay leaf
Olive oil
Salt
Pepper
Paprika (mild or hot)

Sprinkle the chicken with a generous amount of salt, pepper and paprika, then rub the seasoning into the chicken and leave to rest for about 20 minutes.

Peel and roughly chop the garlic.

Heat a little olive oil in a large casserole dish and slowly brown the chicken pieces on both sides. Add the garlic about halfway through this step.

When the chicken is browned, add the brandy and bay leaf.

Cover and cook gently until the chicken is tender, about 30-40 minutes depending on the size of the pieces.

Serve with rice or a salad.

Serves 4

24
Traps

We searched the garden: behind flower-pots, in the shrubs, amongst the wood-pile, in the chicken coop. Nothing.

"Well, that's that, then," said Joe. "They're gone. We'd better tell Sandra and stop her finding new homes for them."

But I wasn't giving up that easily. I thought hard.

"Where could they have gone? Do you think they were stolen? But we haven't told anybody about them, nobody knows they're here..." I was thinking aloud.

I carried on searching until I heard a tiny squeak. I froze and listened again. No, I wasn't imagining it, another squeak. I looked around. Where was it coming from?

"Joe, listen! Did you hear that?"

"Yes, I did..."

So Joe and I played Follow the Squeak which led us to the barbecue. The barbecue was waist high, and below the grill was a metal box that Paco had welded for us. It was a lovely simple design: a box that holds burning charcoal, with grooves to rest one's kebab sticks. There was no doubt, the squeaks were coming from behind the box. I pulled the box forward a few inches, to reveal MumCat and three kittens, all squashed into the tiny space behind.

"What are you doing in there?" I asked Mumcat. "Surely your box with the straw in it is much more comfortable?"

"If that's where she's chosen, that's where we should leave her," said Joe.

"But they'll fall out!" I protested. I really didn't think that MumCat had given her new nursery enough thought.

"The kittens aren't moving around much yet," said Joe. "I don't think it'll be a problem."

We retreated back inside to watch from the kitchen window, and we didn't have long to wait. The kittens hadn't properly found their feet yet, but they could squirm beautifully. Before we could intercept it, one of the big kittens had wriggled to the edge, teetered, then tumbled to the ground with a squawk and an unpleasant dull thud. I ran outside, but MumCat had beaten me to it.

First she gave her baby a good wash, then she scruffed it, and leaped back onto the barbecue, the fat little kitten dangling limply from her mouth. The kitten seemed unhurt in spite of the perilous drop and the undignified landing on the unforgiving paving stones below. I shook my head. No, the barbecue was not a good choice, even Joe agreed.

I reached into the back of the barbecue, and winkled out the kittens, one by one. Then I carried each carefully back to the straw-filled box in the wood-shed. The two girls cried and fought all the way, but the little chap sat in my hands, calmly surveying his surroundings. Unfortunately, MumCat did not agree with my decision. By the time I reached the box with the third kitten, she'd already whisked the first one away, stashed it back in the barbecue and was returning for the second.

"You and I need to talk," I said to MumCat as she collected the last kitten. "This won't do. The barbecue is *not* a good place to raise your family."

So I sat down on the step and MumCat wound herself around my legs, arching her back for strokes. I told her that the barbecue was a foolish place to keep her babies, that they'd keep falling out, there wasn't enough space, etc., etc. She stated that the woodshed was too public, and that she objected to the other village cats disturbing her family during the night. I asked her if she was willing to compromise? How about if I made her a nice bed in the cupboard under the sink, next to the barbecue? I'd jam the cupboard door ajar so she and the kittens could get in and out, and they'd be safe. At least they'd be on ground level and couldn't harm themselves.

"I don't know why you talk to that cat. She's a Spanish cat, she doesn't even speak English," Joe said.

I ignored him. I went inside and collected a couple of old sweaters, to make a comfortable bed in the cupboard. Finally, I lifted the kittens into the cupboard and stood back to watch. MumCat had already checked out the cupboard and now demonstrated her approval. Entering, she flopped down on her side, purring, encircling the kittens. They nuzzled her and settled down to feed while she washed their heads. The new nursery was a success.

I loved the new arrangement because I could see the cupboard clearly from the kitchen. MumCat was the perfect mother and the kittens thrived. Their markings changed even more: the little girls' ears darkening while their coats stayed snowy with haphazard beige streaks. The little boy grew more beautiful every day, blessed with typical Siamese colouring, darker than his sisters. His ears were too big for him, probably borrowed from a bat-eared fox, but I forgave him that. One of the little girls, the naughty one that had tumbled out of the barbecue, developed a comical smudge on her face. She looked as though she'd stuck her nose up a sooty chimney, so Smut seemed an obvious name. Joe, who'd sworn that we wouldn't name these feline scraps, christened the other little girl Beauty. And, for obvious reasons, the little boy became known as Choccy-Paws, abbreviated to Chox unless he was in trouble.

For the first week or so, we saw little of the kittens, but as they became bolder and developed more control of their feet, little faces began to appear, peeping round the cupboard door. Of course, adventurous Smut was the first, followed by Beauty, and Chox a day later. They invented their first game, one that kept them amused for a good proportion of every day. The game was called 'Paws under the Door' and involved one kitten lying on its side outside, swatting at its siblings' paws that fleetingly appeared in the gap under the door. I'd jammed the door slightly ajar with a wooden wedge so there was no risk of squashed paws.

3 weeks, 3 days - Smut and Chox

While our kitten family was thriving, I worried about the other cats in the village. I'm perfectly aware that it's the same all over Spain. The Spanish rarely neuter or spay their own pet cats, so the problem escalates. Cats run wild and their numbers are not controlled. Every spring countless new batches of kittens appear. The weak ones rarely survive but the remainder grow up to produce yet more kittens to add to the feral population.

I wondered how we could help. Even though our finances were limited, couldn't we do something? It was when we were tidying the garage one day that an idea occurred to me.

When we first bought our house, the previous owner had left all his farming paraphernalia. There were scythes, hoes, shovels, a beehive and all sorts of other curious objects we couldn't identify. There was also a cage, which after examination, we established was a trap. It was quite long and narrow, with an entrance that could be hooked open. Any creature that walked inside and touched the mechanism was trapped as the cage door slammed shut. I wondered what sort of creature the previous owner had trapped.

"Joe?"

"Hmm?"

"What do you think of this idea?" I asked, blowing the dust off the trap. "What if we put something tasty in this trap, and try to catch some village cats? We could run them down to the vet, get them neutered, and then set them free again."

Joe stared at me, then gave his nethers a good scratch.

"Do you know how many cats there are in this village? Even if we caught some, it would hardly make much of a difference, would it?"

"I know, but it's a start isn't it?"

"It sounds expensive," he said. "How much does it cost to neuter a cat?"

That troubled look had returned to his eyes. Was it money that was bothering him? I knew things had been tight since the Credit Crisis and that Joe's military pension had shrunk alarmingly. Was it money he was fretting about? Yet again I made a mental note to tackle him about it as soon as an opportunity arose.

"Well, I don't know... I thought I'd ask Sandra at *Alstrays*. I know their vet will do it at cost price. It wouldn't cost much, would it?"

"No, maybe not. How would we set the trap?"

"We could put some ham or something into it, then leave it overnight on that waste ground next to the cemetery. I know we can't afford to do many, but anything would help, wouldn't it? It would stop a few litters of kittens being born."

"Hmm..."

Joe didn't sound convinced but he helped me bait the trap that evening. As the sun lowered in the sky, Joe and I carried the trap and found a good spot on the wasteland. The birds had already gone to bed and the village was deserted. I put a nice lump of ham in the trap, knowing that most cats would find it irresistible.

The next morning I was impatient to see if the trap had been successful. Even as Joe and I approached, we knew we had a result. The trap was the centre of attention for at least a dozen village cats, some circling it, others crouched in the grass, watching. Two cats were actually standing on top of the trap, trying to fish their paws through the bars.

"That's amazing!" I said. "Look, isn't that nice? We've obviously caught a really popular one and all its friends are trying to rescue it! I wonder if it's a female or a tom?"

The cats scattered as we drew close and we were able to see inside the trap.

"Oh! I can see it now! It's a big black and white..."

"Magpie," said Joe.

The poor magpie was living its worst nightmare. First it was trapped in a cage, then tormented by dozens of cats, and finally dreaded humans had arrived to make its life even more miserable. It flapped and threw itself at the cage sides, desperate to escape.

"Oh, poor thing!" I said.

Joe lifted the cage high in the air, sliding the entrance open. The magpie exploded out in a blur of black and white and landed on a branch in the nearest tree, screaming obscenities at us and the cats. Then it preened its ruffled feathers and flapped away.

"We'll try again tonight," I said. "I don't think that magpie will make the same mistake twice."

I could tell Joe wasn't enthusiastic, but that evening we set out for the wasteland again, trap and ham in hand. It was a little later than the night before and the street lights cast long shadows. Being a Friday, the village had filled up for the weekend but we encountered nobody on the way. The Spanish are creatures of habit, and we knew that at eight o'clock most families would be eating their evening meal.

We were just approaching the spot where we'd left the trap the night before, when I sensed we were not alone. I squinted into the night and identified the cause. A shadow pressed against the cemetery wall. Two shadows, to be precise, glued together. I peered into the darkness and recognised the figures.

"Shhh!" I whispered, grabbing Joe's arm.

"What's the matter?"

"We're not alone. Leave the trap here. We don't want to disturb *them.*" I jerked my head in the direction of the cemetery wall.

Joe narrowed his eyes, peering into the dark and understood immediately. "Oh, right! Okay." He set down the trap as quickly and quietly as he could, and we speedily retreated.

"That was Lola Ufarte and Geronimo, wasn't it?" said Joe when we were out of earshot.

"Hmm... Yes, it was Lola Ufarte, but that *wasn't* Geronimo with her."

"It wasn't? Who was it then?"

"Sofía's policeman boyfriend."

"Oh no! Are you sure?"

"I'm afraid so. I'm positive it was him."

"Has Sofía broken up with her boyfriend?"

"No. Carmen-Bethina told me today that Sofía was expecting her boyfriend to come up to the village tonight."

"Well, why is he with Lola Ufarte then?"

"No idea. But I do know Sofía had a bad headache today, Carmen-Bethina told me."

"So, Mr Policeman was at a loose end, and..."

"Yep, looks like Lola Ufarte stepped in and, er, entertained him."

It was a great pity, but we weren't very surprised. Lola Ufarte was a girl who liked to enjoy herself, as my lovely mother-in-law would have said.

"Don't say a word to anybody about this," said Joe. "We mustn't interfere. They'll sort it out for themselves."

So we hugged the information to ourselves, not wanting to be the ones to break such unpleasant news to Sofía.

We got up early next morning to inspect the trap before anyone else found it. The birds were singing lustily and the sky was that clear blue a brand new day brings. Our feet left trails in the dewy grass. I stole a glance at the cemetery wall and saw that the grass there was flattened.

No cats circled the trap today so we reckoned the magpie had learned its lesson. But there was something in the trap.

Unfortunately, it wasn't a cat. It was a hedgehog. It didn't seem distressed at all, gently nosing the gaps between the bars with its pointed snout.

"Oh dear," I said. "I didn't even know there were hedgehogs here in Spain."

Joe rolled his eyes but said nothing. Gently, he opened the entrance to the trap and the hedgehog trundled out. It sniffed the ground in all directions and ambled away, apparently none the worse for wear. At least it had enjoyed a free meal.

"Can we stop this silly game now?" Joe asked. "We're never going to catch a cat."

"Oh, just one more try! We've just been unlucky, that's all. It's a very good trap."

Back at home, I checked out Spanish hedgehogs on the Internet, just out of interest. As usual, *Iberianature.com* told me all I needed to know.

It informed me that there are two hedgehog species in Spain: the European and the Algerian. The European ones are darker in colour and bigger than their Algerian cousins, but not often found along the Mediterranean coast. I concluded, therefore, that ours was Algerian. Apparently, Algerian hedgehogs' spines are softer than those of European hedgehogs and their ears are bigger. I also learned that the Spanish used to capture and eat hedgehogs, though thankfully they are now protected.

Algerian hedgehog
(Picture from Iberianature.com)

The Internet also taught me that the ancient Egyptians believed hedgehog fat cured baldness. I stored that nugget of useless information in my head in case it ever came in useful. You never know, it could be the winning question on some silly TV quiz show.

We waited until Sunday night when the village was quiet before setting the trap again.

"This is the last time," Joe said. "If we don't catch a cat tonight, we're giving up. This is getting ridiculous."

I put a nice big piece of ham in the trap, and we walked away. I prayed it would be third time lucky and crossed my fingers.

Marinated Spanish Beef Kebabs

Spanish beef recipe using traditional Spanish ingredients such as smoked paprika, olive oil and herbs. These kebabs are ideal for the barbecue and are hot and spicy. Other vegetables, such as mushrooms, green peppers, tomatoes, etc., can also be used.

2kg (4.5lb) beef (cubed)
4 garlic cloves
2 teaspoons hot smoked paprika
250ml (15 fl oz) olive oil
250ml (15 fl oz) wine vinegar
1 red bell pepper
1 large onion
Cracked black pepper
Thyme or mixed herbs

Place the cubed beef into a large dish and set aside.
Using a food processor, blend together the garlic, herbs, pepper, vinegar, oil and paprika.
Pour the spicy marinade over the beef and turn well so that all the meat is covered.
Place in the fridge for a minimum of 2 hours.
To make the kebabs, roughly chop the pepper and onion then thread over kebab sticks alternating with the beef.
Retain any excess marinade as this will be used for basting the kebabs while on the grill.
Barbecue the kebabs over hot coals for 10 to 12 minutes turning and basting frequently.
Serve with fresh crispy salad, boiled potatoes, bread and olive oil.

Serves 4

25
Jumping over Babies

There was no doubt about it, we had caught a cat. As Joe and I made our way to the wasteland next morning, the howls of a trapped cat rent the air. Success!

"At last!" I said. "Wow, it's a noisy one! I told you so! I knew we'd catch a cat in the end!"

But my victory dance was short-lived, because there in the trap was MumCat.

"Oh, for goodness sake," I said, exasperated. "Of all the cats in the village, she's probably the best fed. And still she goes and gets herself caught in the trap..."

"Enough," said Joe. "We are not putting that trap out again, I mean it. First a magpie, then a hedgehog and now our own cat. Knowing our luck, we'll catch Fifi next and then there'll be hell to pay." He stomped off leaving me alone with the furious MumCat.

"That was a stupid thing to do," I said to MumCat. "Surely we feed you enough already? This trap is supposed to be for the other village cats, not you. When your kitties are weaned, we'll be taking you to visit the vet anyway."

I opened the trap and MumCat walked out and wound herself round my legs, not one to bear a grudge. I carried the wretched trap back to our garage and hung it back on its nail to gather dust for a few more years.

Each day the kittens grew fluffier, cuter and more comical. As they ventured further from their cupboard, MumCat tried to keep them in order, but Smut in particular was determined to explore. Like small children, every day they learned something new. At first they couldn't climb the step to the higher part of the garden, then Smut, after a few tumbles, mastered it. Beauty quickly followed her sister's example. Poor Chox had to wait a couple of days - he was just too small to pull himself up.

But climbing the steps wasn't enough. They soon discovered that climbing up the flyscreen on our kitchen door was huge fun. Up Smut would go, higher and higher, with Beauty and Choccy-Paws just behind, both trying to catch their sister's tail as it swished just out of reach. Once at the top, they would need rescuing, only to repeat the process a minute later.

Climbing the flyscreen

Of course climbing the garden steps and gaining access to the upper part of the garden meant more things to explore and discover, including the chickens. Outside the chicken coop, all three kittens sat in a row, like spectators at Wimbledon, their heads swivelling from left to right watching the chickens parade along the fence.

Smut was the first to squeeze through the fence into the chicken coop. Once inside, she stood still, poised to escape if necessary. Atilla the Hen, the leader of the flock, stopped scratching in the dirt and marched purposefully over to inspect the furry feline intruder. Smut crouched, eyes huge, but didn't retreat. Atilla towered over her, but Smut the Intrepid Explorer held her ground. Atilla glared down at her, her head on one side. Then she rattled her comb, decided Smut was not worthy of her attention, and turned away. Smut watched her, waited, then slowly, inch by inch, crept deeper into the coop. The other chickens ignored her and Smut gained confidence. She sniffed their food, investigated the walls and water feature, and climbed the fence.

Beauty and Chox watched from the outside, enthralled. Before long, they followed suit and the three of them claimed the chicken coop as a new playground. They romped in the straw, played hide-and-seek in the laying boxes and scrambled up to the roosting perch. The chickens paid them no attention and the kittens were free to come and go as they pleased.

The kittens made certain chores, like sweeping the patio, impossible. I tried to do it when they were asleep, but as soon as they heard the brushing, they were instantly awake and ready to play. As I swept, they pounced and hung on the broom, while MumCat lay on her side and watched her wayward children, her tail swishing. Eventually the little hooligans grew tired of that game, and pounced on her switching tail instead.

The 'no-entry-into-the-house-on-any-account' rule that Joe had insisted upon was broken very early on. The kittens entered the house whenever they pleased and wreaked havoc. We'd be trying to watch television, and they'd pounce on our toes, or run up and down the couch, or climb the floor-length curtains. Usually their antics were far more entertaining than the TV.

Poor Chox always came last. If it was a rough and tumble game, he'd be at the bottom of the pile. If it was hide-and-seek, he'd still be hiding when his big sisters had tired of the game and were playing somewhere else. His sisters learned to lap milk, Chox just stuck his nose in and sneezed.

Every morning as I woke, the first thought on my mind was the kittens. Except for one morning, when, CRASH, an almighty explosion woke us up at 7.00 a.m. Our bedroom was a cave room with no windows, and the noise and vibrations that followed were terrifying.

We knew we lived in an earthquake zone and that, historically, earth tremors were regular occurrences, although our area had suffered no big earthquakes for centuries. Joe worried about it, but I never gave it much thought. During our first summer in El Hoyo, we'd been awoken from our siesta by urgent loudspeaker announcements. Convinced it was an earthquake warning, Joe sprang out of bed in fright and sprinted to the square, only to discover that it was a van selling peaches.

Neighbour's house demolished

This morning, we leaped out of bed and ran into the garden, shaken. Everything looked the same. Swallows wheeled overhead, the kittens pounced on our feet and each other, the birds sang. I remember thinking, *don't birds stop singing during an earthquake?*

Still in our night-wear, we clambered up the metal staircase from the garden to the roof terrace. The Boys in the house opposite stood side by side on their balcony in their matching monogrammed bathrobes, each clutching his own little dog.

"*¿Qué pasa?*" called Joe. "What's happening?"

"*Allí,*" said Roberto, pointing over our shoulders. "There!"

We swung round. A cloud of dust hung in the air and a massive earth-moving machine loomed over the pile of rubble that used to be a house. Yesterday there had been a house on Paco's far side, but today it was gone.

"Honestly!" said Joe, giving himself a scratch. "What with The Monstrosity being built on one side of us, the Ufartes and The Boys always doing stuff to their houses, the Mayor's new house on the other side of the valley, and now this! It's like living on a building site."

"Don't forget we were always working on our house up until recently. It won't take them long to rebuild that house."

And it didn't. Soon a spanky new house had arisen from the rubble of the old one. The owners only occupied it during the summer, so our lives were affected not at all.

I know England has some very strange customs and traditions. I remember the annual cheese-rolling event where runners chase a rolling cheese down a steep hill. Another favourite of mine is the worm-charming contest, where contestants are allocated a staked out area and are encouraged to charm as many worms from the ground as they can in 30 minutes. Some play music, others tap-dance, bounce balls or sing. But for me, the Spanish baby-jumping event is surely the most outrageous.

I'd never heard of it until I saw the Ufarte twins in the street one late May day. As usual, they were they dressed indentically. Both wore party dresses with matching shoes, and ribbons in their hair.

"Well! You two look lovely! Are you going to a party?"

"No, we are going on a holiday. We are going right to the top of Spain!"

"Mama says we can try our holiday clothes on."

"But we must not get dirty." Twin #2 smoothed down her dress and checked her shoes. Twin #1 did the same.

"Are you all going?" I asked.

"Yes, Mama and Papa and..."

"Jorge and Carlos..."

"But not our *abuela*."

"Because she gets tired..."

"*Tía* Lola will stay with *abuela*."

"And our baby brother is coming with us, of course."

"That's why we are going. We are going to stay with Papa's cousin and we are taking our baby brother to *El Colacho*."

"Mama and Papa took *us* to *El Salto de Colacho* when *we* were babies."

"*¿El Salto del Colacho?* What's that?" The Devil's Leap? I'd never heard of it before.

"It's when the devil jumps over babies, silly!" said Twin #1. "Everybody knows that!"

Both twins giggled behind their hands and ran back into their house leaving me to ponder over this information. Later I asked Carmen-Bethina about it, and she explained.

Apparently, this festival takes place in Castrillo de Murcia, and

El Colacho jumping over babies

probably dates back to about 1620. To celebrate Corpus Christi, men dress in yellow and red costumes to signify the devil. Families from all over Spain arrive with babies born during the previous 12 months. The babies are dressed in their best clothes and laid out side by side on mattresses in the street.

Then, wait for it, the devil, known as *El Colacho*, leaps over the babies. This is supposed to cleanse the babies' of sin and guard against evil and illness, thus ensuring them a safe passage through life.

As an added bonus, the organisers of the festival, the shadowy brotherhood of *Santísimo Sacramento de Minerva*, cloaked in black, give chase and terrorise townsfolk and spectators throughout the day.

Fascinated, I researched a little more. I discovered, unsurprisingly, that the festival has been rated one of the most dangerous in the world. It was also alleged that the last Pope asked priests in Spain to distance themselves from *El Salto del Colacho*.

So, the devil was going to jump over the Ufarte baby? Only in Spain...

To begin with, Smut and Beauty were real little scaredy cats. Trying to pick them up was extremely challenging. They scooted away and made it very clear they didn't want to be handled. We persisted because we wanted to prepare them for their future homes. So we put time aside every evening to hold and stroke the girls whether they liked it or not. It was like trying to stroke a twisting, squirming pincushion, but we persevered.

Chox was very different. He loved to be picked up, and his rumble was the first purr I heard from the kittens. He knew that if I was working in the kitchen, he only needed to stand on his hind legs, tap me with his soft front paws, look up and say, "Purrrp?" a few times before I'd stop everything and give him a cuddle.

Smut had a way of completely vanishing, worrying us half to death. She could hide in the smallest of spaces, and often did. Behind the dustbin, in my plant pots, in Joe's pack of beers, anywhere. If we left a drawer open, she'd squirm in and often wriggle over the back of the drawer into the space behind. Or sometimes I'd pull a drawer open, and there she was, curled up fast asleep amongst my underwear.

The day arrived when we lost her completely. For two hours we searched the house and garden: no Smut.

"What if she's got out, and somebody picked her up?"

"No, she wouldn't let anyone pick her up," said Joe, but we widened the search to the street and surrounding neighbourhood. No Smut. We returned, anxious and Smutless.

"Where could she be?"

The answer came from Beauty, who was sitting, fixated by something over our heads. I looked up, and there, high, high above us was Smut peeping down through the leaves of the grapevine.

How to stop kittens climbing trees

"So, you're big enough to climb trees now, are you?" I said to her. "And the grapevine gives you access to all the roofs, and the rest of the village. Not a good idea, young lady, we don't want to lose you."

How do you stop kittens climbing trees? I had a good think about it, then came up with an invention that I may patent. I took a plastic bucket, cut out the base, and wrapped the bucket, upside down round the trunk of the vine, about four feet up. It did the trick. Smut's needle-sharp claws couldn't find a purchase on the bucket's slippery sides. She was successfully grounded.

The time came when we had to take the kittens to the vet for their first inoculations and worming tablets. It was the 16th of June 2010, a date I remember well for two reasons.

Fried Chorizo in Garlic

The Spanish chorizo lends itself to all kinds of dishes. Chorizo is a versatile cured sausages that is good on its own and can also be used in recipes. Chorizo braises well, is good for kebabs and great fried up. In this recipe there is a simple combination of chorizo and garlic lightly fried in olive oil. Delicious Spanish tapas for the summer and ready in under 2 minutes.

2 chorizo sausages (150g or 6oz)
2 garlic cloves
Olive oil
Crusty bread

Take 2 chorizo sausages and slice thinly into 8 to 10 segments each.

Peel the garlic cloves and cut into 8 to 10 slices each.

Heat a drizzle of olive oil in a frying pan and fry the chorizo for 1 minute.

Add the sliced garlic and fry with the chorizo pieces for a further 2 minutes or until the garlic begins to turn golden brown.

Remove the ingredients from the pan. Lay them to rest on a sheet of kitchen towel.

Serve in small tapas bowls along with salad or peppered tomatoes.

Retain the infused olive oil and use for further cooking or enjoy with fresh crusty bread.

26
Soccer and San Juan

The faster and louder a sport is, the more the Spanish adore it, and the inhabitants of El Hoyo were no exception. Small boys on miniature motor bikes careered around the village, imitating their Moto GP heroes, Jorge Lorenzo and Dani Pedrosa. Likewise, most men in the village were avid followers of Formula 1, rooting for their idol, Fernando Alonso. But these exciting sports paled into insignificance compared with every red-blooded Spaniard's first love, FOOTBALL!

Subtle changes were happening in the village. The men talked about one thing only, and discussed it passionately, in the finest detail, often nearly coming to blows when their opinions conflicted. The women rolled their eyes but slowly became more involved as the TV showed little else. Geronimo stopped stalking Lola Ufarte and could be found in a huddle with other men, his knuckles white with passion as he clutched his Real Madrid scarf. The little boys played soccer with more urgency in the square, each sporting red football shirts with 'David Villa' printed on the back.

The cause? The FIFA World Cup, and Spain was in with an excellent chance. On the 16th of June, they were due to play their first game in the contest, against Switzerland.

But first, Joe and I had a vet visit to worry about, and getting all the kittens into the travelling box was a major hurdle. As fast as we put one in, another squirted out. Finally, we succeeded and drove off to rendezvous with Sandra from *Alstrays*, Smut and Beauty howling like banshees, Chox the picture of placidity.

Our kittens' appalling behaviour didn't end there. Sandra had brought other strays and we entered the surgery together. All Sandra's kittens behaved beautifully and their treatment was swift. Even Fleur, a cute little tortoiseshell kitten with a broken leg, purred.

"Ach so, and vat do ve have here?" asked the German nurse, resting her hand on our kittens' crate.

"Three kittens," I said. "Two months old."

The nurse opened the door of our travelling box and lifted Smut out. But Smut was having none of it. She wriggled out of the nurse's grasp, shot across the surgery and into the operating theatre, disappearing under a bank of storage units.

The formidable German nurse was going to stand no nonsense.

"Ach!" she said, and seized a broom, succeeding in hooking Smut out and grabbing her. Of course Smut howled and fought but was powerless in her experienced hands. Inside a minute the medication had been administered. The nurse applied antiseptic to the scratches on her arms, and turned to deal with Beauty. Beauty protested but was no match for the nurse. I heaved a sigh of relief. Chox would be a piece of cake after his hooligan sisters.

"Vell, zis is a very nice cat," said the German nurse as Chox purred in her arms. "He has very beautiful blue eyes. I have written his name on the card, 'Choccy-Paws'."

"What is the meaning of 'Choccy-Paws'?" asked the vet in Spanish.

"Feet of chocolate," explained Sandra and the vet nodded, scratching Chox between the ears and making him purr even louder.

"He'll be no trouble," I said. "He's a lovely little cat."

That day, Chox was not a lovely little cat. He was dreadful.

Events went like this:

Take One: Chox flatly refuses to open his mouth, despite Joe's and my efforts. Attempt fails.

Take Two: Sandra takes Chox and holds him while the nurse prises his mouth open. The vet tries to insert tablet. Phhhhhtttt, Chox spits tablet across room. Attempt fails.

Take Three: Sandra holds Chox. The nurse pulls his mouth open. The vet inserts tablet and blows in Chox's face. Vet holds Chox's mouth closed. Vet releases hold. Phhhhhtttt, Chox spits tablet across room. Attempt fails.

Sandra, Vet and Nurse with Chox

Take Four: "*Donner und Blitz...*" says the nurse. They try again. They lever Chox's jaws open. The vet inserts the tablet and holds Chox's mouth shut for a full minute. Vet releases hold. Phhhhhtttt, Chox spits tablet across room. "This Feet of Chocolate is a bad boy," chuckles the vet. Joe and I are not amused. Attempt fails.

Take Five: "We will have to do the water trick," says the vet. The nurse nods. "Don't vorry," the nurse says to Joe and me. "Sometimes ve must do zis." She goes to the sink and turns the tap on so that it's dripping fast. The nurse and vet turn Chox onto his back, open his mouth, insert tablet and hold him under said tap. Chox gulps. Tablet is swallowed. Success!

The kittens behaved better on the journey home. I think they were exhausted because, when I peeped through the bars, all three were entwined, fast asleep.

When we got back to the village, some unusual activities were unfolding in our street, so we quickly took the kittens through the back gate and into the garden. They seemed none the worse for their adventure and galloped over to MumCat, who gave them all a thorough washing. Then we sauntered outside to find out what was happening.

TV in the street

The villagers were preparing for Spain's first match of the World Cup. Work on The Monstrosity had stopped and the Ufartes had set up a large flatscreen TV in the street, the power cable of which snaked through the window of their house. They'd carried out all their chairs too, and the three-piece suite, and set them down in the road. Papa Ufarte was already on the couch with Geronimo, deep in conversation. Both were growing animated, hands waving as they discussed the forthcoming match.

As a mark of respect, Granny Ufarte had the seat of honour in the front row, although I thought it unlikely that she was Spain's most lively football fan.

Mama Ufarte and Lola drifted in and out of their house, collecting tapas and bread, and laying them out on the table they'd prepared. Lola seemed a little sulky, and I guessed it was because Geronimo was too wrapped up in the approaching game to pay her much attention.

The Ufarte twins, dressed in red shirts and white shorts, were helping, although I noticed they sampled the dishes more enthusiastically than they set them out. Their brothers, Jorge and Scrap, couldn't sit still, and were practicing goal kicks, waiting for the match to begin. Fifi charged after their ball, thankfully too intent on murdering the football to notice Joe.

It was a Wednesday, so Paco and Carmen-Bethina were absent, but I guessed they'd be watching the game in their city home. Carmen-

Bethina had confided in me that Sofía had broken up with her policeman boyfriend. She said that Sofía had discovered that her ex-boyfriend had a 'roving eye' and I wondered if he'd been caught *in flagrante* with Lola Ufarte.

Other villagers strolled down the street carrying their own chairs and packs of beer. Dogs weaved through their legs and cats appeared high on the roofs, always on the lookout for a food opportunity. Soon the street outside our house was packed, the atmosphere heavy with expectancy. Mighty Spain against little Switzerland? Haha! This was going to be a walkover, a slaughter! Switzerland didn't stand a chance! A fine start to the World Cup.

"Come and join us," said Mama Ufarte, waving her one free hand to indicate the chairs and food. Snap-On stared at us from his perch on his mother's hip.

"Thank you, but we'll watch inside," said Joe.

Fifi looked up at the sound of his voice, but we quickly disappeared inside before she decided to charge.

We turned the TV on, settled down, and began to watch the match as much as the kittens would allow. The reason we had chosen to watch it on our own TV was because we wanted to hear the commentary in English. Our satellite dish was massive and we could pick up most British channels.

"Do you know," said Joe, making himself comfortable, "that next month I'm going to be in utter heaven?"

"Why?" I asked, my mouth full of juicy, locally grown peach.

"Because, would you believe it, on my birthday, it's the British Grand Prix, Moto GP...AND...the World Cup final? Wall-to-wall sport! Now, if you were to serve me tapas, naked, it would be the best birthday ever!"

I snorted. As if!

We concentrated on the game. Although we were watching the same game as the villagers outside, our channel delivered it a good few seconds earlier. So when Spain looked as though they were going to score a goal, we shouted encouragement. Seconds later, the villagers shouted encouragement. When Andres Iniesta failed to score, we howled. Seconds later, the villagers howled. It was most disconcerting, like having an echo.

But the blow came in the 52nd minute when, to the world's astonishment, Switzerland scored. The whole of Spain went deathly silent, trying to digest this horror, then groaned in unison. The Spanish players redoubled their efforts but as the final whistle blew, the score remained unchanged: Spain 0, Switzerland 1.

What? Mighty Spain had been beaten by Switzerland? I peeped through our shutters to see what was happening in the street. Outraged,

Papa Ufarte kicked his couch. Geronimo, the picture of misery, sat with his head bowed, hands covering his face. The other villagers were melting away, taking their chairs with them, their lips tight lines of pain. I looked up the street to see men sitting on their doorsteps, elbows on their knees, heads in their hands, eyes downcast in disbelief and shame. Spain was in mourning.

"It's embarrassing," said Joe philosophically, "but not disastrous. Spain will come back fighting, you mark my words."

The phone rang. It was my niece Becky. She was coming to stay for a week and was asking whether we needed anything from England. The answer was 'no' except for something we just couldn't find in Spain.

"Could you bring three catnip mice, please?"

"Sorry for laughing, I thought you said 'catnip mice'!"

"I did."

So I told her the whole story of how we came to be fostering three kittens.

"We're not keeping any of them, of course. We still look after Sylvia and Gravy and we can't take on any more cats."

It was lovely picking Becky up from the airport. She hadn't changed a bit since we last saw her five years before. Attractive, blonde and blue-eyed, she still had the same infectious giggle and fondness for a glass of something cold and alcoholic.

Joe and I were a little concerned that she'd be bored. There were no bars or restaurants in El Hoyo, so how would we keep her entertained?

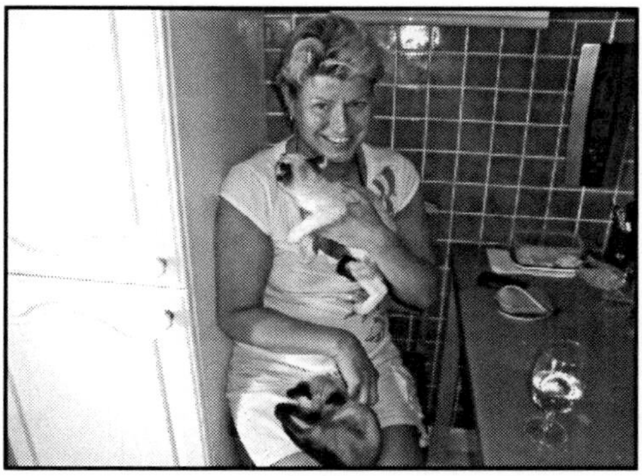

Becky

We needn't have worried because Becky was perfectly happy sunbathing on the roof terrace, working hard on a deep golden tan to take back to England. Being on the roof meant she was on flirting level with the builders who were working on the house on the other side of Paco's. I don't believe the workmen got much building done that week.

Becky loved cats, so she spent lots of quality time with the kittens. The catnip mice were a huge success, particularly with Chox. The girls liked theirs and patted them around the garden a few times, but Chox and his mouse became inseparable. Wherever he went, the mouse went, too. Within 24 hours the mouse was soggy, filthy and misshapen, but Chox didn't care. He'd chew it, bat it, roll on it, or lie on his back and juggle with it using all four paws.

Being such a gregarious little chap, he'd drag the mouse by its ratty, frayed string tail and bring it into the house, dropping it on Joe's bare feet.

"Ewww! Get that disgusting thing out of here!" Joe would yell, kicking it away.

Chox thought this was all part of the game and pounced on his mouse, picking it up again and dropping it on Joe's feet once more.

"Vicky! I'm trying to wash the dishes! Throw that cat and his wretched mouse out!"

I loved the little girls, but Chox was special. He was so full of character, so comical, so affectionate, a joy to be with. When he was sleepy he'd ask to be picked up, and if I sat down, my lap was never empty for long. When I typed, Chox would lie on his back on the desk between me and the keyboard, occasionally patting my cheek with a velvet paw. I refused to think of the day when Chox would leave and I'd never see him again.

Becky's visit coincided with the festival of San Juan. San Juan (St. John) is an important event in the Spanish calendar. It marks midsummer and the shortest night of the year. All day, families prepare by setting up tables and chairs and building huge bonfires on the beach. Rather like the Brits, who hoard their combustible trash ready for Guy Fawkes' night on November the 5th, the Spanish do the same for San Juan. Mountainous piles of wooden pallets, old furniture, logs and bits of timber sprout up on the beach all day. Barbecues are set up and when night falls, the crowds arrive in droves.

We arrived at the beach well before midnight and joined the jostling throngs. Finding a space to park wasn't easy and people were still arriving. The beach was already packed with people of all ages, from tiny babies to ancient grandmothers. A million lights flickered on the water and the sky was inky dark. Waves crashed, bonfires blazed and Spanish guitar music and smoke filled the air. Not having a bonfire of our own, we ordered drinks from a beachside café, sat down and watched.

Some groups were barbecuing, others dancing and singing, but, as midnight approached, the atmosphere changed. Encouraged by cheers and applause, athletic individuals jumped over the smaller bonfires, which, according to legend, cleanses the body and soul. Then midnight struck, and, like lemmings, the revellers, en masse, marched into the sea. It is believed that the water will wash away evil spirits. Fireworks soared into the sky and exploded. It was a magical night.

Becky and I went to the beach next morning expecting to see

the party's aftermath. But at daybreak, as the last party-goers drifted away, tractors had arrived and raked and cleaned the beach until not a scrap of charcoal remained.

Sadly, Becky's visit came to an end, and I waved her goodbye at the airport.

Back in England, I knew Operation Sage & Onion was under way, and I wanted to hear all about it.

Sherried Chorizo

This chorizo tapas recipe is incredibly easy and quick to make and is packed full of flavour. Use spicy chorizos for a fiery kick, accompanied with fino de Jerez sherry. The flavour combination works really well and creates great tapas for the summer.

3 chorizo sausages
1 Spanish onion, diced
3 garlic cloves, chopped
Half teaspoon hot paprika
250ml (half pint) fino de Jerez sherry
Parsley
Cracked black pepper
Olive oil

Lightly fry the onion in olive oil until it begins to brown.
Meanwhile slice the chorizo into half-inch pieces, and add to the softened onions in the pan.

Fry for a further couple of minutes.

Add the garlic, paprika and sherry to the onion and chorizo and cook until the sherry is reduced.

Add a cup of warm water then simmer for 10 minutes.

When the mixture has thickened add the parsley, season with pepper and stir well.

Serve on tapas plates with fresh crusty bread and peppered vine tomatoes with olive oil.

Makes 6 tapas

27
Operation Sage & Onion, and Vuvuzelas

I wasn't present, of course, and had to rely on the accounts of those who were. I was fascinated to hear how Gin Twin Sue would cope with her first-ever pets and the rescue of the ex-battery hens. Her husband had given her a chicken coop for Christmas and, having recovered from the shock, she had registered for some ex-batts way back in January. But she had to wait until the summer when some deserving hens would become available.

Now summer had arrived. Mark, Sue's husband, painted a pretty good picture of events in this letter to me.

Mark wrote: '*West Sussex British Hen Welfare Trust seemed to have run out of ex-battery chooks so we were put in touch with Dorset and went with Gin Twin "Chicken Whisperer" Juliet and Sue to Dorchester (3hr round trip for some aged hens ???). Operation Sage & Onion was under way. There must have been 200-300 to choose from in a large barn so Gin Twins 1 and 2 picked the nearest 3 that "looked nice". We'd come armed with regulation size boxes with regulation size air holes (BHWT are very strict on transportation boxes). Juliet sat in the back talking to the chooks all the way home to keep them settled.*'

The chickens were put into their new coop and the question of names came under discussion. Mark and Sue named one Jalfrezi, Ruth, Sue's daughter, called hers Beaker, while brother Joe's was Lady Henrietta as she already seemed to have assumed the Top Hen slot.

Gin Twins Hen Party

The Gin Twins stayed in the garden with the chickens and a bottle of gin: a Hen Party. To celebrate, Beaker actually laid an egg, albeit a shell-less one that looked as though it had been laid in clingfilm, but an egg nevertheless. A few days later, another egg appeared, a sound one this time, which was eaten for breakfast with much lip-smacking and

Gin Twins carrying chickens

Gin Twin Sue with new pet

appreciation. The girls settled in well, even though Mark's vegetable plot suffered.

But disaster loomed just around the corner.

Mark wrote: *'All went well until one day poor Henrietta looked off colour. No amount of encouraging her with tidbits did any good, and 3 days later she passed away to the Chooks Cloud in heaven (or that's what I told Sue). Juliet, devastated by the news, came round the next day but only burst out laughing when shown a bin-bagged parcel the exact shape of a hen (rigor mortis had set in). I think she still feels bad about laughing.*

Barely a week had gone by when I got a text at work. "Phone home as soon as you can." Sue was in tears - poor Beaker had been ambushed by a fox in broad daylight and was no more. Nothing for it but to get another couple - Kiev and Tikka.

Whereas the first 3 got along together fine, Jalfrezi and Tikka decided that Kiev was the lowest of the low and definitely bottom of the pecking order. They picked on her mercilessly, so much so she was soon a bald oven-ready bloody quivering mess and clearly in imminent risk of death. On to the internet (as you do) to research what could be done, and discovered something called "anti peck" spray that the website said discouraged cannibal behaviour in hens and pigs. This clearly was the stuff to sort the problem and a can was duly acquired from the local small holder store. Unfortunately the first attempt to spray poor Kiev alarmed her so much she flew screeching from the nesting box - have you ever tried to recapture a traumatised chicken? Not easy, but eventually she was back in the coop, where, despite stinking to high heaven of "anti cannibal" spray, was pecked all the more. Back to the internet.

"Badly pecked hens must be segregated in a separate coop" it said. Good advice if you happen to have a spare coop - but we didn't, so muggins had to go to B&Q for wood, wire mesh and a new saw

(couldn't find the old one - shows how much DIY I do). So, 2 days in the garage sawing and nailing with a cold led to a week off work with laryngitis.

Kiev now looks like a hen again, as opposed to road-kill, but still lives a separate life from the others. Her earlier traumas have completely stopped egg production, Jalfrezi seems to have retired from laying, leaving Tikka providing 1 egg every other day. Taking into account the cost of the first coop (£150), Kiev's personal confinement coop (£100), electronic ultrasonic fox deterrent (£40 and clearly didn't work), anti-cannibal spray (£10 also didn't work) plus numerous other food additives, feeds, straw and other pampering; and the average cost of each egg must be a fiver each.

Sorry, didn't mean to write so much.

Cheers,

Mark x'

"Pah!" said Paco, thumping the table with his balled fist. "That daughter of ours is never going to find a husband."

The corners of Carmen-Bethina's mouth turned down sadly as she nodded her head in agreement.

"Perhaps the policeman boyfriend was not the right one for her," I suggested, recalling what we had seen at the cemetery that night. "I'm sure the right one will come along."

"Where will she find a husband?" asked Paco. "She doesn't like anybody in the village. She doesn't like anybody at her work. She doesn't like any of our friends' sons in the city. I think Little Paco will get married before she does."

Little Paco, who was watching TV and sharing the couch with Bianca, pulled a face and shuddered at the thought. He was thirteen now and his only love was football.

"I see the Mayor's new house is finished," said Joe, changing the subject. "How on earth did he get permission to build it out there on rural land?"

"Didn't I tell you he would build a fine new house?" said Paco. "Pah! He is the Mayor, so he can do whatever he likes. On the plans they will call the building an *almacén*." He tapped the side of his nose conspiratorially.

"An *almacén?* An agricultural warehouse? But it looks nothing like a warehouse, it's more like a palace!" Joe was indignant.

"*¡Claro!*" said Paco, leaning forward. "But that's the way they do it out here in Andalucía. They call it an *almacén* even if it has a swimming pool, gardens and luxury bathrooms."

"I see The Monstrosity is almost finished, too," I said. "Twenty-seven apartments! The apartments must be very small inside. And I still don't understand why they painted the whole thing bright yellow. Who is going to buy a poky little yellow apartment in El Hoyo?"

"The foreman told me that most of them are already sold," said Carmen-Bethina, her double chins wobbling.

The conversation moved on to the usual topic, football. World Cup fever had gripped Spain in earnest and nobody escaped. Spain was heaving sighs of relief having won the next two matches against Honduras and Chile. The humiliating defeat by Switzerland was a distant, unpleasant memory, not to be dwelled upon.

The first time I heard the buzz of vuvuzelas, I thought there was something seriously wrong with our TV. It was one of the first games of the World Cup, and the televised stadium vibrated with the hum of thousands of these 'musical' instruments, drowning out the commentary. Joe pointed out the vuvuzelas and explained that they were traditional in South Africa. Originally they were made of kudu horn and were designed to call Africans back to their villages. But now they were being mass produced in their millions. Two feet long and made of plastic, these horns emitted a single note. Every spectator in the South African stadium seemed to have one glued to his lips, and the rest of the world either accepted it, or switched off their television sets.

Complaints flooded in from the viewing public calling for vuvuzelas to be banned, but Sepp Blatter, the president of FIFA, had the last word. *'We should not try to Europeanise an African World Cup ... that is what African and South African football is all about — noise, excitement, dancing, shouting and enjoyment'*. So vuvuzelas became part of the World Cup experience, whether we liked it or not. Vuvuzelas sold in their millions all around the world.

Vuvuzelas had even come to El Hoyo. Every child had one and many adults, too. Little Paco had one, all the Ufarte kids had one, and Geronimo now had one permanently sticking out of his pocket alongside his bottle of San Miguel.

One Saturday, we heard two little taps on our front door. Joe opened it to reveal the Ufarte twins on the doorstep.

"Papa said to give you and *Tía* Veeky these for tomorrow," said Twin #2.

"Papa said that the way England is playing football, they need all the help they can get," said Twin #1.

They pressed two vuvuzelas into Joe's reluctant hands and skipped away, giggling behind their hands, leaving Joe squirming at the reminder of England's lamentable performance to date.

Of course we supported England first, followed by Spain, but our team seemed to lack its customary sparkle, and was performing badly. Of the three matches already played, they'd lost one and drawn two, all against lesser teams. An embarrassing statistic bearing in mind that England had invented the game.

"Shall we take them with us when we go to Judith's and Mother's tomorrow?" I asked.

"Yes, why not? It'll give them a laugh," said Joe. "I don't expect they'll have seen a vuvuzela before except on TV."

We'd been invited to watch England playing Germany at Judith's house the following day. It was a crucial match - if England lost, they were out of the World Cup. And to lose against sporting archenemy Germany would be unthinkable, the epitome of humiliation.

"We Brits must stick together, don't you know," Judith had said on the phone. "Come on over and we'll have a jolly old drinky-poo and watch Old Blighty trounce the Jerries."

Germany was also on my mind for a reason far removed from football. Sandra Marshall had contacted me with news that should have delighted me, but in fact threw me into a deep depression.

To help find homes for them all in Germany, Sandra had asked me for photos of the kittens and MumCat for her blog. In fact, I'd gone one better than that and put together a little movie of them. The response was excellent, and Sandra was confident that homes would soon be offered.

"That's good news, isn't it?" I said dully to Joe. "They'll all go off to Germany next month to their new homes."

Sometimes Joe has a disconcerting knack of seeing right through me. He stared into my face for a few seconds, before speaking.

"It's okay, we'll keep Chox. He can stay with us. He doesn't have to go to Germany."

I threw my arms around him. "Are you sure?" I said. "I thought we'd agreed we couldn't keep any."

"I know, it's probably not very sensible, but Chox is rather special."

"You're staying with us," I whispered into Chox's soft ear later. "You don't have to wear lederhosen and learn to speak German after all."

Chox purred, and I took that to be a signal that he approved.

"Come in! Come in!" roared Judith from within. "Just push the door open, it's not locked. Tyson! Invisible! Fluffy! Half! Leave poor Joe and Vicky alone, they've just come to watch England clobber the Jerries."

Obediently, we pushed the front door open and waded through the dogs who whipped us with their tails and sniffed us with huge interest, probably picking up the scent of our kittens.

Tyson, Invisible, Fluffy and Half led the way to the living room. I smelled the familiar scent of Chanel No.5. Adjusting our eyes to the gloom, we were met by Judith, who planted kisses on our cheeks. Mother was draped on the chaise longue and didn't arise, but smiled welcomingly.

"Mother won't get up," said Judith. "She gets a bit stiff, don't you know. She'll loosen up a bit later after a couple of brandies and one of her herbal cigarettes. Won't you, Mother? Not bad for ninety-one, is she?"

Mother always looked glamourous, but today she looked quite magnificent. She wore a full-length silky blue dress, red shoes and matching belt, and a white lacy shawl thrown jauntily around her shoulders.

"Red, white and blue!" said Judith, catching my look. "Got to be patriotic, haven't we, m'dears? Today we're going to teach those bloody Jerries a lesson they won't forget. Ah, and are those eggs for us? Top hole! So fresh and tasty, aren't they? I see you've brought your own vulva-azaleas, too. Jolly good! We've got ours."

And they had. Mother's manicured hands were curled around hers like birds' claws at roost and Judith's was propped up against her chair, ready and waiting.

We sat down and glasses of local ruby wine were thrust into our hands. The dogs settled down, noses on paws, eyes watchful. As my eyes grew accustomed to the dim light, I discerned all the cat shapes decorating shelves, antique chairs and the grand piano like ornaments. Judith wanted to know all our news from the village.

"I hear the Mayor's house is finished?" she said. Judith's village shared the Mayor with ours. "I hear he's going to have a house-warming party. Typical bloody Spanish, any excuse for a get-together. And how are you coping living next to those Ufartes? And what about those kitties of yours? I'd take 'em like a shot if I could, but we're rather overloaded with animals, don't you know."

She waved her hand to indicate the menagerie, and the dogs lifted their heads. I could see five dogs, but I knew there were another six somewhere in the house. Judith had stuck to her resolve never to have ten dogs, so they still had nine and a Half and one that was Invisible. Half wagged his tail when I looked at him.

"Oh, the kittens are growing fast," I said, "and they've all got homes waiting. But we're keeping Choccy-Paws."

"Oh, excellent!" said Judith. "Jolly good show! That little cat would melt the heart of a bloody snowman. Awfully pleased to hear you're keeping him after all! That's jolly good news, isn't it, Mother?"

But Mother was thoughtfully drawing on her herbal cigarette

and seemed to be in a world of her own.

"It's nearly five o'clock," said Joe, looking at the polished pendulum clock on the mantelpiece. "The match is about to start."

White Bean and Sherry Garlic Dip

A lovely smooth blended dip full of flavour that goes exceptionally well with raw vegetables such as carrots, celery and summer salads. A perfect dip for hot potato wedges with a bite that comes from the garlic and cracked black pepper and hint of sherry vinegar. Great for the tapas table!

2 -to3 large potatoes
200g (7oz) jar of white beans
1 garlic clove
200ml (6 to7 fl oz) water
Pinch of cracked black pepper
250ml (half pint) extra virgin olive oil
Splash of sherry vinegar
Salt to taste

Cut the potatoes into wedges and place into a fryer and cook.

Meanwhile, place all of the other ingredients into a blender and blend for a good 60 seconds until a smooth paste is achieved.

Taste test, adding more garlic or sherry vinegar to achieve your preferred flavour strength. Add a little more olive oil if required.

Pour into a bowl or cazuela.
Serve with the hot potato wedges or salad.

Tip: Add half a teaspoon of hot smoked paprika for an extra smokey flavour.

Serves 2

28
Red and Yellow

Judith leaned forward and switched the TV on, and instantly the room was filled with the buzz of South African vuvuzelas. All the dogs sprang up and started barking.

"Half! Tyson! Sinbad! Fluffy! Pipe down!"

But the dogs only barked harder. Cats lifted their heads in alarm, their ears pricked up, alert.

"Mother! The vulva-azaleas!"

Mother nodded and lifted her vuvuzela to her painted lips. In unison, Judith and her mother blew. The dogs exited the room en masse, almost falling over each other in their rush to evacuate. Mother cackled and took another deep draw of her herbal cigarette.

"Always works!" said Judith, refilling all our glasses and settling down again. "The dogs hate it. That's what we do when they start being a bloody nuisance. They'll go and lie down in the kitchen for a while and give us some peace now. Jolly good invention, those vulva-azalea thingies."

The red wine and the company was a pleasure, but the game was not. By half-time, England's lack-lustre performance had brought the score to Germany 2 - England 0.

"It's not going frightfully well, is it, m'dears?" said Judith emptying her glass of wine down her throat. "Our boys really need to buck their ideas up if they want to win this match."

We all agreed and dissected the match, finding it wanting. If England lost this game, they'd be out of the World Cup without even reaching the quarter finals. Unthinkable. Only Mother didn't comment. She was on her third brandy and lying back on the chaise longue, gazing at the ceiling, humming quietly to herself.

Paul the Psychic Octopus predicting that 'Chickens' would become a bestseller (from Paul Hamilton)

We had a good laugh about Paul the Psychic Octopus. Paul lived in a German Sealife Centre and had become an oracle. His keepers had placed two tasty mussels in separate boxes marked with opposing teams' flags. The box Paul first selected represented the team expected to win. So far, Paul had succeeded every time in choosing the winning flag and had correctly predicted all Germany's results. He'd also predicted Germany to win this game against England.

"Good Lord!" said Judith. "What does a bloody calamari know about soccer?" We all agreed.

"Actually," said Joe. "It's next month I'm really looking forward to. The 11th, to be precise."

"Why's that, dear boy?"

"Lots of reasons. It's my birthday, and it's also the British Grand Prix, Moto GP and the World Cup final. All in one day. I'm going to watch all of them and Vicky's promised to serve me tapas, naked."

"I most certainly did not!"

Judith guffawed and Mother started cackling, but luckily the second half of the match started, drawing the attention away from me.

I'll make no more observations on the sorry match, except to admit that Paul the Psychic Octopus was right yet again and the final score was Germany 4 - England 1. England was out of the World Cup.

Scratch-cards

Joe and I were in the kitchen. I was busy scraping away at two scratch-cards that Carrefour had given us on our last shopping trip while Joe was racking the eggs he'd just collected.

"Joe? Have a look at this! I think this means that if Spain win the World Cup, we win 130 euros!"

Joe snorted. "Huh! There'll be a catch to it. Read the small print."

I put the scratch-card away. Spain had to win the final before we could even think about claiming the prize. Actually, they were in with a very good chance. Spain had beaten both Portugal and Paraguay and were playing Germany next.

Spain and El Hoyo were crazy with World Cup fever. Nobody talked about anything else, and even Carmen-Bethina admitted praying in church for a Spanish victory. Paul the Psychic Octopus had predicted a German defeat which led to death threats from enraged German fans,

Spanish Chorizo and Calamari Salad

If you enjoy seafood and have a passion for Spanish chorizo, then this simple healthy salad is a real Mediterranean treat.

3 large whole squid
A good bunch of baby spinach leaves
150g (6 oz) sliced chorizo sausage
Extra virgin olive oil

Wash and clean the spinach leaves and place in a large bowl or cazuela.
Clean the squid, remove the heads and cut the bodies into large squares.
Score the meat to create a nice criss-cross effect for presentation.
Thinly slice two chorizos.
Fry the squid and chorizo in olive oil for 5 to 6 minutes.
Place over the spinach leaves.
Drizzle with extra virgin olive oil and salt and pepper to taste.

calling upon Paul to be cooked and eaten. Paul had captured the world's imagination and became a celebrity in his own right.

Somebody knocked on our door and Joe put the eggs down.

"That'll be the Ufarte kids," he said. "I promised the boys I'd come and watch them play football in the square." He chuckled, "I think I'll give them a bit of a fright."

He tiptoed to the front door, grabbing a vuvuzela on the way. Then he crouched down. When the knock was repeated, he wrenched it open, lurched forward and blew lustily on the vuvuzela at child height. Except it wasn't the Ufarte boys, it was the Mayor.

In an effort to blow as hard as he could, Joe had squeezed his eyes tight shut, so it was a bit of a shock when he finally opened them.

"*Buenos días, señor* Twead," said the Mayor. "How are you? And how is your lovely wife, señora Beaky?" The Mayor was particularly nasal in his speech, and his Andalucían accent was thick, transforming his '*v's*' to '*b's*'. I had come to terms with being called 'Beaky'.

Joe blinked, recovered himself and lowered the vuvuzela.

"Er, *buenos días*, we're both fine, thank you. I'm sorry about the, er..." He switched the vuvzela to his left hand and extended his right hand to shake. "Please come in, Pancho, Vicky will be pleased to see you."

That was a blatant lie. I never felt comfortable with our Mayor. Perhaps I was imagining it, but I always felt Pancho was undressing me with his eyes.

"Today I will not enter," said Pancho. "Today I am visiting everybody to invite them to a party to celebrate my new house. I would be pleased if you and señora Beaky would attend. It will be in two weeks."

"Oh, thank you, we'd love to come..."

"Before I go, my wife asked me if you are still keeping

chickens. She loves fresh eggs, you know. They are always so tasty."

"Yes, we have six chickens, but they're rather elderly. They don't lay much any more..."

"I know my wife would really appreciate a few fresh eggs." Pancho persisted. He was accustomed to getting what he wanted.

Joe held up a hand, indicating the Mayor should wait, and darted back into the kitchen to put six eggs in a paper bag.

"Very kind," said the Mayor, accepting the bag. "I will see you at my party." He left and headed toward the Ufartes.

"That'll be nice," I said to Joe as I searched through the fridge for something for supper as omelette was clearly no longer an option. "I'll be interested to see the Mayor's new house."

"Huh," grunted Joe. "At least we'll see where our taxes are going."

That evening, Joe and I sat on our roof terrace with a drink. Evenings are beautiful in El Hoyo. When the sun sinks, it paints the sky all shades of pastel pink and the distant ocean glimmers with rosy lights. The pink light bathes the mountain slopes lending mystery to the caves and contours. Squads of swallows wheel overhead, snatching insects on the fly.

MumCat had followed us up the outside staircase and all three kittens had joined us too. They were now big enough to manage the steps, and our roof terrace had become yet another playground for them. They were always more active in the evening, having snoozed most of the day.

As always, Chox shadowed us, while the two girls played together in another corner, pouncing on invisible mice and each other. I remember that particular evening because of Smut, the feisty, adventurous kitten who avoided handling at all costs.

Smut and Beauty played until they began to slow down, exhausted from the rough and tumble with each other. I picked Smut up and smoothed her silky fur, tinged pink by the sunset. I sat down with her and continued stroking, and to my delight, she began to purr. I experimented and lifted my hands away, allowing her to jump off my lap if she wanted, but she didn't. Instead, she nuzzled me, asking for more strokes. Smut was learning to enjoy human company.

Smut

Beauty followed suit a few days later and became very insistent. She usually chose Joe's lap, and she was a wriggler. If he stopped stroking her, she'd butt him with her hard little head and make puddings with her paws, kneading his legs and purring like a pneumatic drill.

As the sun sank lower in the darkening sky, we heard footsteps below us on the street. I put Smut down and leaned over the wall to see whose feet were responsible. It was Nicolas, The Monstrosity's crane operator.

"Hello, Nicolas, it's a beautiful evening, isn't it?" I called down.

Nicholas looked up, recognising me. "Hello! I was just taking a wander around the village. Our work on the apartments is almost finished. We are dismantling the crane tomorrow. In a few weeks we will all be gone."

"I hear most of the apartments are already sold?"

"Yes, that is true. Even in this Credit Crisis, people want to live in El Hoyo. I have the keys, and the electricity is connected. Would you like to see inside one or two?"

"We'd love to! We're coming down." I turned to Joe. "Come on, I'm dying to see how horrible those apartments are inside!"

We ran down the stairs and met Nicolas in the street and together we walked over to The Monstrosity. Nicolas sorted through the massive bunch of keys on his ring, selected one and opened a front door, reaching in to switch on the light. Then he stepped back, allowing us to enter first.

The apartment was *not* poky and cramped as I had expected. On the contrary, it was spacious and well designed with tasteful, modern fittings. The bedrooms were large and airy and the bathroom much bigger than our own. It even had a balcony looking out over the village and mountains.

"Oh!" I said to Joe. "It's really nice! I thought it was going to be really small and cramped."

Discussing it later, Joe and I decided that perhaps it was unfair to call the apartment block 'The Monstrosity' anymore. And perhaps it was a *good* thing that more people moved into El Hoyo. After all, the inhabitants are the life-blood of a village and ensure its survival. Yes, the yellow colour was decidedly awful, but we knew from experience that all colours fade under the Spanish sun.

Joe's birthday, July the 11th, arrived. It was a hot and sticky day, full of promise. Hurrah! Spain's Jorge Lorenzo won the Moto GP championship, and Britain's Lewis Hamilton came second in the British

Formula 1 Grand Prix. Unfortunately, Spain's Alonso wasn't placed. But now the World Cup final approached, Spain versus Holland...

Back in his German Sealife Centre, Paul the Psychic Octopus had been consulted and predicted that Spain would beat Holland. Paul was now much in demand. A businessman from Galicia, Spain, raised €30,000 as a 'transfer fee' to have Paul shipped over to Spain. The Germans refused, even though the Spanish prime minister promised to supply bodyguards to prevent Paul from being assassinated or eaten.

We'd noticed that the villagers had very little interest in Wimbledon, despite the winner, Nadal, being Spanish. But soccer was a very different matter. All day, the excitement mounted. Crates of beer were chilled, tapas prepared, Spanish flags hoisted and by evening, every child and male was wearing a red David Villa shirt.

Marcia's grown up sons climbed onto Marcia's roof with wide paint brushes. Back in the spring they'd sprayed her roof with red waterproof foam, and now they used white paint to write *¡CAMPEONES!* (champions) in huge letters big enough to be read by aeroplanes flying over. I only hoped the statement wasn't premature.

Red and yellow bunting fluttered in the breeze, strung between the four trees in the square. More decorated the entrance to the village, and Spanish flags flapped lazily from hastily erected flagpoles on chimneys. Cars were parked around the square, flags tied to aerials.

Marcia and Uncle Felix sat side by side outside the shop. Marcia never dressed in any colour except black, but even she had made an effort. Uncle Felix had removed his flat cloth cap, and he and Marcia sported matching straw boaters decorated with red and yellow hatbands. Every few minutes, poor Marcia had to get up and hobble painfully up the steps into her shop to serve a steady stream of customers with beer, sweets and potato crisps.

Some prepared to watch the match in their own homes, others, including the Ufartes, joined with friends and relations and set up their televisions in the street. Once again the three-piece suite and extra chairs were hauled out, drinks poured and tables set.

Lola Ufarte was looking extremely patriotic, although I don't believe Spain, or football, was the first thought on any red-blooded male's mind who set eyes upon her. She was wearing a silky mini-dress of red and yellow stripes that clung to every curve and bodily undulation. The dress left little to the imagination, particularly when she leaned over the table she was setting out. Her long tanned legs gleamed as she walked, her hips swaying just a little more than most girls' hips do. Red and yellow bracelets jangled at her wrists, and I noticed her fingernails and toenails were painted with tiny Spanish flags.

"Lola Ufarte is looking the part," observed Joe. "Nice dress."

"Behave yourself," I said. "You're probably three times her age."

"I know, I was just saying..."

I pretended to trip and gave him a sharp enough kick on the ankle to make him hop.

"Ouch! That hurt!"

"Sorry," I said, but I wasn't.

Granny Ufarte sat in her chair, fast asleep, oblivious to the frenzy around her. Her sleeping fingers rested on a vuvuzela on her lap. The Ufarte baby's stroller was parked beside her, whirring red and yellow windmills attached to the handlebars. Fifi's hair had been bunched together out of her eyes and tied with red and yellow ribbons that fluttered as she scampered up and down the street, yapping.

"*Tío* Joe! *Tía* Veeky! Look at us!" yelled the twins as they raced past us. "*Tía* Lola has painted our faces!"

They stopped just long enough for us to admire their red and yellow striped faces, then pelted off again down the street.

People shouted to each other, children screamed and blew their vuvuzelas, dogs barked and weaved in and out of the furniture while the village cats chose high places to sit and watch the activity, wide-eyed.

Geronimo's face was white with anticipation, his fingers gripping the neck of his beer bottle. Geronimo was ready. El Hoyo was ready. Spain was ready. The starting whistle shrilled on countless TV's. The 2010 World Cup Final had begun.

Honey Barbecued Chicken

Spanish chicken recipes often involve cooking chicken on the barbecue. This a summer dish that is light, versatile and goes down well with salads or cold potatoes.

4 skinless chicken breasts
Juice of 1 lemon
2 tablespoons of honey
2 garlic cloves (crushed)
Knob of butter

Melt the butter in a cazuela or pan and cook the garlic for 1 minute.
Mix in the lemon juice and honey, keeping some aside for basting the chicken breasts later.
Marinate the chicken in the mixture for an hour.
Prepare the barbecue creating a good "*brasa*" or even level of hot coals.
Place the chicken on the barbecue and cook for 15 minutes turning frequently.
Baste the chicken generously 2 minutes before serving.

Tip: Serve with a white Rioja and fresh salad drizzled in extra virgin olive oil for a typical summer dish.

29
An Accident and a Party

Joe and I could have joined the Ufartes outside, or sat with Paco, Carmen-Bethina, Sofía, Little Paco and their many relatives next door. But Joe wanted us to watch it in our own home, and, as it was his birthday, I concurred. We'd thrown open our windows and doors so all the noises of the village poured in anyway.

English referee Howard Webb officiated and the ball in play was gold-coloured to echo the gold trophy. The Spanish Royal family, the world, 15.6 million Spanish viewers, plus Joe and I, were transfixed. The match had started.

An exciting game, although not without controversy. A record fourteen yellow warning cards were issued for various offences, each one heralded with roars from El Hoyo. Advice and abuse were hurled at the Spanish players and English referee, and the village groaned with one voice when Holland nearly scored. Half-time came and the score sheet was still blank.

In the second half, the ball was headed past the Dutch goalkeeper. A Spanish goal seemed undeniable. El Hoyo roared. Children screamed 'Goal!' and stampeded in a pack down the street, deaf to the groans from disappointed supporters who'd then seen the goal disallowed.

Full-time, and the score remained at 0-0. Extra-time.... Then finally - 'GOOOOOOAL!!!!' Spain had won the 2010 World Cup! Spain were the soccer champions of the world!

The noise was deafening. Both Granny Ufarte and the baby woke up. The baby stared with astonishment and Granny Ufarte's face split into a happy grin as she blew on her vuvuzela. Papa Ufarte leaped onto the table, feet oblivious to the plates of tapas, fists clenched, roaring, "GOAL!" at the sky. Paco stood on his doorstep with a bundle of fireworks, releasing giant rockets that ripped into the heavens.

Grown men wept, women clung to each other and people blew their vuvuzelas and danced in the street. Children of all ages went berserk and ran round the village shouting, "*¡Campeones! ¡Campeones!*". Entire families piled into their cars and drove round and round the square, blasting their horns, cheering and leaning out of the windows to wave their Spanish flags. Dogs barked and cats fled into derelict buildings to hide. Geronimo dashed away his tears of joy to let off more fireworks that whizzed into the night. The valley was an explosion of elation.

At three o'clock in the morning, Joe and I finally dropped into bed.

"Next time we go shopping, we must remember to take those scratch-cards with us," I said, but Joe was already asleep.

Did Joe enjoy his birthday? YES! Did he enjoy the F1, the Moto GP and the World Cup final? Oh, yes! Did I serve him tapas? Yes, I did. Oh, and I know what you're thinking, did I serve him naked? No way, José...

The next day, Spain carried on partying and revelling in their victory. Paco told us that in a neighbouring village the night before, everyone jumped into the public swimming pool, fully clothed, including three policemen in full uniform.

I don't know if it was the Siamese strain in our kittens' genes, or just that they were unusual, but all three possessed a fascination for water. Cats I've owned in the past avoided water at all costs, except for the odd opportunistic fishing session in a goldfish pond.

These three kittens made watering the garden almost as tricky as sweeping the patio. The first hurdle was unwinding the hose from its reel, the kittens pouncing on every coil as it hit the ground. Next, I would attempt to drag the hose to its watering destination. All three kittens gave chase, grabbing the moving hose with their front paws, rolling onto their backs to juggle with it and try to sink their needle-sharp teeth into it as it writhed.

"Let go!" I said, tugging at the hose. But they refused and I ended up dragging all three little pests along on their backs.

And it didn't stop there. The next game was 'Chicken'. As I aimed my water spurt at the flower beds, all three little horrors crowded to where the water was directed, swiping at the rebounding droplets. I couldn't bear getting them wet so I was forced to aim the water at anything except where I really wanted it to fall. Eventually, they'd tire of the game, and, soggy and exhausted, they scampered to MumCat for a wash and feed. Hence a job that should have taken fifteen minutes took me twice as long every single day.

There was another time that one of the kittens fell foul of water in an unfortunate accident.

I was in the kitchen when I heard a kitten crying. I thought the noise was coming from the garden, that one of the kittens had got stuck somewhere, but I knew that Joe was outside feeding the chickens and that he would sort it out. But the howling persisted, so I put my potato peeler down and went to investigate. The noise wasn't coming from the garden at all, it was coming from the bathroom. It was Smut, of course, Little Miss Adventure. She wasn't supposed to be in the bathroom but had somehow managed to sneak in. She was very tiny at the time but already insatiably curious.

I pushed the door open, and saw the problem right away. Smut had fallen into the toilet. She was standing on her hind paws, waist deep in water, scrabbling in an effort to get out. Being so tiny, she wasn't able to pull herself out. I groaned and reached into the bowl to extract the distressed kitten.

Smut was unharmed, but scared and soaked. Wet cats are not easy to hold, and Smut was not co-operative. She twisted free and shot away, leaving a wet trail across the tiles. Through the house she dashed until finally she hid under our bed. I knelt down and managed to grab her.

"Oh no you don't, young lady," I said as she tried to escape again.

I rubbed her with a towel until her fur looked reasonably dry and clean, then I delivered her to MumCat. MumCat understood the situation immediately and pinned her daughter down with one paw and gave her a thorough washing.

I'd just about finished cleaning the kitten, the house and myself, when Joe came in from the garden.

"Have you only peeled one potato?" he asked. "I've been outside for ages! You must be the slowest potato peeler in the world."

I took a deep breath, then put him straight. Firmly.

The misadventure did not cure Smut of her curiosity, nor did it cure her fascination for water. However, Joe and I made sure that in future, the bathroom door was always kept closed.

Smut and Beauty

But the kittens were not the only ones to be attracted to water. It surprised me how much the chickens enjoyed it.

Of course they always had clean, fresh water to drink in their coop, but their reaction to the hosepipe was notable. As soon as they saw me unravelling it, they made excited little cluckings, and crowded the fence. They paraded up and down against the chicken-wire, pushing, jostling and treading on each other in an effort to be first in the queue. I'd train the water jet into their coop (if the kittens let me) to wash down the walls a little. Immediately, the chickens moved in and drank from the muddy puddles that formed. Then they'd paddle and scratch the ground, turning the soil into slush. Finally, they'd systematically work along the fence, using their long thin tongues to lick up the diamond drops of water caught in the chicken wire.

It was midnight and the live band was in full voice. On the stage erected in the garden, the lead singer swayed her hips and crooned into the microphone. Her backers, dressed in tight leather trousers and flounced red silk shirts, strummed their guitars and smouldered. Villagers nibbled on the tapas and stood chatting in clusters. Elderly couples danced together, while children ran in and out of the huge open entry gates. Fairy lights bedecked the sculpted trees and lit up the ornamental fountain.

It was the Mayor's house-warming party, and I had decided I couldn't wait any longer. I was going to ask Joe outright what was bothering him. It may not have been the best choice of time or place, but I had to know. Too often I had seen his eyes darken and watched him disappear into himself, but I couldn't fathom what was troubling him.

I'd tried hard to puzzle it out. Was it money? Was it homesickness for England? Was it disenchantment with Spain? I honestly didn't know, but I resolved to find out that night.

I had sent Joe to get drinks and was deep in thought when I felt a hand on my shoulder. Warm breath stirred my hair and I turned my head.

"Beaky, you are looking wonderful tonight..."

"Oh! Pancho! I didn't see you there." I backed away slightly, uncomfortable with the Mayor's proximity. He was not discouraged and caught my hand, brushing it with his lips.

"And where is Joe tonight? Surely he has not allowed his beautiful wife to come out alone?"

"No, he's just..."

"I shall look after you, Beaky. It will be my pleasure. Come, you must dance with me. I will show you why we Spanish men are famous for our dancing."

"But Joe is..."

Pancho ignored my protests and steered me onto the dance floor, his hands never leaving the small of my back. The band was finishing an energetic, pulsating number and the guests on the dance-floor paused, out of breath, applauding the musicians. Pancho waved to the stage and made a hand-signal to the band: slow the music down. They nodded and struck up again, this time with a moody, romantic piece. Many of the dancers drifted away, leaving Pancho and myself highly visible.

"Beaky," Pancho breathed into my ear. "I do not think Joe knows how lucky he is to have a woman like you." He clasped me tightly to him, the hand on my back splayed, fingers massaging. "A vibrant woman like you deserves more attention... If you ever need to talk, you know where to find me at the Town Hall."

My eyes bored through the crowd, desperately searching for Joe. Pancho was pressing me uncomfortably close to his body and I was forced to concentrate hard in order to avoid stepping on his toes.

"Beaky, I noticed you from the moment you moved into El Hoyo. Such eyes! The colour of the sea..."

This was getting ridiculous. "Pancho, I'm sorry but..."

"Say no more, my little Beaky! I know you are a woman of honour. But all women have needs, just as we men do, and I..."

"Oh! There's Joe!" I tore myself from Pancho's hot embrace. "Thank you for the dance, Pancho, but I must go." I fled, leaving Pancho standing, bewildered and disappointed.

"Where did you get to?" I snapped when I reached Joe.

"What do you mean? You asked me to get you a drink! What's the matter? Did you get lonely?"

"No! I... Oh, never mind..." I took the glass from Joe and sipped it gratefully. "Joe, can we find somewhere quiet? I want to talk to you."

Joe looked surprised but nodded and led the way to the edge of the garden, near a clump of trees, a good distance away from the noise and bustle of the party. We were about to settle on a bench when we both heard a man's whisper wafting from the shadows.

"You are a such a beautiful thing, like a lovely butterfly that dances on the flowers... All day I can think of nothing but you..."

Joe and I stared at each other and I stifled a giggle.

"Every night when I lay my head on my pillow to sleep, I think only about you..."

Joe mouthed a name, "Nicolas, the crane operator," and I nodded. Yes, I agreed, it certainly sounded like him.

"When I see you across a crowded room, my two knees go weak. Oh, come to me, my beautiful little butterfly..."

There was a rustle, then a seductive giggle which Joe and I also recognised. We looked at each other, amused, then mouthed simultaneously, "Lola Ufarte!"

We tiptoed away from the lovers and found an alternative quiet spot, a bench near a bush of scented jasmine. The heavens were a dome of dark velvet, spangled with a million stars like the flowers of the jasmine bush. The music thumped away in the distance, vibrating through the warm air. If only I could just lean my head back and enjoy the night, but I'd brought Joe here for a purpose. I turned to face him.

"Well, what do you want to talk about?" he asked, avoiding my eyes. I sensed he already knew.

I took his hand and forced him to make eye contact. “Joe, look at me. I want you to be totally honest with me, I want you to tell me the truth. I *know* there’s something bothering you, so don’t tell me there isn’t. We’re supposed to be partners, and I need to know what the matter is, however bad it is.”

Joe looked at me, then at the stars, then sighed deeply.

Orce Chicken and Chorizo

Chicken and chorizo is one of those classic Spanish combinations that goes down really well either as simple tapas, a starter or as a main meal. Use strong spicy chorizos for an extra kick. Cooked in less than 15 minutes.

1 chicken breast or de-boned leg
8 garlic cloves, skins left on
100g (4 oz) chorizo
8 peppercorns
100ml (3.4 fl oz) red wine
Olive oil

Heat a splash of olive oil in the frying pan.
Cut the chicken into bite-size pieces and brown in the frying pan.
Leaving the skins on, crush each garlic cloves roughly and throw in with the chicken pieces, fry for 5 minutes.
Meanwhile, slice some chorizo thinly and add to the chicken along with the peppercorns.
Add the red wine and continue to cook until it is reduced by half. Stir and turn the chicken, then cover. Turn down the heat and leave to simmer for 10 minutes.
Once the chicken is cooked, serve on tapas plates with fresh salad and crusty bread.

Serves 3 to 4

30
A Bombshell and a Puzzle

"It's not easy to explain," he said at last.

"Try, I'm listening."

Still he said nothing, and my eyes searched his face for clues.

"Joe, talk to me. Is it money?"

He shook his head. "No. Well, maybe partly."

"Are you tired of living in Spain?"

"Oh no, it's not that!"

"Well, then what is it? Are you sick? Joe, you *have* to tell me."

Joe looked down at my hand in his and traced a pattern on my palm with the tip of his finger. I held my breath.

"It's a kind of mixture of things," he said eventually. "I suppose mostly, it's the children."

"Children? What children? Our children? The Ufartes?"

"No, no. Not them. It's children in general. And it's to do with my birthday."

Now I was really confused. "Joe, explain. I don't understand."

So Joe started explaining in detail, and slowly I began to understand.

"I've just had my 59th birthday, and now I'm racing toward my 60th. I love it here in El Hoyo, but I feel useless. It's okay for you because you're quite happy writing, but I want to do something constructive, too." He paused and sighed again.

"Well, why don't you start writing the book you always said you'd write?"

"No, that's not enough. I want to go back to teaching, being with kids in the classroom one last time. Being useful."

"But you haven't taught in a school since 1989!"

"I know. I just feel *now* is my last chance. I'll never get a teaching job when I'm sixty years old. But it's not just that, it's also because of money. My pension is just not stretching as far as it used to. We get a third less income every month since the Credit Crisis and the disastrous foreign exchange rates. We need more of an income to cope with the bills."

"But where would you teach?" An icy hand had clutched my heart and a thousand questions crowded into my mind.

"I don't know. Not England. Maybe China, or the Middle East? Somewhere where they pay well. You could stay here and write."

"What? On my own?"

"Well, you don't want to go back to teaching, do you?"

"No, but I don't want to stay here alone."

My hands were shaking. No! This couldn't be happening. Joe leaving? Not now when life was so good.

"Well, you managed very well when we first came out here to Spain, remember? You were here for months on your own before I could come out. And the house was a mess then, no bathroom or kitchen, remember?"

"Yes, but..."

"I doubt I would get a teaching job anyway, at my age. It was just a thought..."

We talked through the night, not noticing that most of the guests had already left and the band had packed up. When we got home, we talked again. I slept fitfully.

In the morning, I felt lightheaded and agitated, but I had to set aside the hideous thoughts that plagued me because there were important jobs to do. We had an appointment with Sandra at the vet's for all three kittens, plus MumCat. The kittens were successfully weaned and it was time for MumCat to be sterilised, ensuring she would bring no more unwanted kittens into the world. The kittens needed vaccinations and the vet would issue pet passports so that the girls could travel to their new homes in Germany. We wanted Chox to have a pet passport, too, in case he ever travelled with us.

I felt like a zombie going through the motions. Catch the kittens, put them in their crate. Catch MumCat, put her in her crate. Check they all had water. Lock the house and leave. Drive to the vet. It was like being on autopilot; my body worked but my mind was detached and churning.

As usual, Sandra had brought an assortment of other cats and kittens that needed attention, including a massive orange tomcat that bulged out of the crate he was being carried in. His name was Big Boy and he was being tested for diseases before they attempted to re-home him. Then it was our turn.

"Ah, I remember you," said the vet to Chox. "You are Feet of Chocolate, no?"

Fortunately, this time, none of our kittens misbehaved and we left MumCat in the surgery to be operated on. One of Sandra's cats was also being sterilised, so Sandra, Joe and I went to kill time in a nearby cafe. Sandra told us tales of all the latest cats she had rescued and the antics of her own.

Sandra and her husband lived in an apartment with a balcony, and one of their cats kept getting them into trouble. The people in the next apartment had plastic flowers and plastic trailing ivy on their balcony, and Sandra's cat would systematically destroy the arrangements, much to their neighbour's annoyance and Sandra's embarrassment.

I listened, but wasn't really paying attention. I kept stealing glances at Joe. Was he serious, or was this just a passing whim? Would he really leave me and Chox and our house and chickens to go and teach in some strange country? How would he manage on his own? How would I manage? An hour later, we returned to the vet who handed over a semi-conscious MumCat.

Back at home, I couldn't settle. I tried to write but the kittens were being particularly naughty, as though they sensed some future upheaval in their lives. Chox decided he wanted to type, causing pages of Greek to appear on the monitor. Smut and Beauty squeezed behind my desk and began pulling on the cables, resulting in the computer and router sliding backwards away from me.

"Enough!" I said to the little monsters and banished them outside.

MumCat was still sleeping off her operation. She had a row of fearsome looking stitches in the centre of a bald patch down her side, where she'd been shaved. We had to keep her in solitary confinement, so shut her in the bathroom upstairs to give her time to recover. We'd been told to keep the kittens away from her for a few days.

When I'm anxious or preoccupied, I pace. I must have tramped several miles, pacing up and down the kitchen, trying to come to terms with Joe's bombshell. Joe was in the garden, pretending to read a book. He'd been out there for over an hour, and I hadn't yet seen him turn a single page.

To clear my head, I started writing one of my famous lists.

<u>For</u>
Probably Joe's last chance to work
Satisfy Joe's wish to feel useful and work with kids
Earn some money

<u>Against</u>
Don't want to live on my own
Will miss him desperately

I chewed the end of my pencil. Lists normally come naturally to me, but this one was not flowing. I looked out over the mountains and imagined not being able call Joe to grab the binoculars to watch mountain goats, or an eagle in the sky. I silently cursed him. *Why did you have to turn our lives upside down when we're so happy and comfortable here?* I knew I could just put my foot down, say no, refuse to go along with it, but the damage had been done. Joe had poured his heart out to me, and I had to make the right decision. Let him go, or what? *Selfish, selfish, selfish,* a voice kept repeating in my head. Joe had come to Spain to please me. Wasn't it time I did something to please him?

I marched outside. "Joe?"

"Uh huh?"

"I think you should go and search on the Internet. See if you can find any teaching jobs abroad."

Slowly, Joe closed his book and locked me in a steady gaze.

"Are you sure?"

"Yes, I'm sure. Perhaps you can find a job somewhere warm. A temporary contract just for six months or so, I think I could manage that long without you if I had to. I'll just get on with writing the *Chickens* sequel. I'll be okay. It isn't forever."

"Right!"

Secretly, I doubted there were any jobs to be found. In fact I was banking on that.

Chox and Beauty asleep on keyboard

The kittens were growing fast and were the picture of health. My Facebook and Twitter friends looked at photos I'd posted up and told me that Smut and Beauty looked like Snowshoe cats, a term I hadn't heard before. Their fur was longer than Chox's and silkier, and their colouring was unusual. They were mostly white, but had beige streaks, brown ears and tails and beautiful powder-blue eyes.

Choccy-Paws, once the runt of the litter, had made up for lost time and was now just as big as his sisters. He had the same huge blue eyes, but his markings were all Siamese. He was by far the calmest of the three and the most affectionate. Wherever I went, Chox came too, even just to sit under the grapevine, or to hang clothes on the washing line.

All three were becoming very independent, and the fact that MumCat was locked in the upstairs bathroom, recovering from her operation, didn't seem to bother them at all.

Smut was the only kitten who had learned to climb over the bucket I'd fixed to the grapevine trunk, and she was now able to leave the garden at will. Beauty and Chox would sit side by side, staring up into the canopy, watching her, but they hadn't yet succeeded in negotiating the bucket obstacle.

I was forever worried that a villager might catch Smut and carry her away, but there was nothing I could do to prevent it. My niece Becky had given all three kittens sparkly collars that I hoped would indicate that our kittens were owned, if found. But being so small, Smut slipped out of her new collar immediately, and short of confining her to the house, I'd run out of ideas to stop her escaping from the garden.

In August, our grapevine was a thick thatch of bright green, so dense that the sun could not penetrate it. When in full leaf, it provided shade and privacy, and even The Boys standing on their roof terrace looking down into our garden couldn't see us. Thanks to Uncle Felix and his pruning expertise, and Joe with his sulphur, massive bunches of grapes hung down, heavy and delicious. Each bunch was the size of a rugby ball, packed with more purple, delicious grapes than we could ever eat.

Our grapevine in summer

Our grapevine provided a leafy roof that stretched from the kitchen door to the barbecue area. We set out a long table and chairs beneath, allowing us to sit outside even on the hottest of days.

We wove lengths of fairy lights through the grapevine and on a hot summer night, the tiny lights twinkled through the leaves and reflected off the purple grapes. For me, it was the perfect place to enjoy a meal, better than any restaurant in the world, particularly if Joe had barbecued and I didn't need to cook.

The kittens enjoyed barbecues as much as we did. When Joe opened the cupboard under the barbecue where the kittens were raised, and pulled out the sack of coals, the kittens appeared from nowhere. As he poured out the coals, they would sit and watch, ears pricked, eyes huge. They knew that before long, some delicious fishy or meaty morsels would be coming their way.

But now, we didn't have a barbecue planned. All three kittens were safely asleep on one of the living room chairs. Joe was busy working on his résumé. He hadn't needed to provide a C.V. for many, many years, so it was taking quite a long time to put one together. I didn't mind; any delay was welcome.

I went outside and looked up at the grapes. Most had already blushed from green to deep purple and I thought that they might now be ready to eat. Something caught my eye amongst the leaves. It wasn't green or purple, this thing was black.

Puzzled, I climbed onto a chair, reached up and pulled it down. It was a wispy bit of nothing, a little piece of gossamer fabric. I held it up to examine it. It was a thong.

I inspected it further and marvelled. Had I *ever* worn anything quite so small and wispy when I was young? Embroidered in tiny fancy letters was the word *Lunes*, the Spanish word for 'Monday', but apart from that, there were no clues.

How had it got there? Whose undergarment was it? I hooked it over one finger and carried it in to Joe, who was poring over his computer. He looked up.

"What's that?" he asked, swivelling his chair round and leaning forward to look. "It's a thong, isn't it? Very nice! Go and put it on, I can finish this C.V. later..."

"Don't be ridiculous! It's not mine!"

"Well, whose is it then?"

"I don't know! I found it in the branches of the grapevine."

"What? How did it get there?"

"I don't know. Your guess is as good as mine."

"Do you think the wind blew it there?"

"That's possible, I suppose. I don't know how else it could have got there."

Joe stood up. "Show me where you found it," he said.

I led him outside and pointed. He squinted up into the branches.

"What's that?" he said. "Good gracious! I think it's another one!"

Barbecued Spanish Lamb

Barbecued lamb is a real treat in the summer time, especially when prepared with a good marinade. This delicate, yet flavoursome, marinade is best left for at least three hours to infuse. Use lamb chops or a leg of lamb cut into steaks, or a full leg that has been boned and flattened.

1 leg of lamb, cut into thick chops
Generous handful of fresh mint
1 onion, peeled and grated
1 clove of garlic, peeled and crushed
Dry mustard
Freshly ground black pepper
200g butter

Rub each chop with the pepper and dry mustard then place a layer of mint leaves in a large shallow dish. Add the lamb and cover with grated onion and more mint leaves. Leave in the fridge for at least three hours.

In a saucepan, combine the butter and garlic and cook gently for 5 minutes then add a little more fresh chopped mint and simmer for a few minutes more.

Remove the lamb from the dish, removing all of the mint leaves, and place on the barbecue grill.

Brush the lamb with the garlic butter sauce during cooking, about 6 to 8 minutes each side.

Serve immediately with a sprinkle of salt for juicy, succulent lamb with a delicate hint of mint and garlic.

31
Joe's Shame

Being six feet tall, Joe had no problem reaching up into the grapevine. He parted the leaves and plucked out another thong, shocking pink and shiny. This one was embroidered with the word *Sabado*, Saturday.

Joe and I looked at each other, trying to fathom the mystery.

"Beats me how they got into our grapevine," Joe said at last.

It's funny how useless pieces of information that have been filed away in one's brain, surface when you least expect it. I've often surprised myself by being able to answer a random Mastermind question correctly, having no idea how I knew it. I suddenly remembered something I had read, or perhaps seen on the TV about cats that were chronic thieves.

"Joe, I think it may have been a cat."

Joe raised his eyebrows. "A *cat*? What *are* you talking about?"

"Cats have been known to steal stuff, like washing off clothes-lines."

"Never!"

"Yes, honestly! I remember reading it somewhere. There really are some cats that like to steal clothes and underwear."

To prove the point, I went on the Internet and searched. Sure enough, there were plenty of cases reported. Interestingly, many of the culprits were Siamese.

"Listen to this," I said, reading aloud. "'*...in the past three years, this cat has stolen over 600 items, amassing a growing pile of loot at home, ABC News reported. He's not choosy. Stolen goods include towels, stuffed animals, gloves, socks, shoes, spongy footballs. He stole a Converse sneaker and returned later for the other one, the station said. He lifted a neighbor's bikini bottom drying outside, and came back for the top a few minutes later.*' There, you see! It's one of our cats that's turned to crime."

"But MumCat is locked upstairs, recuperating. And the kittens can't climb over the bucket..."

"Smut can..."

Realisation dawned. Smut! I knew Smut was an excellent climber, but I didn't know she was a criminal. So Smut was a kleptocat? It was hard to believe.

"I think I can guess who the thongs belong to," I said.

"Me, too," said Joe. "Lola Ufarte."

I nodded. I couldn't imagine anybody I knew, apart from Lola

Ufarte, who would wear such insubstantial under-garments.

Few people in the village had gardens or any outdoor space of their own. We were lucky with our garden and roof terraces, which gave us plenty of space for a clothes-line. In the summer, Carmen-Bethina hung her enormous white drawers to dry on the burglar bars outside her window, and the Ufartes also used their window bars as a drying rack. Joe and I always averted our eyes when we walked past, considering it rude to stare at other people's laundry.

"So what do we do?" Joe asked.

"Try and keep an eye on Smut, I suppose," I said.

"No, I meant about the thongs."

"We'll have to take them back and explain," I said.

"*You* will, you mean. I'm not taking them back." Joe was adamant.

"That's not fair, why does it have to be me?" I really didn't want to be lumbered with the embarrassing task. I grabbed a euro coin. "Look, we'll toss for it. If it lands with the king of Spain up, you go. Okay?"

"Hang on a second. Is this a case of heads you win, tails I lose?"

"No. I won't cheat."

"Okay."

I tossed the euro into the air and allowed it to drop. It rolled away, wavered, then settled. The king of Spain smiled at me.

Joe looked at it unhappily. "Best of three?" he asked hopefully.

"No, we agreed, so you've got the job. Just go round to the Ufartes and explain. Tell them the truth." I began to giggle. "And you'd better be quick!"

"Why?"

"Because it's Friday today. We've got Lola's Saturday pair here, so she won't have anything to wear tomorrow."

Joe was far from amused but grabbed the little wisps and set off down the street.

I opened my emails and waited for him to return. One was from Sandra Marshall of *Alstrays*, concerning the re-homing of the kittens in Germany.

Hi Victoria,
Your little girls already have an adoptant! Kerstin in Germany put their photos and your great video up on their website this morning, and within 2 hours somebody had reserved them! This is great as when they travel to Germany they will go straight to their new home, and they'll be together.
I wasn't sure if you had named them. We have called the one with the black on her nose Milly, and the other one Mia.

Sandra x

Of course I was delighted that Smut and Beauty already had homes to go to. Even better, they'd be together. But I was dreading parting with them, and hearing their new names, however pretty, just drove home the fact that they weren't ours, and that they'd soon be leaving for ever. Thank goodness Chox was staying with us. Imagining him in some other house, snoozing on somebody else's lap, bringing his dreadful catnip mouse to a complete stranger, was just too painful.

"Well, girls," I said to Smut and Beauty. "You'd better brush up on your German. You've got a lovely new home waiting for you."

Joe stamped into the house, and his expression banished all thoughts of the kittens' future from my mind. He was empty-handed so I assumed he had found the rightful owner.

"How did it go?" I asked.

Joe's mouth was set in a grim line, and he gave himself a vigorous scratch down below.

"Well? What happened?" Obviously it hadn't gone well.

Joe's reply was too punctuated with four letter words for me to reproduce verbatim, so I shall try to recreate the sorry scene as he reported it, minus the expletives.

Apparently, he'd reached the Ufarte's house, but was reluctant to knock on their front door for two reasons. Firstly, he was embarrassed clutching the thongs, and secondly, he certainly didn't want another incident with Fifi. Since laundry was already hanging on their burglar bars, he decided to drape the thongs alongside the other bits and pieces drying there and swiftly leave. A good plan.

So he looked up and down the street. Nobody there, all clear. Good! He leaned forward and furtively peeped through the window, hoping nobody was home. To his horror, Lola Ufarte was looking right back at him.

Both of them jumped in fright, then Lola vanished, and the front door was wrenched open.

"Excuse me? What exactly are you doing?" she asked, head on one side, hands on her hips, bracelets jingling furiously.

"Oh! I was just..."

Lola looked at Joe and then at the thongs he was still clutching.

"Have you been stealing my underwear?" she demanded, raising her pencilled eyebrows.

"No, I was just..."

"You naughty man! Never would I have imagined you were the type of man to take ladies' underwear! *¡Madre mía!*"

"But I..."

"And why were you peeping through my window? *¡Madre mía!*

You are a moron!"

"No, no! I was just..."

"*¡Madre mía!* What would your wife say if I told her what I caught you doing?"

"Vicky? Oh, Vicky knows all about..."

"She knows? Your wife knows? And she does not mind? *¡Madre mía!* You English have very strange customs! Here in Spain it is not acceptable to steal ladies' underwear. And does she know you are a moron?"

I'd been listening to the story unfold with my hand over my mouth, and at this point interrupted. "Lola Ufarte called you a moron?"

Joe shrugged. "Yes, she said I was a moron! She refused to listen to why I was holding those blasted thongs of hers. When I tried to tell her I was putting them back, not stealing them, she just said, 'Oh, yes, I'm sure you were...' in a really sarcastic tone."

Joe was so indignant, so outraged, that it took all my wifely skills plus a generous medicinal brandy to calm him. As he simmered down, still spluttering and cursing, I checked something.

"Joe, it's okay, I don't think Lola Ufarte called you a 'moron'. I've just looked it up in the Spanish/English dictionary."

"She didn't? What did she call me then?"

"Well, actually... It wasn't 'moron'. I think what Lola probably said was, 'mirón', which roughly translates into English as 'Peeping Tom'. I think she was actually calling you a pervert."

"WHAT?"

It took some considerable time and another large medicinal brandy before I was able to bring Joe back from the stratosphere. I promised to visit Lola and explain, in order to restore Joe's bruised reputation.

Enough time had passed since MumCat's operation, and she was healing nicely. She'd been shut upstairs away from her unruly kittens for her own sake, but we felt she was now sufficiently recovered to be let out. She ran down the stairs, through the kitchen and out of the back door, calling her children.

Smut, Beauty and Chox were absolutely delighted to see their mum. They mewed their welcome and circled her, leaning into her and rubbing themselves against her sides. They sniffed her surgical stitches while she washed each kitten furiously, catching up on lost time. Then she lay on her side and allowed them to feed, her raspy tongue scrubbing their heads as they butted against her. A happy reunion.

We received another email from Sandra Marshall:

Family reunion

Hi Vicky and Joe,
Good news! Kerstin in Germany has found a home for MumCat! The brother of one of the girls who works for the charity in Germany that finds homes for our cats, wants a lovely female cat to be a friend to his male. He is just about to move to a new apartment, where she will be able to go outside if she wants ... no big roads ... only a brook at the end of the garden.
This sounds perfect so I would like to send her with her girls. What do you think? I definitely think this would be a more secure life for her and she would get all the attention she needs and have her own home.
Sandra x

So, thanks to Sandra's work, MumCat and the girl kittens all had homes waiting, but I still felt unhappy and tense. Until Joe gave up his silly notion of working abroad I couldn't settle. I honestly didn't think he'd find a job, but I wanted him to find that out for himself. Then we could wash our hands of the idea and get on with our life in Spain. After all, it was already August, and the school year started in September. It was highly unlikely that any school would offer him the position of Maths or Physics teacher this late. Wasn't it?

But life has a way of refusing to pan out the way you expect. The day came when Joe came into the kitchen, his eyes wide.

32
The End, and a Beginning

I put down the plates I was holding and gave Joe my full attention, my heart already filled with dread. Joe scratched himself down below and I knew the news was bad.

"Vicky, there's an international school in the Middle East that's trying to fill a vacancy for a Maths and Physics teacher starting in September. They've expressed an interest in me."

"Really?" That's all I could manage.

"Yep. I've had an email from the principal there. Her name's Daryna and she's new to the school, and she says she's keen to recruit some older teachers as most of the staff are very young and inexperienced."

"Really?" My ability to form sentences seemed to have deserted me.

"Yes. The contract is for one year."

"A year? A whole year?"

Joe nodded. "The pay is pretty good, and they provide the airfare out there and back again. Plus free private medical insurance, and they give you an apartment, and free transport to and from the school. No taxes, either."

"Really?" Not only had my powers of speech failed me, but my knees felt weak too. I sat down heavily.

"She wants me to scan my qualifications and send them in an email to the school office. Are you okay? You look a bit pale."

"I'm fine."

A whole year? Joe would be away for a whole year. *No!* This was happening too fast.

"Well, what do you think? Shall I go ahead and submit all the bits and pieces they want?"

No! You can't leave me for a year! That's what I wanted to scream, but instead I spoke calmly. "It's totally up to you. If you like the look of the job, go ahead."

Chox put his front paws on my lap, asking to be picked up. I scooped him up and stroked him absently, scratching his ears and chin the way he loved.

Joe went back to his computer, leaving me to try and clear my head. What did I want? To stay on my own for a year without Joe? *No!* Well then, should I stop him going? *No.* And then I knew the answer, and I hated it. I would have to go, too. I would have to leave everything for a year and go with Joe to the Middle East. He needed me, and I needed him. We were a partnership.

I put Chox down and walked slowly into the living room where Joe was bent over his computer, typing furiously.

"Joe, I think I should go with you. It's only for a year, after all. I think we should lock up the house, and go together."

Joe swung round on his chair, and took my hands. His eyes bored into mine, and I could see hope and relief in his.

"You'll come too? Have you thought carefully about this?"

"Yes, like you said before, it's just a wallet-fattening exercise, it's not forever, and it would be an amazing experience. We'd just lock up our house for a year. We could take Chox with us, he's got a passport. You could teach, and I would look after Chox and write." I hadn't thought this through properly, but it sounded feasible. "Perhaps they have a part-time teaching vacancy for me? I might consider that, as long as I still have plenty of time to write."

"Hold on," said Joe. "I'll find out. Daryna's kindly offered to help me with my application. She knows what the owners of the school are looking for." He typed quickly and then read his words aloud.

Dear Daryna,
It is many years since I have applied for a teaching position and I have consequently struggled to write the letter of application. I therefore heartily welcome your comments and suggestions before I send it. Please know, however, that I have total confidence in my ability to teach and long to get back into the classroom.
Also, I wonder whether it is worth mentioning that my wife is a fully qualified and experienced English teacher? She is not looking for a teaching position, (she is an author) but could be prevailed upon to help out occasionally, should the need arise, as she was also a substitute teacher for many years.
Thank you for your encouragement and I await your thoughts,
Joe

"Good. Let's see what she says. We've always liked Dubai, haven't we? I think teaching in Dubai wouldn't be too bad at all." I was doing my best to be as positive as I could.

"Who said anything about Dubai? This school is in Bahrain."

"Is it? I don't know anything about Bahrain. Where's that?"

"It's next to Saudi Arabia I think... Actually I'm not sure exactly."

So I pulled out our huge old Atlas from the bookcase and opened it at the Middle East. After some searching, we found the Kingdom of Bahrain, a tiny teardrop of an island in the Persian Gulf, connected to Saudi Arabia by a causeway.

"It's not very big," I said, peering at the map.

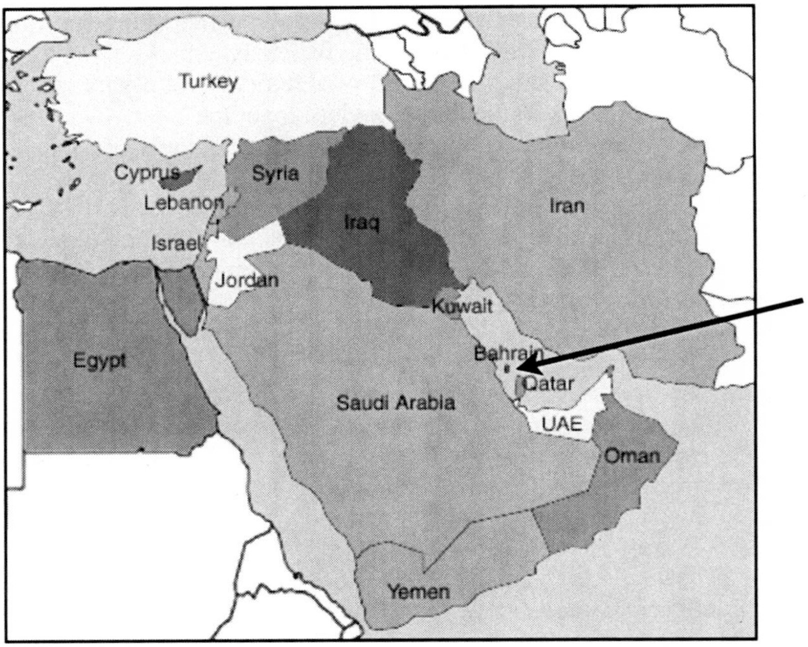

"Ah, but it has a Formula 1 track," said Joe, happily. "Imagine, we'll be able to watch the Grand Prix live!"

"How strictly Muslim is it? I suppose alcohol is illegal?" I would miss Paco's wine. "And what's the name of the school?"

"It's called the American Specialist School," said Joe, "in the capital, Manama."

"Are you quite sure? American Specialist School? That's spells ASS! Somebody hasn't thought that through very carefully!" We both laughed.

The next 24 hours were a blur of fact-finding. Daryna filled in many gaps by telling us about the school and the apartment we would be given if we were offered jobs. We found out that the students were mostly Arab, and that the school had three separate units: Kindergarten, Middle School and High School.

I acted superbly, feigning enthusiasm, but really I clung to the hope that Joe wouldn't get the job, that his age would be against him. I simply couldn't imagine packing up and working in the Middle East. I hoped that this was all just a flash in the pan and that we'd continue to wake up as usual to ordinary days in El Hoyo. I wanted to hear Uncle Felix's mule clattering up the street, see the swallows circling overhead, feel the mountain breeze on my face.

But the die was cast. The next day, job offers arrived. ASS offered Joe a position as Maths and Physics teacher in the High School, and I was offered English in the Middle School. Part-time jobs were not an option. We were asked to print and sign our letters of acceptance, scan them and send them back within 24 hours. I was in a state of shock.

"We can still change our minds," Joe said, but the pen was already poised over the contract, ready to sign.

"No, sign it. If we don't, we may regret it for ever. Sign."

Joe signed with a flourish and passed the pen to me. I gripped it and signed my name with numb fingers. The deed was done.

Lists, lists, lists. No time to wallow in regrets. No time to write. No time to think too hard about what we were leaving behind. Two weeks to pack up the house, to sort the cats and chickens. Two weeks to tell everybody and prepare for the year ahead.

To Do
Dig out suitcases
Find decent working clothes
Dig out teaching resources
Find out more about the syllabuses we'll be teaching
Find out more about Bahrain
Get haircuts
Buy travelling crate for Chox and get his paperwork done
Claim the prize for our scratch-card because Spain won the World Cup
Take cats to pick-up point for journey to Germany
Ask Paco to look after chickens
Buy enough chicken grain for a year
Tell our kids, Gin Twins and other friends
Make house secure for winter

Every night I dropped into bed exhausted, both mentally and physically. I felt I was caught in a tsunami propelling me into unfamiliar territory, with no brakes, no turning around. Flocks of butterflies danced permanently in my chest: the fear of the unknown.

And yet I was excited, too. Coming to live in Spain had been a huge adventure. House swapping, both in the USA and Australia, had been another adventure. But this was probably going to be the biggest adventure of them all.

And then something else happened that upset me far more than anything else had. It became clear that Choccy-Paws could not share our adventure, would not accompany us to the Middle East.

The paperwork was complicated, and we would need an import license. Although Bahrain was rabies-free, Chox would have to go into quarantine. Daryna told us that our school-owned apartment in Bahrain was not yet finished, and that, initially, we'd have to live in a hotel. Neither the hotel nor the school allowed pets. The obstacles were too great. We would have to find a home for Chox after all.

We didn't know anybody prepared to take him for a year. Judith and Mother's house was already full to overflowing with animals, and none of our Spanish friends liked cats.

My tears dropped onto Chox as he lay on his back on my lap, his soft paws waving in the air. I tickled his tummy. I couldn't bear to give him away. But common sense told me that it wouldn't be fair to leave him all day on his own in an apartment in Bahrain. He'd have no garden, no company, and he'd have to spend time in quarantine as well.

"I'm sorry, Chox, I've let you down," I whispered into his silky ear. Chox patted my cheek, oblivious.

Barbecued Pork with Orange and Ginger

4 to 6 thin pork fillets
2 tablespoons mustard
2 teaspoons ground ginger
Juice of 1 orange
2 tablespoons olive oil
Salt to season

In a large shallow dish, mix together the ginger, orange juice, mustard and olive oil and season with a little salt.
Add the pork fillets and leave to marinate in the fridge, turning occasionally for up to 2 hours.
Cook on a barbecue for 5 minutes each side until cooked through and tender.

33
Epilogue

Time was short, and like robots, we worked through my lists.

Dig out suitcases. Not only did they need digging out, but they needed serious dusting down and airing.

Find decent working clothes. Many of our old clothes didn't fit anymore or had been attacked by moths, or were just plain inappropriate. Research told me that as Bahrain was a Muslim country, I'd have to wear sleeves at all times, and long skirts or trousers. Joe's old suits no longer fitted him as his waistline had definitely expanded during our years in Spain. However, Daryna reassured us that tailor-made clothes in Bahrain were inexpensive and plentiful.

Dig out teaching resources. I found a box of lesson plans and resources, but they were yellowed with age and smelled musty. I decided to take the barest minimum, and Joe selected only a book on Calculus for packing.

Find out more about the syllabuses we'll be teaching. Not easy. Not even Daryna seemed to know. We had no idea how well the students spoke English, or what the standard of education was like. Time would tell.

Find out more about Bahrain. That didn't take long. The island was tiny, and its main tourist attractions seemed to be the many glitzy shopping malls, and the Tree of Life, an ancient tree that grew miraculously in the desert, quite alone. How it found enough water to survive was a mystery. Joe made a point of reminding me about the Formula 1 racing track.

I also checked the political situation and was relieved to read that Bahrain was an extremely peaceful country, ruled by a King. There was other good news. Although fiercely Muslim, Bahrain was well known for its tolerance. Unlike its close neighbour, Saudi Arabia, women were permitted to drive cars, and even alcohol was freely available for non-Muslims and visitors.

Get haircuts. Joe's was easy. By now I was an expert with the hair clippers. I treated myself to an appointment at a swanky salon in the city. I couldn't face Juanita and her fearsome assistant Olga, and I didn't want to arrive in Bahrain with raven-black caterpillar eyebrows.

Buy travelling crate for Chox and get his paperwork done. Alas, no longer necessary. Sadly, I crossed that one off the list. I spent as much time with him as I could, treasuring each moment, knowing that soon I would only have photographs and memories to remind me of him.

Take cats to pick-up point for journey to Germany. Sandra Marshall from *Alstrays* had understood the situation immediately and was convinced that finding a home for Chox would not be difficult. He would travel with his mother and sisters to new homes in Germany. The meeting point was to be a Repsol petrol station, at 10.30 in the morning.

I buried my face in Chox's warm fur, knowing that our time together was over. Some other lucky person would play with him in the future. Other hands would stroke his fur and scratch behind his ears. After this morning, I would never see my beautiful, gentle Choccy-Paws again. The pain in my heart was indescribable.

Chox

We successfully lured all the cats into their travelling crates with slices of ham, and firmly secured the boxes. The hand-over at the Repsol garage was swift, intentionally so. Even Joe was abnormally quiet. We turned our backs and drove away leaving our little cat family behind.

Claim the prize for our scratch-card because Spain won the World Cup. We queued at the Carrefour Customer Care counter, winning scratch-card in hand.

"Good morning. We've come to claim our prize because Spain won the World Cup," I said.

"Good morning. May I see the card?"

"We've never won anything on a scratch-card before. I think 130 euros is a lovely prize!" Joe handed it to the assistant, smiling. The lady examined the card and turned it over.

"I am sorry," she said, "But I am afraid you have won nothing."

"We haven't? Why not?"

"If you read the small print here, and here, you will see that this is not a winning ticket." She stabbed at the offending print with a long red fingernail.

Joe snatched the scratch-card back and we both stared at it. The print was too small and too Spanish for us to understand.

"Oh, well," Joe said at last. "That's that then." He tore up the card into little pieces and left it on the counter.

Ask Paco to look after chickens. Joe and I went next door to break the news and ask the favour.

"You are leaving El Hoyo?" Carmen-Bethina repeated.

"You are going where?" asked Paco, gaping at us.

"The Kingdom of Bahrain, in the Middle East."

"But why?"

"They pay well, and it's just for one year."

"*¡Madre mía!*" said Carmen-Bethina, both hands up to her face, eyes round with astonishment.

"The school will give us an apartment, and pay for our flights, and medical care. And there are no taxes. We'll be able to save some money."

"No taxis?"

"Not *taxis*, no taxes."

"But the Middle East is a dangerous place!"

"Oh no, not the Kingdom of Bahrain. Bahrain is very peaceful and safe. They never have any trouble there."

"*¡Madre mía!* A whole year!"

"So, would you mind looking after the chickens for us? They still lay eggs occasionally."

"No problem at all. Do not worry about them, and Uncle Felix and I will look after your grapevine."

"The grapes this year are fantastic, thanks to you. But we won't be tasting any. They're not quite ripe and we'll be gone before they're ready to eat," I said.

"Never mind," said Carmen-Bethina, putting her arm round my shoulder. "The year will go fast. You will taste next year's grapes."

Buy enough chicken grain for a year. Joe left me packing and drove off to collect three huge sacks of grain, more than enough for six elderly chickens for a year. Another job ticked off.

Tell our kids, Gin Twins and other friends. Our kids took the news well, accustomed to our globe-trotting adventures. The Gin Twins were surprised. They had already booked flights for their October trip to El Hoyo. We wouldn't be there, but they decided they'd still come, collecting the keys from Paco when they arrived.

The news spread round the village like influenza, "Have you heard? The English are going to Arabia!" and we were questioned daily.

"What is Arabic food like?" asked Mama Ufarte.

"Will you have to wear a head-dress?" asked Lola Ufarte.

"Why do you have to go away?" asked Twin #1.

"Will you come back one day?" said Twin #2.

"Shall I keep all your post for you?" asked Marcia.

"Do they have soccer teams out there?" asked Geronimo.

Make house secure for winter. With the memory of the persistent rains of last winter still fresh in our minds, Joe packed sandbags against our doors. We checked all the windows and locks.

Daryna, the principal of the High School, had been emailing me daily from Bahrain, and her letters were a fascinating glimpse of the life we were about to lead.

Dear Vicky,
You will like Manama - it is spotless and a real desert which is sort of beautiful. Get ready for a sauna though - when you walk out it curls your hair and steams the creases out of your clothes. The sheer aridity of the land, the steaminess of the air and the intensity of the heat make the need for air conditioning an absolute necessity. 15 minutes outside and the body is waning.
Food seems to be quite inexpensive but other things are like Europe - pricey.
I am being told again and again the kids in this school are hard to motivate and lazy - what can we do to light a fire? Your little darlings in the Middle School probably haven't been corrupted yet by the lassitude. It's so much easier to motivate the little ones - stickers, candies, games all work. The older ones want ...... I don't know what. So we have our work cut out for us.
How many more sleeps? Tonight, and tomorrow - and hasta la vista baby!
D.

Suddenly, it was the night before we were leaving, and Joe and I took a drink up to the roof terrace to watch the sun going down behind the mountains. Gradually the sky tinged pink, salmon and coral, a fantasy backdrop for the countless diving swallows. The mountain tops were lit with fiery hues and the distant sea sparkled with orange embers. Then the sun slipped away, and the swallows disappeared to be replaced by flitting bats.

The Ufartes were out in force, swirling, hand-clapping and dancing to Papa Ufarte's guitar. I saw the twins scampering up the street, Fifi leading the way. Their brothers were absent, probably playing football in the square, but Granny Ufarte was dozing in her customary chair.

When the mosquitos started to bite in earnest, we slipped back indoors. Neither of us had said a word, too lost in our own thoughts.

At 5 o'clock the next morning, Paco's fist thumped on our front door.

"English! Are you ready? Time to go to the airport!"

We loaded Paco's Range Rover with our luggage. Carmen-Bethina stood in the street in her bathrobe, curlers in her hair. Bianca wagged her tail and trotted off to sniff lamp-posts.

"Don't worry about anything," said Carmen-Bethina, as we

hugged goodbye. "The year will fly past and you will soon be back home in El Hoyo. Oh, and have you heard? That no-good Lola Ufarte has run away with one of the workers from The Monstrosity!"

"No! Really? With Nicolas the crane operator, I suppose?"

"No, it was that nice foreman. I heard he left his tools, said nothing to anybody, and just took off!"

"Good heavens!" I said. "Well, I didn't expect that!"

"And still our Sofía has no husband," mourned Carmen-Bethina.

"Hey, Sofía may be married by the time we get back!"

"Pah!" said Paco, slamming his fist down hard on the bonnet of the Range Rover. "That would be a miracle! Now we must go, or you will miss the plane!"

It was the 21st August 2010. The Arab Spring, a violent, revolutionary wave of protests and uprisings, was poised to erupt and sweep across the Arab world. Bahrain was destined to make world news headlines and we two old fools were heading right smack-bang into the middle of it.

To be continued...

Connect with Victoria

Email:
TopHen@VictoriaTwead.com

Facebook: https://www.facebook.com/VictoriaTwead

Victoria's website:
www.VictoriaTwead.com

Free Stuff and Village Updates monthly newsletter and draw:
http://bit.ly/5U9F2k

Video Links you may enjoy

Kittens born in the street outside our home:
http://vimeo.com/29115371

(*My favourite!*) **The YouTube that found the kittens new homes:**
http://bit.ly/na9uMQ

Chickens, Mules and Two Old Fools **book trailer:**
http://youtu.be/1s9KbJEmrHs

The Gin Twins stacking logs:
http://bit.ly/n5r1Id

Jumping Over Babies:
http://youtu.be/fdj4fL_ua7Q

Other Links

Orce Serrano Hams: http://www.orceserranohams.com

Alstrays: http://almerimarlifestrays.com/

Grazamela Guide - Processionary Caterpillars: http://bit.ly/oPIglh

Eye On Spain: http://www.eyeonspain.com

British Hen Welfare Trust: http://www.bhwt.org.uk/

Meet our friends, Gayle and Iain

Gayle and Iain run an online Spanish delicatessen, *Orce Serrano Hams,* from the village of Orce in Granada. They specialise in sourcing the finest artisan cured meats and Spanish favourites such as terracotta cookware, spices, liqueurs and accessories for the Spanish ham.

The young family moved to rural Andalucía in 2004. "We fell in love with the area and the idea of cave living," said Gayle. "So we sold up everything and returned with all of our possessions packed into two cars and a caravan. We were ready for an adventure!"

The first four months were spent renovating the cave house which didn't have any water, electricity or even floors. "It was hard work but very exciting and two-year-old Joshua loved every minute of his new rustic lifestyle. Then, one evening, while enjoying a beer and tapas, we looked more closely at the hams hanging up and had an idea. We loved Serrano ham but had never seen it in the UK. Perhaps we could introduce it? After much research, *Orce Serrano Hams* was born."

The Serrano, or mountain ham, is the cured hind leg of white pigs. "All our hams and sausages come from local producers who still do things traditionally," says Gayle. "We research new products, even commissioning our own super spicy '*Orce Fire Chorizo*' made by our local butcher. The villagers have been a huge help and we cooked so many new dishes, we started to put recipes onto our website."

Five years on, both business and family expanded. Baby Nico was born, and two more German Shepherd dogs joined Otto. "Not everything revolves around work, of course!" adds Gayle. "We're so lucky to be surrounded by open countryside, fantastic for the kids and dogs. We love our Spanish life and feel very much at home."

www.orceserranohams.com

Also in the 'Old Fools' series by Victoria Twead

'Chickens, Mules and Two Old Fools'

Perhaps if Joe and Vicky had known what relocating to a tiny village tucked in the Alpujarra mountains would really be like, they might have hesitated...

Vicky and Joe's story is packed with irreverent humour, animals, eccentric characters and sunshine.

'A truly hilarious page-turner.'

The Telegraph: 'a charming and funny expat tale'

The Catalunya Chronicle: 'Weeks later, you will be standing at your kitchen window doing the dishes and recall some fleeting scene with chickens or mules or two old fools and laugh out loud all over again.'

'Two Old Fools - Olé!'

Vicky and Joe have finished fixing up their house and look forward to peaceful days enjoying their retirement. Then the fish van arrives, and instead of delivering fresh fish, disgorges the Ufarte family. The peace of El Hoyo is shattered.

Packed with badly behaved humans and animals, irreverent humour and sunshine, 'Two Old Fools - Olé!' will make you laugh out loud, while the mouth-watering Spanish recipes will have you reaching for your saucepan.

Coming 2012/13 - **'Two Old Fools on a Camel'**

Cat Family Update

News from Germany

MumCat (now named Calypso):

An email snippet from one of the German re-homers - *"now she is for one week in her new home: the people are SO happy, they say, that they never have had such a lovely cat ! she is coming in the morning into the bed and is going on for a little sleep with her parents ...and she was with them in the garden already, they have a little sea in the garden, she loved it but then she went back with them into the house :o)"*

Smut and Beauty (now named Milly and Mia):

The new German owners were afraid that they may be allergic to the sisters, but all was well. Beauty and Smut live together, and judging by the photos, are very happy, settled and spoiled.

Choccy-Paws:

Chox developed a stomach complaint, but was adopted by a lady who understood such things, her own cat having the same condition. He is doing well and continues to charm everyone he meets.

Email: TopHen@VictoriaTwead.com

Website: www.VictoriaTwead.com

Lightning Source UK Ltd.
Milton Keynes UK
UKOW041818211112

202566UK00001B/63/P

9 781908 603555